Praise for *That Near-Death Thing*

'Rick Broadbent's raw, tender book comes close to the heart of the mystery'   *Sunday Telegraph*

'A thrilling ride "inside the helmets" of four victory-hungry daredevils'   Megan Walsh, *The Times*

'I'll have a soft spot for *That Near-Death Thing* by Rick Broadbent, a terrific piece of work on the Isle of Man TT'
Frank Keating, *Observer*

'A great read'   *Independent*

'Broadbent skilfully weaves in the history of TT racing as this quartet of riders lap the 37.75-mile course . . . by the end you might not share these men's passion but you begin to understand, even admire it'
Simon Redfern, *Independent on Sunday*

'What possesses man to risk his life and limb in search of the next high? . . . *Times* journalist and author Broadbent has come closer than ever to answering that question'
Press Association

'I seem to have consumed every TT-related book/article/ video clip so far, but this one is a cracker . . . perhaps the best of all'   *Motorsport*

'There are 242 corners on the TT course and this book leaves you with the impression that death is lurking round every one'   *Sport*

Rick Broadbent is a sports writer at *The Times*, and the author of books on boxing and football. His MotoGP Motorcycle World Championship book *Ring of Fire* was a *Sunday Times* Sports Book of the Year, shortlisted for the William Hill Sports Book of the Year award in 2009 and described by Murray Walker as 'stunning'.

By Rick Broadbent

The Big If
Ring of Fire
That Near-Death Thing

That Near-Death Thing

Inside the Most Dangerous Race in the World

Rick Broadbent

For Erin and Sam – climb your own mountains
(but not on bikes).

An Orion paperback

First published in Great Britain in 2012
by Orion
This paperback edition published in 2013
by Orion Books Ltd,
Orion House, 5 Upper St Martin's Lane,
London WC2H 9EA

An Hachette UK company

9 10

A CIP catalogue record for this book is available
from the British Library.

ISBN 978-1-4091-3897-6

Designed in Warnock by Geoff Green Book Design, Cambridge

Printed and bound in Great Britain by
CPI Group (UK) Ltd, Croydon, CR0 4YY

www.orionbooks.co.uk

'No need to act tough
It scares me just enough
Love gets dangerous'
BILLY BRAGG

'Racing is life. Anything that happens before or
after is just waiting'
STEVE MCQUEEN

Acknowledgements

Many people helped me in my attempts to bring *That Near-Death Thing* to life. Foremost among them were Conor Cummins and Guy Martin, two fascinating and contrasting characters. John McGuinness, Michael Dunlop and William Dunlop were also generous with their time. The supporting cast was long, but special thanks go to Bridget Dobbs, Milky Quayle, Michael Clague, Marcus de Matas, Carole Cummins, Philip Neill, Cath Davis, Steve Christian and Stephen Davison, the last of those both for his excellent pictures and for the tour of Armoy. Most of all I am indebted to Simon Crellin for his help, ideas, enthusiasm and contacts.

I am grateful to Guy for giving me permission to use his blogs and to the archives of various newspapers, magazines and broadcasters, especially *Motorcycle News*, the *Belfast Telegraph*, Manx Radio and ITV4.

David Luxton, my agent, did his job with his usual calm, while Ian Preece at Orion was a creative editor. I also think Richard Norgate's cover is great and totally in keeping with the feel of the book. Tim Hallissey at *The Times* also deserves mention for having the foresight and imagination to let his writers cover events in the leftfield. Thanks also to Billy Bragg for giving his permission for me to use the quotation from his song 'Love Gets Dangerous'.

Writing a book is always a labour of love, requiring gas and air and much screaming, so special thanks to Debs, Erin and Sam. And Sam, I promise we will go fishing soon.

PART ONE
WAITING

Prologue

Broken Men

(spring 2011)

The broken man pushes a leftover calzone around a plate in Paparazzi and falls off the Verandah. Blacked-out memories and a green-stained cat's eye, a dark rubber scar and a drystone wall. This was the path of his descent, retold by others and borne witness by the five broken vertebrae and ten-inch rods in his back. 'It was when I had to sign the consent forms that it made me think,' he says. 'They said these are the risks. I thought, "Brace yourself". The surgeon said, "There is a risk of paralysis, there is a risk of blindness and there is a risk of mortality".' He smiles. 'I thought, "For crying out loud".'

He drives a fork through the maw of mince and tomato. There is a faraway cadence to his words. Thick black eyebrows sit on a wrinkled brow. Even now, after all this time, you can feel the frustration and the depression oozing out of him as meat through burnt dough. The waiter asks how he is and he drags up a smile. He sips his orange juice. Could have been worse, he convinces himself, but he is the broken man when once he was the leader. Out there in front, on the wall-lined lanes, snaking a 200mph path between jagged edges and downy valleys.

His phone rings and jumps around the table like an upturned insect. He excuses himself and picks up. He puts one finger in an ear and listens with the other. I talk to the waiter and we are both drifting. Back up the stairs, along the Douglas seafront, past the flaking paintwork, rising above the tumbleweed town and its sprawling cemetery, up the Mountain, to the dark rubber scar and drystone wall. We are standing at the Verandah and, once again, we are watching Conor Cummins fall and bounce and break. He puts the phone down and the smile is bigger. 'That was my surgeon,' he says. He goes back to his calzone. 'I'm off to Spain.'

Guy Martin is sitting in an old blacksmith's cottage in Lincolnshire, a bespoke, half-built motorcycle shrinking the room, Pulp Fiction stills on the wall. 'The buzz from that was just unbeatable,' he says. 'That moment between crashing and almost dying. That's raised the benchmark. I want to get back to that point. Money can't buy it.' He pauses. 'Who's that?' he says and points to an iPod docking station. I tell him it's Nirvana. 'Good lad,' he says in a scattergun accent flecked with clipped vowels and lilting optimism. 'Fucking great band. Shame about the singer.'

His legs are still splattered with mud from an evening's mountain biking. Well-thumbed copies of a steam engine magazine nestle alongside an atlas where he has been plotting his route across Cuba. 'Communism,' he muses. 'There's a time and a place for it. Castro's way. That whole Karl Marx thing. Fascinating. I always thought he was the man who put it into practice but he was the ideologist. Now

Lenin, he took the ideology and turned it into communism. So I want to go to Cuba.' His thoughts attack his sentences, truncating them and sending his monologues off in other directions, over verbal Mountains and Verandahs. 'I won't stay in Havana. Did you know my dad named me after Guy Gibson, the Dam Buster pilot? Hey, people call us heroes and that. Oh fuck off. No one's a hero. Well, them boys were. I ain't clever. My brother is clever. Oh, I love this song. What's this, then?'

It is almost 11 p.m. and Martin is buzzing. He talks of his detractors and his BBC television show which is about to launch. He says he only did it because of the silly-money offer, but would rather just be at home with his spanners. 'Mind you, we're all one spanner short of a full set, aren't we? Not mad, really, but different. Everything's been so sanitised with bloody PC nonsense and health and safety that there's nothing else, is there? If it was dead safe I wouldn't do it. And I do get off on the pain. I look back on my crash and, yeah, it did hurt. I had to dig my teeth out of my nose. My chest was caving in and they put this drain in, threaded it through so you could feel it moving around your innards. Hey, hey. That's life. Can't wait to go back.'

In the foyer of The Claremont Hotel, covered in dustsheets as the workmen whitewash walls, a bulky figure is hopping from foot to foot. He has the most famous name on the island – Dunlop, part man, part myth. 'Hate flying,' he says as he gets over the trauma of having taken a tiny propeller plane from Northern Ireland. 'Terrifies me.'

It is three years since Michael Dunlop got back on the bike in the immediate aftermath of a horrendous family tragedy. How he did it cuts to his core. Eight years before that his uncle Joey won a hat-trick of races at the Isle of Man TT. He was 48 and fans, already in thrall to his legend, drank Douglas Bay dry. The next month he crashed into road-side trees during a race in Tallinn, Estonia, and died.

He is bullish and blunt. 'He's got a fuck-you attitude' someone says. 'He's got this rage against the world.' Dunlop is scared of flying but he likes fear so much that some of the other riders think he is a liability in a sport that is an accident waiting to happen. 'It's the danger aspect,' he says. 'It's the trees and brick walls. You have to find the edge of your barrier line and that's the hardest thing you'll ever do in your life. To find it at Handley's with two brick walls flying at you is madness. It's a thin line. A pencil line. If you go over, then it could be over.'

It is a baking hot day and two grey seals poke their heads out of the swirling tide around the Calf of Man. Two riders are chatting. One is John McGuinness, a man approaching middle age at pace; the other is Ian Hutchinson, a prodigy whom the old stager has helped to the summit. Now the prodigy needs help again. He hobbles to the very tip of the island and looks out towards the haven of the nature reserve. He sits down carefully and holds his leg, as he has done so often in the past six months, and shields his eyes. 'I don't feel guilt,' he says. The voice is soft Yorkshire, almost effeminate. 'My parents never wanted me to do this, but what else was there?' He points to a large gull, waddling towards us. 'Careful.' He flicks a hand and the bird flies off. Then he shows me his cage, rolling up the baggy black trouser covering his left leg and revealing the metal scaffolding holding him together. 'I suppose this was my mother's worst night-mare. They were in Spain when it happened. I guess that was a difficult call to take.'

He looks and sounds fragile, but it is less than a year since Ian Hutchinson was the king of the Mountain. He had everything that they all dreamed of and more, even more than McGuinness. A decade after browbeating his parents into reluctant acceptance, new history was inked. While others shared a hospital ward and wondered if they would ride or walk again, Hutchinson went out on the town. He ended the night in Colours nightclub. 'I got pissed,' he admits. 'Well, you've got to, haven't you?'

Then, two weeks after being invincible, a rival ran over his leg after his bike had deposited him in the centre of another, safer race track. 'The pain was so intense I could barely feel it,' he almost whispers. They wanted to amputate his leg, but Hutchinson told them he was a racer and he needed it. 'I wasn't bothered about walking or anything, but I needed to get back on the bike. Nothing else mattered.' Hutchinson rolls down his trouser leg and hides his frailty. It is a matter of weeks until the first race and it looks impossible. I wonder how any of them will do it. Conor, Guy, Michael, John and Hutchy. Could they really put the pieces back together? It was a hell of a puzzle, but the solving of it would be mesmerising.

REWIND

Ten months earlier

First Race TT 2010, 5 June
Superbike

'I'd describe it as being strapped to an Exocet missile,' says Milky Quayle. As ever he is bubbling, a natural raconteur with Milky Bar Kid lenses and freckles that mean only his partner ever calls him Richard. He won at the TT course, back in 2002, the first Manxman to do so for decades, and now he takes newcomers around the circuit, explaining its traps and treasures. His crash in 2003 means he knows both sides. Now it is my turn and so we are off in his car, pretending it is a bike. It is an exhilirating ride.

He explains: 'It's so rapidly fast and just wants to spit you off everywhere. Obviously, there are a lot more rider aids now, but it's just like being on the back of a missile that wants to rip you off, which is why you have to be so fit and strong. The mindset is different to the short circuit lads because there's often only you racing around here. It's like your own personal race track. It just happens to be the best one in the world and you have it all to yourself. Amazing. You have to really concentrate. I would always be looking for the person in front of me, for the sight of leathers or a helmet or the back of a bike. That's why nobody wants to go first, because they are all chasing you. I was No 4 when I won. Happy days.'

Quayle starts the car and we are off.

Okay, this is the start. Bray Hill. You're clicking sixth gear and you want to run your elbow on this hedge here. That straightens the course. One lad, a back marker, cut his leathers open here because he took too much of the hedge. We had to go down and trim it a bit more. I said, 'If you can't see that hedge there's something wrong with you'. At the top of Bray Hill is St Ninian's Crossroads. See where that Scenic is? There's a little crest so give the handlebars a tug otherwise they tend to flutter.

Now this palm tree on the right and that tree in the distance are your focal points. You know the kerb sticks out a bit, so that gives you a good point of entry into the top of Bray Hill. Don't come over to the left too early because these road junctions unsettle the bike. Now come over, but not too far because there's a jump. I line myself up at these yellow lines, look to the right, lean over and then pick the bike up at the very last minute. Push the tank, pulling three or four Gs through here. Knocks the wind out of you. You come up over Ago's Leap, playing with the throttle, sixth gear, land a wheelie, nice and you're off to the next one.

There is no warm-up here. Suspension is hard. The whole bike feels loose and horrible. You're riding the storm. Now you come to Quarter Bridge, where Barry Sheene fell off. There's a big house with a gable end and that's your braking point. Down one gear to fifth, use your chest as a brake, get your head out of the bubble.

Now this next section, Braddan Bridge, is another one. Almost a mile and a half into the circuit now and this is the first left-hand bend. Crazy, isn't it? Have to be gentle here. If you're too aggressive it washes the front out and you're straight into the hedge. Now go hard on the gas and run out of Braddan Bridge. Watch this wall. I don't think I've ever met anyone who has hit it, but you have to be careful. Now off to Union Mills and at this point, two miles into the 37 and three-quarters, my race has not even started ...

The scouts are getting ready. The enormous scoreboard that runs alongside the finishing straight is a work of art. Each rider has a clock next to his number. G stands for Glen Helen, R for Ramsey and B for Bungalow. When the arrow turns to a letter the rider has passed that checkpoint. Lap times are painted on bits of wood. They are passed through holes in the scoreboard and placed in the right position.

Lights are switched on when a rider is approaching the Grandstand. It is a triumph of old-fashioned teamwork, the scouts toiling away between the black screen and the cemetery wall.

There will be five races on different size, and spec, of bike. The top riders enter all the races. They have been practising for a week now, in evening sessions on closed roads. They are tense and quiet.

Michael Dunlop boils the kettle in his motorhome. The first race is coming and he seems bothered. There is no doubt he is fast, but there are issues festering through his mind. He is tired too, because he has been tinkering with his bike into the wee small hours. The patches on his leathers tell the story – Team Hardship, Street Sweep. He is in the big paddock, but there are no fancy awnings here. 'You know you see the smile on the newcomer boys' faces and that's how it used to be for me too,' he says wearily. 'Pure fun

13

of it. The trouble is now if I don't win then I don't enjoy the TT.'

That is the price of success. The previous year, 2009, Dunlop won the second Supersport race on his privately entered 600cc Yamaha. It was his spare bike. He was on the way up and was an ebullient figure afterwards. 'The Dunlops are back on the road again,' he shouted. 'I know my dad and Joey were with me all the way round.'

A year on and reality had bitten. Money was still tight and the competition was being ratcheted up. 'It's hard when you know you can win one. I can't go and relax anymore. First year here, you do the whole learning thing. It's really exciting. But when that's gone, if you don't get results then you're screwed. I enjoy practice now more than anything. You can do your own thing then. It's like the old days. But when it comes to the race and you see P5 on your board you think, "Fuck me, what am I doing?" You start to get annoyed with yourself.'

He is annoyed with his brother, William too, just a few yards away from him, over a dirt path, in his own tent. The riders flit in and out of these tented flaps like soldiers on a medieval battlefield. I know how close the brothers are, but Michael openly talks of a rift. 'It got to the stage where certain people tried to drive us apart and he's fallen into that trap,' he says. 'So I've decided to go my own way. He walked into a big trap and that sort of screwed me. Sometimes you have to sit down and realise what family is, but in this life you're for one man or you're for no man. He goes his way and I go mine.' I ask someone close to them what is going on and I am told: 'You know what they're like – he'd fight anyone if they said anything bad against William, but it's different for him.'

Guy Martin is here in his retro black leathers. He is all smiles and wearing the expression of someone who might be preparing to drive a combine harvester in Kirmington. I suspect Dunlop wishes he could affect the same air of nonchalance that Martin managed after the previous year's TT. Then he blogged: 'Straight off the ferry on Saturday morn I thought, "Where to now? Farm, mow grass, chill out or work on trucks? I know, I'll work on trucks". So straight down to the wagon yard, but my dad works like a good 'un and had got everything finished, so that was it. I ended up in the Polish truck drivers' caravan with Chris the transport manager, drinking home-made vodka and eating Polish sausage. Not a mention of motorbikes, just plenty of slurping, piss-taking and garlic dip.' His conclusion to the 2009 TT? 'Milk always in first.'

Conor Cummins is dressed in purple and green, a smile lifting his face as a camera invades his space. 'Go on Conor, son,' someone shouts. His mother just thinks it. 'I will give anyone the time of day,' he says. 'I'll give my rivals a nod, but the closer you get to the start the less there is of that and rightly so. It's a competitive environment. Some riders say stuff, but I don't succumb to any of that rubbish. It's not me. I do it on the track. That's where it should be done.'

John McGuinness walks past the pram where his baby daughter Maisie is sleeping and makes his way to the grid. Nobody knows this course quite like him. 'Which bit's my favourite? Start line to start line. I like it all really.' He pauses. 'Well, I don't like May Hill. Whitegates. I don't like Tower Bends. I *hate* Tower Bends. I'm not that keen on Laurel Bank. It's not that I don't like it; it's just I go through at the same pace as everyone else. It's all happening that fast that you don't have a favourite place. It's all happening subconsciously. It's bang, bang, bang, gear change, gear change. You don't think, "Ooh, I'm looking forward to the Ballacrye jump when you're coming out of the Cronky straight." Practice week is hard work. Tense and nervous. You get a bit of forearm pump, legs are hurting a bit on the steering pegs. By the end you've had enough, but even if it carried on you would find auxilliary batteries from somewhere. You can't afford to take your eye off the ball for one second. Not until you've crossed the line in the last race.'

The first race of the 2010 TT, short for Tourist Trophy, starts with the riders strapped to the backs of Exocet misiles on the top of Bray Hill. They line up one by one and are waved off down the hill, across St Ninian's Crossroads, where the Scenic had been earlier, and as they go over the little crest, they give the handlebars a tug to stop the bike from fluttering. Bruce Anstey, the veteran Kiwi, is the first man away with a target on his back. McGuinness follows him. One by one they are counted out and onto the course, taking in towns and churches and pubs and Mountain, climbing almost 1,400 feet to the top of Snaefell and negotiating 264 bends, while avoiding the telegraph poles and walls and the memories of more than 230 people killed on this unique sporting route.

McGuinness wastes little time in getting past Anstey, but then his bike slows to a halt, the victim of mechanical trouble. A year's wait has got off to the most frustrating start. Martin is a flash of black and silver on his Honda, liveried in uber-cool Sixties' chic, but he has Michael Dunlop wobbling behind him, threatening to take both men down. 'I watched him last night and he was flat out in the holding area,' Milky Quayle says of Dunlop from his perch in the commentary box. Towards the end of the first lap Cameron Donald misses a corner. He carries on through the barriers, but then finds the slip road closed. With no option he arcs his bike back to the true track, but has to wait for Martin, Dunlop and Cummins to pass through. 'I thought I could get through but the barriers were shut,' Donald said afterwards. 'Then I thought I'd play it safe and let them go.'

It is Cummins who soon takes the race by the scruff of the neck. Although close on the roads, the actual time, taking into account the staggered starts, means he is in a class of his own. The lead is 8.03 seconds. He laps the course at 131.5mph. The pubs echo with excitement in Ramsey.

The riders come in for their first pit stops. Cummins throws back his head and gulps from a red and yellow bottle. Keith Amor changes his helmet. Bikes are refuelled. Encouragement given. There is still mist on parts of the course, but Cummins' lead grows. After four of the six laps he is 21.77 seconds clear. Carole, his mother, sits on the wall by the shed in the paddock and tries to contain her optimism. So does Billy, his father, out on the course, unseen and innocuous. And then, as it so often does at the TT, it goes wrong. Cummins struggles to get the bike fired up, crawls away from his second pit stop and, in a matter of seconds, an hour's hard work is ruined. Soon afterwards, with reality biting, he breaks down for good at Laurel Bank. This is the TT, its variations, rugged roads and 264 corners taking a huge toll on fragile machinery. In Cummins' absence the stage is left for Ian Hutchinson to claim the first race of the 2010 TT festival.

One

John

A couple of silhouettes are digging in the mudflats of Morecambe Bay, where the sand turns from brown to milky beige. It is a picture of bliss, a sun-bleached morning in a northern town, a fish and chip shop bustling into life for lunchtime, the statue of Eric Bartholomew on guard with bronzed binoculars around his neck. The comedian was a keen ornithologist and liked to look out over the cockle beds to spot waders and oystercatchers.

The Bay has a dark side, though, out there covered by the whitening tide. In February 2004 a group of Chinese workers were collecting cockles on the sand flats near Hest Bank. They would get £5 for every 25 kilograms they bagged. It was 9.30 p.m. when the tide returned, silent and fast. The workers, all illegal immigrants, were cut off. They panicked. Most tried to swim for their lives, but the water was iced and unforgiving. Four climbed onto their truck, but it was engulfed by the sea. The cries went unheard, the other pickers having long since departed, tapping an unheaded warning on their watches as they went.

A total of 23 people were killed that night. Most died of hypothermia, some from drowning. The gang-master got 14 years for manslaughter. Six years later a human skull was found near Silverdale Point. It belonged to the last of the Chinese cockle-pickers, a 37-year-old woman named Liu Qin Ying, whose husband also died in the disaster, leaving their son an orphan at home in China.

That was the last time that Morecambe was big news. It is a sleepy town of grey pebbledash and old glory. But a short walk from the Bay is a house on a corner, where a huge motorhome is squeezed into the drive, and where a man in the kitchen picks up the phone.

'Hello, mother. How are you doing? Yes, him with all the dosh. If it's a weekend it's probably a write-off. Town clerk's been on the phone and wants to give me some award. I don't know. I don't know what he's planning. All they want is to be giving me six months free council tax. That would be better than some bleeding brass cup or tankard or summat. Right mother, I'll have to go. I'm busy with some other chap. Alright. See you. Bye bye.'

I am sitting at the table with John McGuinness. He is

slightly overweight for a sports star, with jagged, stained teeth and receding, unstyled hair. He's the local hero who never left. He is still rooted in Morecambe, its tics and tones inflecting his language, his affection in the old place seeping from him. He is pragmatic enough to say 'I don't know what pragmatic means' and will never move. There is a black racing motorbike in the hallway – 'I love that bike.' He is building a trophy cabinet in the downstairs room – 'Feel that. The trophies are getting lighter. Not the same quality.' The garage is a museum of motorcycling; there is a bit of Joey Dunlop's bike, an old Triumph, a raft of helmets from all his successes – 'See the scuff marks on that one, that's where I fell off at Daytona.'

His talent has taken him all around the world, but he is synonymous with the Tourist Trophy. He is the world's best at taming those treacherous country roads; at everything from riding down Bray Hill and seemingly off the edge of the world to surviving the swirling gales of Windy Corner; from asking departed friends for help in Crosby to emerging from blood-soaked bird strikes on the Mountain. As he sits in his neat kitchen, looking at his privet hedge while sausage rolls bake in the oven, it is hard to imagine that he has made it through, flirting with disaster in the last great race.

The TT is a twisted mongrel of an event and is loved and reviled in equal measure. It splits opinion, divides families and wrecks lives. Hundreds have been lost since that first race in 1907, when the riders got acid burns due to chemicals sprayed on the road to combat the dust. Most of the casualties have been riders, but some were marshals and others spectators. For years the fatal attraction has been a difficult subject, hushed away by the organisers as the anti-

TT brigade grew more militant in its banning calls. I wanted to know what drove these people to ride the TT. What made them tick? Why did they keep returning to an island that had seen so much heartache as well as fleeting glory? And of all the top riders to have seen the dark underbelly, none of the current crop has merged reality and immortality quite like McGuinness.

The legend was made on the Isle of Man, but the man comes from Morecambe and that is where his story starts. 'I lived on Granville Road down the other end of Morecambe,' he says. 'My dad had a bike shop two miles away on the White Lund industrial estate. It was just a lock-up, not a dealership. That was how it was. In the early Seventies bikes were everywhere, weren't they? Lambrettas and Vespas, bits and pieces. I lived with my nana for a lot of years when I was younger. I was close to my dad, but my mum and dad split up, as they do, and the stepmother came in, and, well, you don't take orders from your stepmother. I was 13. I wasn't rebelling. It's just something you blank out. It happens every day, everywhere and so you just get on with life, but when it came to the divorce settlement the kids had to get something and I got my Kawasaki KL. That was when I was 17. That was when I started my career.'

The need to earn a living was drilled into McGuinness by his father, John senior. So he got a paper round and he worked nights in a butcher's to make enough money to buy a crash helmet. Already, the bug had bitten and unleashed a nascent passion. It had started when he was only three and his dad bought him an Italjet mini-bike. 'He put the stabilisers on and made me some little jumps, but I soon had the stabilisers off. I thought I was Evel Knievel. He was my hero. I had the stars and stripes uniform and did jumps. Here, hang on a minute.'

He wanders off and the rest of the house suddenly buzzes with life. There is Becky, McGuinness' childhood sweet-heart-turned-partner, and Maisie, who he says is 'high-maintenance, but in a good way, not screaming, but into everything'. There are plenty of knocks on the door and his mobile phone is rarely quiet. He flicks me a laminated newspaper cutting and answers the phone. 'It's an Isle of Man number,' he says, which clearly gives it precedence.

'Hello. It is. Yeah. How you doing? Yeah, I read it on the internet. Some chap wants to put me forward for an MBE. Well, for what other people have got MBEs for I should get ten. Only joking. Aye, well I've not flitted about the country. I'm Morecambe born and bred and am pretty proud of the old place. If I got the MBE it would be the icing on the cake, but I'm an MBE anyway – I'm a motorbike expert.'

The clipping from the *Daily Mirror*, 1973, shows McGuinness in his dark Evel Knievel garb. He is jumping toy buses. The tabloid wonders whether one day the infant McGuinness might emulate his hero. The adult is not so easily seduced by sentiment. He puts the phone down. 'He was an evil old bastard,' he says of his former idol. 'Snake Canyon was a joke, but it was all over for him when he battered his manager. They say you shouldn't meet your heroes and sometimes they're right because they can be total arseholes.'

With both his parents working, the boy McGuinness would accompany his father to White Lund and roam around the estate on his Italjet. 'Nobody cared back then. Do it now and there would be police helicopters out, but it was just, "Oh, there's John on his bike".' On one occasion he went too far, tearing off along Stanley Road before being frog-marched home by the local police.

Becky says he was naughty at school. 'I was just the gobs-hite in the corner. I never shut up. People say they are the best years of your life and you should remember them, but I don't. Just odd bits and pieces. I remember my English teacher saying I was a waste of time. I remember whenever there was a project I would take in my bike and talk about my 125cc Suzuki. I remember not being very physical and so I did not do rugby or cricket or anything like that. I had a bit of asthma and so I would always be on the sidelines, talking with the other dickheads who didn't want to do it.'

His younger brother, Andrew, was the rebel. 'He was the one who had to be put on a rein,' McGuinness says. 'He would stick his hand in the lion's cage while I would be standing back. Whatever he was not meant to touch, Andrew would have his hands on it. He's still much the same now. On his first day at school he said, "I don't like this", and that was it. He went off the rails, but he's still my brother and if I ever needed anything then he would be there. He lives local. I've also got a stepbrother and a step-sister. The brother is in the RAF. It's funny because while I'm flying around the TT course, he's flown two trips to Afghanistan.'

John left school at 16 and wanted to be a mechanic, only for his father to put him straight on that one. 'Forget that, it's a mug's game,' he said to his son. McGuinness senior had worked on the gas rigs and knew how hard it was out on the sea, in the black and cold of anonymous nights. 'Get your-self into the building trade,' he said.

So he did. He signed up to a course at Morecambe and Lancs College. 'I was 16 but I spent most of my time messing around on my AP 50 which I'd bought for 90 quid with money from my paper round. I kept it in my nana's shed. I bought a single seat for it, painted it with an aerosol can. It was my only pride and joy. I spent hundreds of hours tinkering with it. Then I went around one day and someone had burnt down the shed. I couldn't believe it. I mean my nana was frail and it was one of those old council houses where the shed is connected to the house. It was out of order, but they never pursued it and we never got to the bottom of it. My nana was alright but it was a frightener. Fire gets rid of a lot of things. The bike was burnt to a cinder. Gone.'

He got on with his course after that. 'I served my time and did three years. It was okay. You meet different people. My granddad said you had to work to get in the system and so I did. We called it ET for Extra Tenner off your dole. Finally, I got my trade and my credentials. I thought now I'm going to get going and will be making £500 a week, but it was the end of Thatcher and the country was on its ringpiece. And that's when I started mussel-picking.'

So two decades before the tragedy that would see Morecambe emblazoned across the papers, McGuinness began working the mudflats too. 'We'd chip them out of the beds and rake them out of the sand. There's a technique to it. Then you put them in a riddle and tread them in there a bit. There are pools everywhere so you have to wash them. It's hard work. Becky's dad is a fisherman. He makes a living shrimping and bits and pieces. He has not got a right lot, but he's a great old boy. He had a consortium with a few others back then and they'd take the big boat out. We had a big 1968 Nuffield tractor too and used to work away. I was getting six quid a bag and would do eight bags a day. I'd been working my balls off for 50 quid a week with the trowels and all of a sudden I've got 400 sheets coming in and I'm thinking I've hit the jackpot.'

The tide can turn in every way. One day McGuinness was out on the flats with Becky. He was already well-versed in the whims of the sea, but for some reason, on that occasion, he chanced his arm too much. 'Mussel-picking is very dangerous, but not if you know what you are doing and don't get greedy,' he says. This time he did. 'The tide comes in twice a day and it depends on weather, wind and height. If it's a 10.5-metre tide you've got twice as much water, so it comes in with much more force. You have to keep ahead of it. Sometimes you might think, "Why am I going now?" because everything looks fine. But just go; it's not worth it.'

The water came in fast that night. It started to circle around them. McGuinness picked up Becky and carried her through the swirling current. She insists it was fear of what her father would say that prompted the rescue. Cold and scared they made it to safety, but it had been a cautionary lesson about risk and reward, and for a man who would come to live on the edge, it was a valuable one. 'Five minutes can make all the difference,' McGuinness says as he drifts back to the near-misses of far-off days. 'You have to know when to go and the way to go. It looks peaceful and tranquil, but matey boy can be walking along with the kids and they're gone. Tides. Quicksand. The Chinese would have been okay if they had survival suits. If they could have floated in they would have been fine, but it was the cold that killed them.'

Misfortune seemed to follow McGuinness in those formative years. The recession had put paid to one livelihood and now his second career foundered. 'There was some rare, microscopic worm in the beds and so they shut them down.' He shakes his head. 'So what if it put 50 lads out of work, as long as the worm was alright.' Becky is just as incredulous. 'My dad did it for a living and they did *that*.' They clearly share their pragmatism. 'It's like enduro riding now,' McGuinness mocks. 'People don't want you to do this because the world's only for us miserable bastards who walk around with a stick.'

His neighbour is another whose world view he struggles to comprehend. 'I feel sorry for her. She lives in an enormous house. I built a garage for my bikes and she protested and said it devalued her house by ten grand. Meanwhile, her garden is completely overgrown. There's been a cardboard box with eight plastic bottles in the window from the day she moved in. People take a double take when they walk past and ask if anyone lives there. I say, "They do actually". And she says I'm devaluing her house. It's a sorry way to live. I'd rather be dead. She might as well be gone to where you go. She's wasting good oxygen for other people. It's a pointless way to live. She never enjoys herself. She never smiles.'

He knows this sounds harsh but I would come to realise that TT racers struggle to accept those who waste their allotted time. 'Sometimes I feel responsible, but people have motorbikes and kids and lives. It's funny. I have the freedom of Morecambe and Lancaster and I can drive my sheep over Skerton Bridge and graze them anywhere, but I can't put a drive in my own garden without a problem.' He sighs. 'There used to be a bit more power that came with the freedom; when they were chopping the heads off people you used to be on the committee.'

We go back to old Morecambe and his life after the beds were closed. McGuinness went back to his trowels. He worked with Mick Stainton, a man who would go on and win a raft of awards and build Wayne Rooney's mansion.

McGuinness hated the work but liked the dedication. One of the first jobs they did together was converting a garage front to a house. Stainton looked at McGuinness' work, stormed over and kicked down his first wall. 'That's fucking crap,' he roared. 'Somebody's got to look at that for the rest of their life so take a bit longer and do it right.' 'I respected him for that,' says McGuinness. 'There was no argument, because he was right. It was an honest job. I took a lot of pride in some of the work we did after that, but I hated it. I was always thinking and scheming because I didn't want to be there. I wanted to be racing.'

For McGuinness, motorbikes had become an escape from daily drudgery. He built walls by day and broke them down at night. Motorbikes offered both the exotic and excitement. The pain of his burnt bike had hurt like a bereavement. He was being sucked in. His father raced for fun and they travelled to local venues such as Aintree and Oulton Park, but he was really hooked, line and sinker, when he went to the Isle of Man in 1982.

For McGuinness, it was like gate-crashing a private club. Most boys were into footballers or pop stars, but he stepped off the ferry in Douglas Bay and was smitten. For the first time McGuinness saw the jaded windows of the Victorian B&Bs that skirted the promenade, the imposing Douglas Head, the Tower of Refuge, built in the 19th century after a number of shipwrecks and stocked thereafter with bread and water to aid the stranded, and above all, the beginnings of the black-green Mountain. His father was racing at Jurby, an old RAF airfield converted to a race track on the northern edge of the island. 'I watched him race at Jurby and it was like a sledgehammer,' he says. 'It was the noise, the smell, the bumps, the whole thing just sparked off something in me.

It was the year Ron Haslam won the Formula One race.'

Haslam was between tragedies. A blunt, affable figure muffled by sideboard sideburns, his brother Phil had been killed racing at Scarborough eight years earlier. He was clipped by a rider, struck a metal bridge and was thrown into the path of a friend called Steve Machin. Two weeks after that Machin, himself, was killed racing. Ron carried on the family tradition, but two years after that race in 1982, when he was watched by the young McGuinness, another of his brothers died in a sidecar crash at Assen. 'I jumped over the fence and ran to where I could see the marshals gathering,' Haslam would tell me. 'I got there at the same time that the ambulance arrived. I could see "Babe" and rushed up to him, but turned away instantly. I knew straight away. It was an accident that just happened. Another one. Fate.' Hindsight is cruel and as Haslam stood on the podium that day in 1982, who could know the misery that lay ahead? It was the same for all racers, their dreams and lives resting upon feckless fate.

The annual pilgrimage to the Isle of Man became the focal point of McGuinness' year. He counted down the weeks until it was time to take the ferry with his father. The trouble was the Jurby races would finish midway through practice week for the TT. It meant he missed the actual TT races, which see riders compete over the same circuit with different sized bikes, a format that is largely the same today with the riders taking part in five races.

'We'd maybe get two days of the TT in and then we'd go home and I'd be kicking and screaming,' McGuinness recalls. So he started going on his own instead, skiving off school and travelling over on his BMX Fireblade freestyler. 'They used to let you on the ferries to buy a programme and then walk off. I'd stay on. I'd get to the Isle of Man and pedal round like mad on my pushbike. It was different then. There was no health and safety. Kids didn't get kidnapped. I'd sneak back alongside the blind side of a van while they were taking the tickets, and get home that way. I was mesmerised.'

At home he erected a mini shrine to Joey Dunlop. The Ballymoney rider would become the greatest star of the TT with a record 26 wins. He was shy and quiet, with a mop of greasy hair and an ever-present cigarette. In 1982 he had still only won two TT races, but McGuinness began to worship him, developing his shrine – 'it was a bit anal really' – and the infatuation grew in tandem with Dunlop's rise.

It is interesting to see a grown man and modern-day hero revert to his 'gobshite youth' before your eyes, but McGuinness loves the history of his trade. There is a vintage black-and-white photo of old bikers on his kitchen wall and a crate of cuttings on a shelf, and for a while he is the rookie biker again, standing at a corner called Bedstead, because they used to erect fences from old beds, watching the bright yellow helmet of Joey Dunlop race down the Mountain like a late-night comet.

By 1986 the Dunlop shrine covered most of McGuinness's bedroom wall. The Ulsterman had won a hat-trick of TT races the previous year and was the undisputed star turn. The pubs and clubs throbbed to his feats. McGuinness cycled to Bedstead once more. 'There were no houses there then. It was just fields. The view was great.'

The Formula One race was postponed for two days due to the weather and was eventually reduced to four laps (150 miles). To McGuinness' delight, his hero won. Maybe that surge of enthusiasm was why the quiet teenager decided to go down Bray Hill, the steep road leading away from the start and into the cauldron, and find Dunlop's small garage at the bottom. 'I went down there and went up to him. I got my picture signed. I was not a confident boy and so I don't really know what made me do it, but I looked up at him and said, "I'll stand on the podium with you one day". He was not a man of many words but he looked back at me for a bit and then gave a bit of a grunt.'

The selective editing of the TT rider means McGuinness can happily drift over the mussel beds of Morecambe to the muscle-bound machismo of Douglas Bay, 1986. The romance forged in youth is rekindled by the broken bed frames. And so he stays there and sees the yellow helmet and does not remember one of the most calamitous trage-dies in the TT's history.

That happened when the rescue helicopter neared Bal-laugh Bridge to airlift a rider who had just crashed. The nose of the spinning blades spooked a horse which leapt a fence and bolted down the middle of the TT course. Gene McDonnell was the unlucky Irishman who happened to be in the wrong place at the wrong time. He ploughed into the horse at around 160mph, slewed into a garage forecourt and disappeared in a fireball. By the time the TT had ended, four racers would have been killed. But still the racing went on, inviting allegations, of callousness and inhumanity, but inspiring unforgettable images in the head of a Morecambe teenager.

He pursued his sport after that trip. 'Me and Becky would go racing. Beg, borrow and steal. I had no tax, no insurance and no MOT. We did what we could. Part-worn tyres, part-worn pistons, absolutely on the balls of your arse.'

Becky looks over at Maisie as she clouts her dad with a

pink balloon. She shakes her head. 'Maisie, you're absolutely off your trolley.'

McGuinness is thinking about his own parents now because an ursine figure is coming up the drive. 'You know what my mother says to me before every TT?' He is smiling with a degree of incredulity. 'She says, "Don't go too fast ... and make sure you win." Thanks mum. She's clever, though, my mum, not like me. She works for a chemical factory. I missed my chemistry exam at school in 1988 because I was at the TT and thought I'd rather stay and watch the 600 race. I said, "I'm not going home". I thought I'd probably learn more from watching that race. And I probably did.'

John senior has a rough, deep voice doused in experi-ence. It is a lived-in voice. I tell him I want to know what makes his son tick and he says he does too. They have been a team for a long time and I can only imagine what it is like as a father to see your son ride at 200mph next to stone walls. They quickly start to reminisce. McGuinness senior loved the golden era, when Mike Hailwood would be chauf-feured to races in his father's Bentley. Hailwood was an Everyman; rich and well-educated at Pangbourne Naval College, but ready to rough it in any race or paddock. He dallied in the world of cars and raced in Formula One for a while, almost killing himself but getting the George Medal for pulling another driver, Clay Regazzoni, out of a flaming car. Mike the Bike was the greatest, right up until Giacomo Agostini came along with his film star looks and that Italian charisma which seduced women all over the world.

'He tried to drill mother, didn't he?' McGuinness junior says.

'It would have been 1969,' his father replies without missing a beat and providing further proof that TT men are different. 'It was the era of miniskirts. We were walking down the prom in Douglas when I hear this rumble and a yellow Lamborghini soft top pulls up. Birds in the back. Ago's driving and he looks over at us and shouts, "You want to come to party". I can't believe it and say something like, "Who, me?" He says, "No, not you. The girl".'

'You should have buggered off,' his son tells him. 'I'd have been better looking and I'd have been the world champion.'

'Aye, you'd have had jet black hair.'

'I'd have been alright – I'd have looked like a smoothy.'

Both agree that the man they would have most liked to meet would have been Hailwood. He famously dragged himself from retirement and a ten-year exile to win the TT in 1978. It was the mother of all comebacks. McGuinness senior then repeats the line he has obviously shared with his son. 'Sometimes it's best not to meet your heroes because they turn out to be tossers, but Hailwood always gave people the time of day. Not like Phil Read. Yeah, Hailwood – amazing really, how it ended for him.'

He is drifting but he has a point. Having endured the most vicious era of motorcycling racing, when racers would tick off their crashes because they reasoned everyone had three a year and that six riders would be killed, and having won the George Cross for bravery, Hailwood was killed in 1981 when he was hit by a lorry while collecting fish and chips.

Father and son talk about other old riders. 'Stan Woods. Married two women didn't he? Married a French bird. And then blew the lot. Died a miserable old man. Ernst Degner. Died in very strange circumstances. He took the MZ plans to Suzuki. They say he topped himself, but people reckon he got his throat cut. The old secret service gave him a portion. Santiago Herrero. Got killed at the TT. That's why no

Spanish rider can do the TT. They won't allow it. The Spanish have to do it on a Portuguese licence.'

They even talk about the 1936 George Formby film, *No Limit*, in which the hero plays the ukulele and wins the TT. 'My old man knows that film word for word,' McGuinness junior says. 'Look at that – 1936 and what's changed? You get your own bike, build it in your shed, you write a letter to the factory, they rubbish you, you go to the Isle of Man, you meet a tart, you ride round in practice, you go fast, you win. I mean what's changed?'

'Not a lot,' the old man concurs. 'Hey, there's a big write-up of Joey in *Motorcycle News*. Tux has done it.'

It is intriguing to hear these two bike men flit back and forth in time. Before long they are in John's early days, scrimping and saving and negotiating. 'I remember when we went to buy this TZ and we were told it came with all sorts of spares and parts and data. We went in and shook hands and asked where the spares were. They showed us three sprockets. I said to John, "We're going, mate". He said, "You what?" I said, "It's not what they promised". I could feel him saying, "What are you doing you daft sod?", but we were halfway out the door when they came running out and said, "Don't take any notice". We got loads of cranks, barrels, pistons and stuff. I've never seen John panic as much. He thought he'd lost his TZ.'

The relationship could be fractious. On another occasion they came to blows at a race at Donington Park. 'There was a steady build-up,' McGuinness senior says. 'He did a crank in qualifying and just scraped into the race. I said …

'Right let's get the engine out. Where's the spare crank?'

John shrugged.

'Didn't you load it?'

'No.'

Things escalated.

'I thought I was ready for a shot at the title,' McGuinness says when remembering how he took on his father. 'Big mistake. But I got my best result of the year the day after.'

His father leans over and looks at a book on the table. 'He was treating that throttle like he was ringing my fucking neck.'

John junior got friendly with some other rising stars such as David Jefferies, but it was always a struggle. 'DJ had his big Yankee motorhome and we were in a loaf of bread caravan,' McGuinness says. 'I looked at him and thought he had it all. But he could deliver the goods too. We got pally.'

McGuinness and Becky would travel to the circuits and race there, but it was racing on the open roads that really got the adrenaline pumping. So in 1994 they went to the North West 200, a race run on narrow roads in Northern Ireland and a traditional warm-up for the TT. 'I had 80 quid in my pocket and it got nicked. That was all I had to get home. I went to the organisers and they gave me the 80 quid. Imagine anyone doing that for you now, but road racing is a community. I've never forgotten that generosity.'

McGuinness raced at the TT for the first time in 1996. He was 15th in the lightweight class. The following year he made the podium in the lightweight race won by Joey Dunlop. The prediction he had made to Dunlop at the bottom of Bray Hill all those years ago rushed around his mind. 'I said, "Do you remember when I said I'd stand on the podium with you?" It did not register at all. I thought there might have been a little glimmer. It shows how big something can be for someone and yet it can be nothing to someone else. It was the same two years later when I won my first TT.

David Jefferies did the hat-trick that year, winning the senior to boot. I remembered me and him talking about the TT when we started out and him saying, 'Fuck that, I'm not doing that!' Now we were winners and I expected there to be a bolt of lightning or something. It felt like something else should happen. But I guess in the whole scheme of things, with what goes on in the world, it's a grain of sand. Look at all the other aggro in the world and it's just a bike race. Okay it's the most famous bike race in the world, but it's still a grain of sand.'

Now another decade has gone and McGuinness is the Dunlop of his age. He is the most successful TT rider on the planet, but the clock is ticking to the end of his career and the next TT when he will mow the lawn and check the finances. Just in case anything bad happens. He is pushing 40 and knows younger, hungrier men are clinging to his coat-tails. Can he still win? 'You never know.'

There is a cast list of usurpers who are like the 1999 McGuinness. Guy Martin, the people's favourite with his wolfish mien and eccentricities. 'If he ever wins then I think they'll erect a statue to him, but it's just not happening for him,' McGuinness says. Conor Cummins, the local hero from the Isle of Man, plotting his dreams across Morecambe Bay. 'A nice lad.' And there are the Dunlops, Michael and William, nephews of the great Joey. 'They are the coming force. When all the pieces of the jigsaw come together Michael's going to be fairly unbeatable. He's a bit wild and he tries to intimidate. He's got this don't care attitude. He's like, "I don't care if I go through a hedge", but I'll bet you everything I have that, deep inside, he does. You have to care about what's behind that hedge. But that's Michael. He looks a bit loose and dangerous, but people work in different ways.'

The nerves and hopes and fears are bubbling in a smelting pot. McGuinness tucks into a sausage roll and picks up the phone again. It is a friend with news of the flats he rents. McGuinness has one too, but it is bane and he struggles to understand the lack of respect shown by some tenants. 'Iron dropped on the carpet. Burnt a hole. No apology. Ferret shit on the wall. It's amazing how some people choose to live, isn't it?'

Now this flat-out jump is great, a lovely, smooth surface, gorgeous like a motorway. Only thing I have to watch out out for is I need to pull the bike really straight so it does not get too loose. Nice little wheelie, sixth gear, out of the bubble, down one gear, use chest as brake, just to get underneath this bank. Now downhill. It really sucks you in. Knee on the kerb but you can't get back on the gas too early. Guess why? Because there's a trap. There. Feel it? Spits you out of the seat. You have to be gentle with that and the depression by the Post Office.

Second Race TT 2010, 7 June
Supersport

*I*an Hutchinson is delighted with his victory in the Super-bike race, although as Jamie Whitham, the former racer who is covering the TT for ITV, pointed out: 'He's not one given to massive shows of emotion.' He gripes about having no grip at the start but speaks of the weight lifting from his shoulders when a four-second deficit turned into a 34-second advantage.

Michael Dunlop walks from the podium through a side door at the back of the press office and into the press conference room. The boards bearing sponsor names teeter behind him. Cameron Donald joins him. He has been elevated to third place after Guy Martin was handed a 30-second penalty for speeding in the pit lane. For the first time a limit of 60kph has been introduced. Martin had been a tenth of a kph too fast.

'The Ginger Hall section was madness,' Dunlop, the second place man, mutters, looking to the floor as is often his way when speaking. 'I didn't care but I think it was touch and go for some of the lads. There were a lot of slides out there, but that's the way I like it; it keeps the heart going.' With every race and press conference, Dunlop enhanced the image of the devil-may-care outsider. 'Yeah, the 130mph lap is something everyone wishes for. I'd love to be in top spot but there's two factory bikes ahead of me. Everyone says you need factory bikes. You don't; you need good lads. My sponsor has worked his nuts off and has been shipping in engines all week. Everyone said I was not ready when I won [the 2009 Supersport]. I was only 21. I knew in my own head. A couple of clicks can make all the difference.'

Donald is happy with third, after running off the circuit and a year on from the crash that had threatened his career. 'This day 12 months ago I was sitting in Nobles Hospital and thinking racing might be over so it's pretty sweet,' he says.

Conor Cummins is phlegmatic as he talks to his mum about the race, while Martin is in a simmering strop in a motorhome. He slumps in a seat and mutters injustices. The sense of grievance will fester all the way through to the end of the next race, in two days' time, when he will be second to Hutchinson in the opening Supersport race. Martin will want to boycott that podium celebration, a time-honoured tradition, but will turn up briefly for the sake of his mechanics. Some of his rivals snigger at what they see as a stage-managed hissy fit. He has just ridden superbly to finish three seconds adrift of Hutchinson after 150 miles of racing, but he is living in the past. Martin cannot care less what anyone thinks and later he will tell me why he was so appalled.

'It's crap sometimes. The clerk of the course puts you on to one fella and he puts you into another, but to get done for 0.112kph, do me a favour. I was pissing in the wind talking to them but I thought, "What goes around comes around." I am not an arsehole. I wasn't doing it [the podium boycott] for the sake of it, but if they can be awkward then why can't I? You have to have facts.'

The fact is he was over the limit in the second race. 'Yeah, but there has to be tolerance,' he says, his voice quickening with his mounting anger. 'I think you could really sort of take it to heart and say the fuckers don't like me because I speak my mind. I do things my way and don't conform to what they want. I don't do all the pressers. You know, I'm not doing it purposely to get attention.'

But wasn't all this just giving fuel to those critics who saw him as a bit of a prima donna? 'I don't need motorbikes and that's what gets 'em. That's the problem right there. I have enough jobs. I don't need to race motorbikes to make money. I do it as a hobby. I'm not complaining. I do alright out of it, course I do, but what do you want me to do? The other lads used to get at me for going to work, but we race bikes at weekends so what do they want me to do on Monday morning?'

He is veering off track, just as Donald did in the first race, but he has other complaints too. The dream syndicate with Wilson Craig, a craggy Irishman, is not quite what he had hoped for. Martin likes input into his machines, but Craig has his own men. And then there is the row with his father, Ian, who has reneged on a promise to come to the Isle of Man. 'Yeah, he should be here,' Martin muses. 'Made up some cock-and-bull story.' Cock of the north or cock and bull? The jury is still out on Martin too.

Two

Guy

'Her dog is called Cooper, but he hangs out with two cats called Richard Spanksville and Margo du Pape. Now Richard Spanksville is pimping out Margo du Pape, and Cooper appears to be the thickest Boxer known to man, but the truth is he's only playing the part of a thick Boxer because really he's an FBI undercover agent.'

Guy Martin looks at me and senses confusion. 'That was her ringing. I'll call her back.' And so the most popular figure in road racing, a man who delights in pricking away the hubris of his peers, is calling his fiancée about the cats.

'Now then, alreet mate, what's going on with Richard Spanksville and Margo du Pape?' He nods sagely and fixes me a look of gravitas. 'He was grooming her, but he's turned over a new leaf. He's rowing for Blaydon. Any other news on that front? What's Cooper doing? Ah. He's looking for Gaddafi. On high alert for September 11. What else? He spends most of the day snoring. I'll ring you in a bit lass. Thanks for the information.'

It is a snapshot of why some people do not get Guy Martin. He has not yet won a TT race, but his peculiarities mean he is far and away the best-loved rider. He has a prime-time BBC One show in the pipeline, a comfortable travelogue where he will take a canal boat to touchstones of the Industrial Revolution, and is the central figure in the forthcoming film, *TT3D*, a documentary that will break records and fuel the antipathy some of those with better records feel towards him.

Martin is unimpressed by the suggestion that he needs to impress. As he sits in his rented room at the top of a Lincolnshire hill, he clearly revels in the fact that he works as a truck fitter and only plays at motorcycle racing. It is only one of myriad passions, alongside stationary engines, downhill mountain biking, the Second World War and tea, yet he is the one the big sponsors are sniffing around; he is the one being asked to front TV programmes and sign book deals – he has turned down all of the latter. It is either a damning indictment of the cult of celebrity or proof of an engaging personality. Martin seemingly has it all, delighting in winding up both rivals and the assortment of clocks and cranks that litter his coffee table. He has it all except the TT win he needs.

He is weary of having to explain the appeal of the TT to laymen. 'It's so fast and long, the thick end of 200mph, sucking the rabbits out of the hedges,' he says. 'But really, I was driving down the dual carriageway and saw a guy about my age, in a people carrier, kids in the back, bonnet up, steam coming out of the engine, wife at his side giving him all that. What's he do at the weekend? Mow the grass? Wash the car? I mean, how can I explain something like this to someone like that? It's just not in his DNA.'

Even the Grand Prix racers are an alien breed to him. 'Racing round a track is like going round Morrisons car park in comparison.' He sips his tea. He loves his tea. He is a member of the Tea Appreciation Society and has the T-shirt to prove it. Fans send him boxes of the stuff, different derivatives and rare blends. 'Go through history and tea plays a major part,' he says. 'You had the British troops using it to camouflage themselves in India because they realised their red jackets made them stand out like a pair of tits on a donkey. It's part of what Englishness is all about.

'I've been on teams where they all whoop and holler and go in for high fives and chest slapping. I had to say to them, "Look fellas, we're English". I hate all this Americanised stuff. Most of them do it at the TT. McGuinness is very British, but Hutchy and the Dunlops do it. And it's not like Einstein's just discovered $E = MC$ squared or Darwin's got to the bottom of the theory of evolution; it's only a race, mate. It's good that it means so much to them, but if that's all they've got in their lives then, fuck me, they are not seeing the big picture. I want to win the TT and it will happen – because when I say I'll do something I do it – but when I do there will a firm handshake and a stiff upper lip.'

There is a theory peddled by his detractors that Martin is

something of a chancer and that his working-class hero shtick is at odds with the Aston Martin that has 50 miles on the clock. However, for him socialism is in the mind rather than the garage and so he juggles his road racing and growing fame with 60-hour weeks fixing trucks.

He is also more interested in other spheres than most sportsmen, his super-caffeinated brain running over subjects as an engorged stream of consciousness, whether it be the whys and wherefores of the Sixties space race or the science of monkey trapping. 'During the 1960s there was a bit of a dick-measuring exercise going on between the Russians and the Americans. Fair enough, the Russians knew they couldn't beat the Americans in the arms race. Who could? Look at the Cuban missile job. So, the Russians thought they'd win the space race. So there they are in Moscow, getting everything sorted, but the Yanks are a bit far ahead and just need a pen to write in zero gravity. So $1.5 million and a good few man hours later, they find a solution. Phew – how could they ever get by without one? In the meantime the Russians decided they'd use a pencil.'

And: 'My sister Kate was only telling me the other day about monkey trapping. Do you know they used to cut the top off a coconut, tie it to the ground and fill it with food to catch monkeys? The monkey would put his hand in, fill it with food, but then couldn't get it out due to it being full of the food. The monkey, not being the sharpest tool in the box, never thought of letting go of the food. The greedy little bugger would just struggle along. Monkey brain eh?'

Martin looks as distinctive as he sounds. He has intense features, an angular jaw and pronounced cheekbones framed by dead-ferret sideburns and febrile hair. His voice is marinated in a Lincolnshire lilt and his sentences accelerate and often plough straight through punctuation into a clucking laugh.

His ancestry is just as colourful. 'My granddad was Latvian, from just outside Riga. Fucking hell, he was a double-hard bastard. He died about ten year ago. He was huge. Incredibly tall. Could not speak much English, but he was a real grafter. He was a builder first, but in the war he worked as a farmer. Then he got captured by the Germans and so he went to fight for them. Him and his mate had enough and so one night they escaped through the bottom of Russia on the axle of a train. Two days they spent on that. Then they got captured by the Americans and were brought to England as prisoners of war. That's how he met my gran. Now my other granddad, Jack Martin, was a Royal Marine and was on the beaches on D-Day. They used to joke with each other about how they had fought on different sides. They got on alright. I'd like to go back to Latvia and see where Walter came from, but I guess it's probably all westernised now and not at all like the old eastern bloc he'd have known.'

This nearness of history fascinates Martin. He is proud of his grandfathers, on both sides of the family and war, and more interested in the nuances of warfare than your average 20-something. Hence, he is the only TT rider, indeed sportsman, who has ever decided to write about Operation Chariot. 'Code name for the British commando raid on the French port of St Nazaire on 28 March 1942 on a 356-metre long Normandy dry dock. The 257 Army Commandos and 345 Royal Navy took part.' He writes about the attack in minute detail, culminating in the paragraph: 'Of the 611 Commandos who went into action, 169 lost their lives, 200 were captured and five escaped and made it safely back to England through Spain. Five men were awarded the

Victoria Cross, one posthumously, for outstanding heroism.' It is fair to say this is not the usual PR fodder put up on a sporting website. Why did he do it? 'These stories make me so proud,' he says.

Guy Martin grew up in Kirmington, a tiny village in Lincolnshire, and loved his primary school, just down the high street from The Marrowbone and Cleaver. 'There were 18 kids there and one teacher, Mr Acum. He was the man. An absolute legend. We used to have a maths test every Friday morning, but that was the only academic thing we ever did. Everything else was stuff like teaching us how to light bonfires. He had a putting green out the back of the school and he used to get us all working on keeping that in good shape. We were dead practical kids as a result. On sports day we used to have a fast bike race and a slow bike race. No other school did that. He was crackers. But that sort of made us.

'He taught the juniors and his missus taught the infants. But then I went to secondary school, the Vale of Ancholme, and hated it. I went from 18 kids to 400 and I did not have any proper mates. I was always getting detention. Not for anything bad, just for being shit. I couldn't get out of there fast enough. All I wanted was to build stuff. I'd get home and start working on my lawnmower engines. I'd build them and tune them. I had my 50cc moped and would spend hours on that. I was only 14, but I was getting it ready for when I was old enough to take it on the road.'

Like many racers, engine oil was the sap of the family tree. 'My dad raced at the TT and was given the number 69. This was at a time before oral sex had been discovered in England. In Lincolnshire anyway. So when some French riders came up smiling and sniggering "Soixante-neuf", my dad and his mate didn't hear them properly and didn't know what they were on about. They looked at each other saying, "Wath-on-Dearne? That's near Doncaster".'

His father was a truck mechanic. 'Still is.' They are still working together. Martin has just moved out of the farm where he lived for ten years and into the old blacksmith's forge in Caistor, on the Viking Way. Someone is building his house. 'Very slowly.' He loves dissecting trucks with surgical precision, but still yearns for the days spent farming wheat, barley and rape in Kirmington. Now he is planning to spend his weekends back on the farm, back helping Mr and Mrs Lancaster, surrogate parents and his would-be in-laws as he dated the girl he always refers to as 'the farmer's daughter'.

'I never got to drive the combine,' he says with palpable regret. 'That's when you know you've made it on the farm. The potato harvester runs and pulls them out of the field, and I'd follow in the tractor and they put them in the back in boxes. I loved farming but it would fry my head if that's all I did. Even now, when I'm doing an 80-hour week on the trucks, I still do my motorbikes and I still do my telly. I could never just pick one part of my life and do one thing. People keep saying you're spreading yourself too thin, but I like my life and so I will keep doing it.'

If road racing, fronted by the TT, is an anachronism, Martin is dragging it, kicking and screaming, into the modern age. Most of those who watch it like its cultish status. It is a Masonic society cast into geographical isolation in the Irish Sea. But Martin is prime-time and transcends these boundaries. He has a frivolous side, but he knows the dangers of racing motorcycles on the roads, especially at the TT, which is longer, harder and, bluntly put, deadlier. 'You can't replicate the buzz,' he says. 'It's that near-death thing. I plan to win one and quit. Tick the box and move on. I've never taken drugs but I think I'd need something to replace it.' He pauses. 'But I know there isn't really anything.'

When Martin was 12 he would do three paper rounds and then cycle the seven miles from Kirmington to his father's garage in Caistor, a stone's throw from the old blacksmith's forge where we are sitting. 'We had to earn our own money,' he says. 'We never had it given, never had pocket money.' His father raced for 15 years, another of the journeymen living on the margins. His son was bereft of ambition. He lived in the moment, as people with boundless enthusiasm always do, and kept tuning his moped. 'It would get to 80-odd miles an hour,' he says. 'I got it going real good. Bit too good, actually.'

When he was 16 he went to his sister's 18th birthday party; the morning after he was on his moped when he ran headlong into a car. 'I walked away from it because I was pissed and flexible. I was badly hungover and, to be fair, I think that's what caused the crash. I thought, "That's getting a bit near" and so I thought I'd better go racing. I did not start because I wanted to win races; I went because I wanted to build bikes. I wasn't bothered where I finished.'

It must have been hard to see how this figure in the middle of every pack would one day become one of the leaders. He had modest means and results, but with only his friend, Johnny, as an accomplice, he enjoyed himself. There was no pressure then, no sponsors to please, no PR days to attend, no fans. 'I'm not ungrateful,' he says of his current status, before scrutinising his words for leaks. 'Well, actually, I suppose I am.'

In his second year of racing on the circuits, he improved. He even won a couple of races. 'I was nowt spectacular.' But then something clicked. 'Me and Johnny would chuck it in the van and just go and race. And it began to work. I never thought I could have a career because I was still working. I would finish work and go racing and then finish racing and go to work. I'd think, "Some of you are doing this professionally". I would get off on that. I still get off on it now. I'm just fucking about at it really; them boys are at it full-time and they let a dickhead like me beat them. I think it's funny.'

He knows these sort of comments grate on his rivals at the TT, but he loves playing with people, inverting hackneyed ideas and lighting bonfires under platitudes. The world of road racing seems a natural fit, with its mortality framed by walls and houses and lamp posts rather than softened by the run-off areas, safety barriers and smooth tarmac of the tracks. When you start racing on the roads, the talent is similar, but the courage is multiplied. The odds are suddenly stacked against you and so it becomes an underworld of underdogs.

'I was doing alright on the circuits,' Martin says. 'I was getting on the podium. Ruffling a few feathers. I thought I could do something with this. Then I went to Rockingham.' That day at the Northampton circuit in 2002 would change everything. 'I ran across a chicane. It was dead common to do that. They said that if you gained time and position then you would get a ten-second penalty. Fair enough. But I lost time and position and they still docked me ten seconds. I said, "What the fuck are you doing? Look, it says here". Now this fella would not listen to me. He was a musty chap, as old as the hills, must have been 90-odd. He said I'd have to appeal so I did. I went to see the organiser and he was being dead cocky so I slammed his laptop shut on his fingers and went to lamp him. Somebody had to pull me away.'

He got one more weekend's racing in before the Auto

Cycle Union took his licence away. A tribunal followed. 'They asked me what I'd have done if there had been a wall where the chicane was. Come on, man. If there was a wall then we wouldn't be racing. I was mouthy but I was right. When I know I'm right I will stick my neck out and let them know. To appeal you had to pay £120. I wrote them a cheque, but I could tell it was going to make no difference. I wasn't getting the licence back. So I went home and cancelled the cheque. That really annoyed them. That's why they banned me.'

If it started with a fist then that was apposite for what followed. It was also a line drawn in the sand between the warring sides in the Guy Martin debate. To the antis he is more egotistical than eccentric, a man whose desire to be different is fuelled by idiocy rather than idiosyncrasy. To the vastly greater lobby of supporters, he is the last of the mavericks, a lupine V-sign to conformity.

After the fist he went road racing in Ireland, forced there by the intransigency of the biking establishment. Even now he does not have an ACU licence. 'I have an Irish one,' he smiles, wallowing in the situation. 'Since then the ACU have tried to get me to do loads of PR things for them, but I've said, "No". He who laughs last laughs loudest. But the blokes in Ireland have always been brilliant. Over there it's all about helping you.

'The weekend after losing my licence I went to Ireland for my first proper road race. I finished second in the 600 and beat McGuinness and all them boys, first time out. I won three races in Ireland out of the back of the van. There was just me and my brother and a mate called James. I came away with six or seven grand and thought, "Bloody hell, I could make money out of this". I thought, right, I know what

I'm doing in 2003 now. And that's what I've been doing ever since.'

Martin is engaging company, and the barbs and brickbats seem ironic given that he appears to be among the most trenchantly honest of sportsmen. He openly tells me about his BBC deal and what he thinks of other sports people. 'Footballers? Poofters chasing a bag of wind.' He may work for the BBC but there is no pretence at toeing any establishment line.

And yes, he really does get off on pain and admits he would not be so drawn to the TT if not for the danger. Such talk has often been taboo at the TT where, for decades, its own establishment looked suspiciously at anyone who highlighted the death toll. More than 200 deaths were explained away by comparisons with other dangerous sports such as equestrianism and boxing. Why should the TT be held to any different account, they bristled, not realising that the danger was actually part of the attraction and the drip-feed of disaster, horrible as it was, served to highlight that. Like it or not Martin, with his candid remarks about the buzz of near-death experiences, has cut to the truth, ugly and otherwise. For him the TT is sport distilled to its purest form, a race against rivals but more importantly a test of the self. He does not talk about boxing or equestrianism, but likens it to mountain-climbing, both in its essentiality and irrelevance. It is one man's battle against his own fears and insecurities.

'I think some people have forgotten we go racing because we love it. They see glamour. That's why we are having retro black leathers this year. No fancy-named sponsors. If I'd just wanted to stand out, I'd have painted the bike salmon pink with a dysentery brown stripe; it's about making people remember why we are here. I want to go to the grave having won one; I'm not bothered about all the shit that comes with it.'

In his fledgling days Martin was often warned by more seasoned riders. Men like Martin Finnegan and Adrian Archibald would offer advice that was noted and duly ignored. 'They said, "Keep riding like that and it will catch up with you". And they were bloody well right.' It did not take long. The accident happened at the Southern 100, a post-TT meeting on the south of the Isle of Man in 2003. Unlike its more famous cousin, the Southern 100 is not a time trial, but a race over a four-mile circuit in Castletown with the riders all starting at the same time, rubbing shoulders and fairings along the narrowest of roads. It is run from a ramshackle hut by a warm-hearted grouse named Phil Edge and the paddock is a field. 'It was my first time there and I was beating the big boys,' Martin says. 'But it's a dangerous hole and I was riding like a dickhead. The thing is I could not give a fuck. I was flat out. I put a hard move on someone and got it wrong and hit a wall. I ended up in hospital for a couple of weeks. They had to screw me bloody leg and ankle together. I thought, "Those boys said it would catch up with me and it did".'

What goes around comes around and the probabilities mean the racers play pass-the-parcel with calamity. Throw in testosterone and youth and it can be a recipe for disaster. Martin walked away from his bone-breaking epiphany. So did Cameron Donald, a handsome Aussie with an armful of tattoos. 'I thought the same thing about him,' Martin says. 'It's going to catch up with you. This was maybe a few years ago. I didn't say it to his face. I mean, who am I to talk to him like that? He's won at the TT, he's older than me, more experienced. It's how you deal with it when it catches you.

How you come out of it. Cameron has struggled since his crash. Me, I was a fair old mess. The leg was bent backwards and the bone was hanging out. They would not let me race for six weeks because of all the metal they put in. Well, I went to race at Scarborough on the first day back and I could hardly walk. But I beat them all, McGuinness and the lot, beat them with a broken leg. I thought, "Fuck you".'

He takes another tea break. The kitchen is littered with mountain bikes and a racer. He moves with a curious waddle, like a determined duck. His scattergun brain is always firing. 'If the space shuttle moves faster than the speed of light and turns its headlights on does that mean you can't see them?' He talks about how his friend has told him that a donkey can see all four of its feet when it moves forward and that this is tied into Darwin's theory of evolution.

Then he is back to his sofa and back on the bike, the Royston Vasey place sign on a mantelpiece. 'Do you know where that's from? It's the *League of Gentlemen*, but it's the real name of Roy Chubby Brown, the comedian.' The year after his accident he went to the TT for the first time. By then he was living in Ireland with Johnny where a former racer named Uel Duncan helped him out. Duncan had been paralysed in a crash at the Ulster Grand Prix four years earlier. 'I broke every rib in my body, back and front, I dislocated my arm, I broke my ankle, I punctured my lungs, stuff like that,' Duncan said of that day.

It was still a struggle for Martin, though, so when he took the ferry to the Isle of Man, he got a job painting houses for £10 an hour. 'I would be up at 6 a.m. to go painting high up scaffolding and then go practising at night. So I'd earn £100 before I got on the bike, but then I had to pay Johnny and pay for tyres.'

The TT is a curious event even in how success is rated. Of the five races the last, the Senior, is the most prestigious. Riders set off at ten-second intervals and it is the overall time for the race distance that wins. It means that the first bike to finish the race does not necessarily win it. Landmark lap times have come to be regarded as huge accolades – the first 100mph lap and now the first 130mph. These are key parts of TT lore and legend.

Martin made the brash statement that he felt he would lap the 37.73-mile circuit at an average of 120mph by the time he finished his debut in 2004. Given it is widely accepted that it takes three years to learn the course, it sounded fanciful. 'It come dead easy,' he says. 'My first ever lap was 113mph. I knew exactly what I was doing. I was so cocksure. I would never mean to mouth off, saying I'm going to do this or that, but I was so confident in myself. They gave me an orange bib because I was new and told me to get cracking.' By the end of the fortnight, Martin had finished seventh in the Senior race with a lap time of 120.07 seconds. It was comfortably a record for a newcomer. 'David Jefferies, a legend, did 116. People asked what I thought I could do and so I told them.'

At the TT there are three paddocks. The first lies in the shadow of the Grandstand, across the start line from the cemetery where the deceased riders are remembered on a wall of plaques. This paddock is for the elite, with sponsored awnings, cash-backed teams and prefabricated work areas. The second is a concrete yard for the privateers, the men and women doing it on a shoestring. Finally, there is a muddy field leading down to Douglas seafront for the waifs and strays. Martin and Johnny got there early that first year and camped by the shower block in the second paddock.

Sidecar racers, long considered second-class citizens by the two-wheel riders, worked on their curious machines next door. Martin befriended a Cocker Spaniel. He was a world away from celebrity status.

He clearly has a lot of affection for the early days at the TT. 'My mates would all come over and stay. I've never been much of a shagger, but Benny would bring a different bird back every night. Johnny had to clamber over them to get to the loo. It would get cramped in the truck, because there'd be half a dozen mates over for race week. I slept in the back because I had to get up to paint houses and did not want to deal with that lot coming back pissed up at 3 a.m., dragging women with them. Now I can laugh about it, but at the time I thought they were a bunch of dickheads. And the women too, racer chasers we call them, not bothered who, just what. I've never had the joys of that sort of business. Not interested.

'In the winters I'd go home from Ireland and work for my dad. Then from Thursday to Saturday I'd work collecting glasses at the Chicago Rock Café in Grimsby. The staff had to dance on tables whenever one of four songs came on. Even now when I hear *Build Me Up Buttercup* I'm away. When I wasn't doing that I worked down the docks driving a coal truck. The coal would come in from open casts in Poland and South Africa. They'd bring it to Immingham and then it would go to the power stations. It meant I'd start work with my dad at 5.30 a.m., go through 'til 4 p.m., start the coal job at 6 p.m. and then do either a 12 or 24-hour shift. I started on ProPlus to help, but then got hold of EPO, the blood-boosting drug the cyclists use. A bloke I knew got it from Canada. Good stuff. Kept you going.'

From these odd origins Martin fashioned a unique form

of popularity that has since become a phenomenon. He says he never went looking for it. Does not even want it. But his near misses – at the TT in 2009 he was second twice – only made him more seductive. He hates casual talk of sporting heroes, especially the suggestion that he is one himself, and so goes back to a favourite topic to refute such misnomers.

'I was named after Guy Gibson who led the Dam Busters. What a boy. Now I respect people in those situations, people who were sticking their necks on the line every night, and some of them did three or four tours. They were double hardcore bastards. There are lots of theories about how he died, but I think he topped himself. He was on his last flight and knew the war was coming to an end. He had a job lined up giving talks in the US, but I don't think he could cope with the idea of leading a normal life. He could not live without the buzz.'

There is an obvious parallel with Martin and his fellow TT risk-takers, but he does not draw it. Instead, he says he wishes he could go back to the old days. 'Now look at me and the rest of my mates – they have all grown up, Benny and Johnny, even my younger sister, Kate. I'm the only one who has not grown up. I've probably got less responsibilities now than I did when I was 16. Back then I always had to get money for petrol for my bike; I was always cutting it fine. Now I've got a bob or two and have zero hassles. But I need to grow up. I do. I need to grow up.'

The clock is ticking for Martin too. The TT is coming and he knows he will be the centre of attention, even though he has not won a race there yet. The next year, 2011, has to be the year. 'It will come and then I'll retire.' He is 28. Ten years younger than McGuinness, five older than Cummins, seven older than Michael Dunlop. All want the same thing. All will take their chances on the meanest streets in sport.

The mention of Dunlop rouses Martin from his reverie. 'I've said it to Michael, himself, but it will catch up with him. Might take a year or might take three, but it will catch up with him. There's a lot of bravado, but he's wild and he's got the mouth and all. He's cocky as fuck, but he's not a bad person. It's not like he's not going to shag me granny. But he's got a big chip on his shoulder, about what I do not know.' He catches himself because we both know it cannot be easy being Michael Dunlop. 'Maybe it was what happened to his dad,' Martin says. 'I mean, what Michael did that day at the North West ...' The words trail off. Fripperies about his fiancée's felines are lost as he shakes his head and puffs out his cheeks. 'Incredible.'

Ballagarey. Affectionately known as Ballascary. Why? Because it is. Throwing gears at it, fast as you can do, the bike is doing wheelies. It's the most important and dangerous corner on the circuit. This is the boy. Get it right and you're going to make some serious time. Get it wrong and it's going to kill you.

Third & Fourth Races TT 2010, 7–10 June
Superstock & Supersport

The week proceeds in similar fashion. Ian Hutchinson keeps on winning on board his Padgetts bikes. Nobody begrudges Clive Padgett his success. A charming man with a damaged hand that betrays his former career, he is a stickler for detail. He also listens to his riders, trusting them and doing his best to give them what they want. If Hutchinson was prepared to spend the winter at Jim Moodie's house, slaughtering himself in the gym for the sake of extra unseen gains, then Padgett would give him the bike he craved. It is a deal that is working its way towards record-breaking feats.

The third race of TT 2010, the Superstock, is held on the afternoon after the first Supersport race. The Superstocks are the most similar to the bikes that the punters can buy. There are strict rules about modifications. For some this is the most attractive class because these are not highly-tuned thoroughbred bikes, and so it is the easiest class in which to squint and put yourself on the seat whizzing by. For others the bigger bikes that are used in the Superbike and Senior races are the real draw. Hutchinson is the common denominator. Once again, he looks fluid on his orange and white bike, peerlessly weaving a silk thread through the Mountain artery. This time the opposition comes from Ryan Farquhar, who has bought and built his own bike. Conor Cummins too, is exhibiting the rich form that had almost given him his maiden TT win on Saturday. 'Wow, that was impressive,' Steve Parrish says in the commentary box as Cummins sails past Cameron Donald on the Verandah.

Farquhar leads by nine seconds at the halfway stage, but the TT is flushed with pitfalls. A disaster in the pits erases his advantage, just as it had for Cummins on Saturday, and now Hutchinson is back in the box seat. He is smooth over the Mountain and nobody can dent his armour when surrounded by the green and black of wild heights. So he wins again. This time the margin is a mere 1.32 seconds. Farquhar is second, Cummins third. Farquhar is emotional. Hutchinson, though, is not. There is talk of matching the record four wins in a week, but not from him. He is living in the moment, divorced from the past and future, and so it is just another win.

Things are not going as smoothly as Cummins would have liked, but he has his podium and his form in the opening race of TT week had shown everyone that he was on the rise. 'I'm not blowing smoke up my arse, but from the beginning of the third lap in that first race, the Superbike, I had no clutch. No clutch and yet I was still able to pull time on the rest. That shows how well I was going. So to get within reach of Glen Helen and the bike just to expire like that, I was gutted. That's the appropriate word. But even after that I thought, "I've shown I can lead". A few things obviously need to go my way in order to win a race. You get niggly little problems, gear ratios, suspension, set-up. Well, potentially, everything can go wrong here.'

Even in the Superstock race, where he has just finished third, he had been hit by gremlins. 'I was very lucky to finish the race,' he admits. 'A component basically came off the bike and we finished without it. It seems like every race something is going against us. I was not sure I could get it over the Mountain. I was praying all the way over.'

All around the paddock and the island the little histories of the TT were being played out. Riders raced, fans drunk, mechanics toiled inside muddy tents. They were all bonded by the shared love and pain of the TT, all fighting personal battles, from Cummins and his ailing bikes to the bearded giant sitting in the centre of the The Quids Inn, swigging what was probably pure alcohol from a bottle in his paw, sniffing another dubious-looking substance straight off his ham of an arm.

Steve Christian had his own battles. He was the producer behind the *TT3D* film being shot over the course of the fortnight. He had lived next door to the TT course as a boy and knew the two faces of the race. 'I loved it as a kid,' he said. 'But then, during my late teens and early 20s, I was always hearing about death and destruction, all the bad things. People were winning races by seven minutes.' He moved into the film business and became a huge success. He worked with the likes of Johnny Depp, Christian Bale and Renee Zellweger, but would regularly receive scripts from people interested in making a film about the TT. 'Most of the people coming up with ideas had not even been here,' he said. 'The classic Hollywood version was about a 16-year-old girl who would win the TT. That would have seen us get completely slaughtered.'

Then he had the lightbulb moment. 'Why fake it?' he said. 'I'd seen about 25 scripts, at least one a year, some with big names, some without, but they did not get what the TT is about. And it's about guys who stand on the line, sling their leg over the bike and go down the hill. Guys who do what most of us want to do, not necessarily the TT but to live our lives like that, to have the balls to do something we really want to do. That's the story.

'It's all about ordinary guys doing extraordinary things. Whether you're Hailwood, Dunlop, McGuinness or Martin, whether you're dead or alive, you're gone in the blink of an eye compared with the TT. Two world wars and the TT endures. That's what we are trying to get across with this film. We are trying to get across the enduring nature of the Isle of Man. This mythical aura. It's been here for centuries, but for two weeks these guys try to come and tame the beast and the island flicks them away.'

Christian knew his film was going to be controversial because he was not going to shy away from the dark side. Hutchinson was only part of the equation as he helped himself to a fourth win in the second of the Supersport races, three days later. It looked easy on paper, but this time the winning margin after 150 miles was 1.4 seconds. Michael Dunlop was the unfortunate runner-up, so close to getting the victory that he wanted to silence those who never mentioned him without talking of Uncle Joey. Keith Amor was third, followed by Guy Martin, John McGuinness and Conor Cummins.

But down the paddock the TT took one of its horrible lurches into pitch black as Paul Dobbs, a rider who never truly had the chance to win a TT, was killed. In some of the video reviews of 2010, Dobbs would not be mentioned. The cynical view is that this is airbrushing history. Others would maintain that death is a byproduct of freewill and the TT should not be judged. Life goes on and wallowing in the tragic is the stuff of sensationalism. But Christian had no intention of pandering to the bike audience and so it would not be long, when Dobbs' widow, Bridget, had issued an extraordinary statement that went to the heart of madness, that he would fire off an email to her. 'I emailed her out of the blue and said, "You don't know me from Adam, but would you mind if we brought some cameras to the funeral?" As soon as I pressed the send button I regretted it. I thought what if she sends it to the TT organisers? They could kill the film. I waited four days and worried. What if they sent it to *The Sun*. I could see the story – "This is what they do on the Isle of Man. Look at these callous bastards".'

Three
Michael

The bike was not running well as it neared Mather's Cross. He had complained about it to John, his sponsor, saying it only felt right in top gear, that the rest was a fight. It might even be in danger of seizing. It was that fast section where it all went wrong. The inquest would hear that Robert Dunlop had inadvertently hit the front brake instead of the clutch. Darren Burns had just been overtaken by the Mighty Micro and would tell how it was as if Dunlop had hit a brick wall such was the force with which he was thrown from his bike. Burns could not avoid running over him. William Dunlop arrived quickly on his bike. He saw his father, rushed nearer and crumbled. He was restrained by Mervyn White, the clerk of the course. That was Thursday, 15 May, 2008.

On Friday Stephen Davison, a photographer who had got to know the Dunlops over the years, went up to the house to pay his respects. It was a striking building on farm land gathered around a grey turret. It brought back memories of the night in 2000 when they had brought Joey back from Estonia in a hearse. On that occasion the blackened vehicle had hummed into a deserted Ballymoney and arrived at the funeral parlour on the top of the high street. Davison remembered thinking how odd it was that the last time he had seen Joey was a mere ten yards away, across the road, in the town hall, the star of a civic reception to mark his 26th TT win. Now he was a few yards and days and a world away. 'I remember it being deathly quiet and then suddenly as the hearse turned the last corner there was a rising wailing.' That was the family. And now the family, the most fabled in Irish motorsport, was dealing with further tragic consequences of life-affirming rushes.

On the Saturday, William and Michael, two of Robert's three sons, left their father in his coffin at home and went back to the paddock. William was in his leathers. He had made his mind up quickly that, less than 48 hours after the death of his father in practice for the North West 200, he was going to compete in the race. Davison saw him walk out of a room at the track and move towards a fence. Then it was as if the bones had been sucked from his body and he slumped against it. Davison assumed the emotion had caught up with William, but he was wrong. The boy was distraught because he had just been told that he was not going to be allowed to race.

'They voted three to two against,' William would tell me. 'Well, the first thing was these people didn't know what they were talking about. They were all about saying how much they would help us after my dad, but when we went to the meeting they did that. I was devastated. I could not believe it. I was determined to ride, but thought that was that. And then the boy who sponsored me said they were ignorant pillocks and took the bike down anyway. I didn't realise my bike was on the grid until I got a phone call.'

Back then, in the Spring of 2008, Michael was 20, three years younger than his brother. More belligerent, he made his mind up to race too. 'I said to the boys, "Let's get that thing out". I went down there. William's bike was already there. They didn't have the balls to take us off.'

It was a thankless position for the organisers. Damned if they did not, they knew they would be damned if they did and something else went wrong. In the end the Dunlops and the massed crowd, roaring their approval, settled the matter. 'I saw the boys who'd made the decision looking at each other, thinking to themselves, "We're screwed", Michael would say. 'They were wondering what they could do, but it was too far gone. But they were not worried about safety; it was their own personal appearance that was going to be damned.'

That is a harsh assessment given that the organisers were caught in the middle of a personal nightmare. Racing seemed secondary to the grieving process, but as it turned out they were the same thing. So the race would be run over four laps of the nine-mile circuit on roads that formed the

Triangle between the towns of Coleraine, Portrush and Portstewart. John McGuinness was the favourite after qualifying on pole position. He could only look at the two young Dunlops and wonder whether it was right. Life always carried on after racing tragedies, but this was something else. This was near to the bone, a 200mph wake rather than the grief by proxy that was the ordinary way of moving on.

'It was one of the ballsiest things I have ever seen,' McGuinness said when we discussed it. 'I was behind Robert when he had his accident. I could not really see what happened, but there was a puff of smoke, another lad involved. I always remember Robert looking over his shoulder and winking at me; three minutes later he was dead. Now for Michael to come back and do what he did ...'

It was a tight race. Michael skirted the lush verges and hard walls. He gained time through Mather's Cross and became embroiled in a three-way battle with McGuinness and a rider named Chris Elkin. He did not know that William had been forced to retire on his warm-up lap, but rode hard and fast, as always. It was both sublime and ridiculous. Michael lapped at an average of just under 110mph on a course where the top speed would soon rise to 204mph. There was no room for self-pity or even sentiment with the bushes and hedges and people blurring by. The TV commentators were astounded.

You couldn't write the script for this.

Elkin looked to have the faster straight-line speed and so Dunlop did his best to hit the brakes late and to cling on to his slipstream. A record crowd sweated in the sunshine by the side of the Giant's Causeway.

I was speaking to Robert earlier in the week and he was tipping both of his boys for the podium. When the flag lifts everyone forgets everything.

McGuinness seemed to be biding his time in third place on his Padgetts Honda, watching Elkin and Dunlop race side by side and wheel to wheel. And then Dunlop's bike sent up a puff of smoke into York. Breath was bated by this week's trauma. Dunlop's wheel locked. Elkin recognised the danger and pulled up. Within little more than a second, both men had come close to falling and had risen.

This has to be the best race he has ever done in his life. He is doing it for dad.

It was at Metropole where the race was won. Elkin ran wide and Dunlop pounced. And then he was away, over Black Hill and under the bridge.

It's unbelievable. He looks like he's trying to ring the throttle right off the bike.

When the Grandstand saw his white bike with its black No 3 draw into focus on the last lap, the noise was thunderous. He crossed the line and then collapsed in a heap, an epicentre for back-slappers and those whose mourning had been momentarily suspended by sporting gold. That was Saturday. The funeral was Sunday. 'Some dickhead in a suit said I wasn't mentally right to race,' Michael would tell me. 'I said I'd never been mentally right.'

We are sitting in Clouds coffee shop on Ballymoney High Street, a short downhill walk from the town hall and funeral parlour, a longer one up from Joey's bar and the memorial garden, where he sits astride a bronze motorcycle. They have been hard to track down. Their uncle was famously unimpressed by journalists and William and Michael are following suit. Joey mended bikes, rode bikes and had the dirty black fingernails and rolled-up sleeves of the working class hero. When he moved out of the tiny grey bungalow by the bridge in Armoy, the new inhabitants found a bunch of trophies buried in the sand in the garden; Joey had given his cups to the local kids to play with and they had been lost and forgotten. The celebrity status afforded to Guy Martin would have been anathema to him.

The new Dunlops are the same. They are road racers, not show ponies, local boys not local heroes. Michael, in particular, does not care for the spotlight that comes from winning. 'I can't understand why people want to know all this shit,' he says. William is more reserved, more polite. Physically they do not look like brothers. Michael is short and squat with a cold front of aggression. William is taller and leaner with soft, watery eyes. The family remains protective of its legacy. Gaining access to the Dunlops is like an undercover mission, the myths and legend swirling around the reality locked behind Ballymoney doors. There is an air of suspicion when an outsider enquires.

It all started in Armoy, a tiny County Antrim village a midnight flit from Ballymoney. It is a happily haunted ghost town on the River Bush, between two of the nine glens of Antrim. It was here that David Wallace found himself in the late 1970s. Wallace was a film-maker working in the school market, and had three ideas for a feature that would help him escape. One was about the harvest, another about protestant and Catholic poetry. The third was commissioned.

It was to be a documentary about Irish road racers. He quickly found the Armoy Armada, a trio of friends scraping by on broken bones and splintering dreams, and recorded a beautiful film of underground high-fliers.

There was Big Frank Kennedy, a gentle giant whose job selling cars foundered on the fact he chose to shut up and go racing every Saturday. He was too honest to be a good salesman too. 'Yes, that's a lot of money,' he would sympathise with customers. Mervyn Robinson had wild, lank hair and a threadbare red jumper. His situation gave Wallace a dramatic storyline as he had recently crashed and suffered concussion. His vision was affected and Robinson was wondering whether he would be able to continue. 'Mervyn borrowed £5 from his mum to buy his first racer,' said the voiceover in *The Road Racers*. 'Even marriage and a child could not stop him racing.' Finally, there was Joey Dunlop. In those days he looked every inch the rebel racer, black and silver leathers, rock star hair and grubby good looks. 'To be a road racer is to be something special,' the voiceover added. So they practised on the local roads, illegally, looking out for police cars, children sitting on bridges, laughing as the racers tore by at 160mph.

The road racing scene in Ireland looks breathtakingly amateurish. 'We've just had a dog run across the road,' said the announcer at one race. 'Please, a particular warning to dog owners, if you value your pet.' It was a hobby bound in shoe and heartstring, kaleidoscopic colour seeping through the muddy glamour.

It was not a lucrative existence. Dunlop reasoned the £20 prize money was not much for risking your neck, but it was already obvious he had something special. 'Big Frank lacks Joey's single-minded approach,' agreed the voiceover. 'His racing is sometimes brilliant and sometimes mediocre. With a new baby on the way and a house half built, his wife thinks it is high time he should give up racing.'

So did the Church of God which Kennedy attended every Sunday and which took a 'dim view of a man who risks his life.' Even the doctor looked less than sympathetic as he examined Kennedy's healing collarbone. The strapping was basic by modern standards, a tightly-bound bandage criss-crossing his back and shoulders, but soon he was on the phone, his green shirt open to his belly button, a camouflage fishing cap on his head, phone to his chin. He is asking a sponsor for parts. As with his cars, he is not selling himself well. 'Aye, it's a lot of money.'

Joey harvests peat for warmth and has little money, his only sponsor the dole. Mervyn thinks about quitting, leafing through his old cuttings with headlines such as 'The Rising Star' and 'Mighty Merv, the one to beat'. The sadness is palpable.

They go to The Glen Dale pub. The bar is a dirty brown, coloured by flickering red lights. The friends swig pints. They are the froth of small beer dreams. Robinson ponders retirement through a beer bottom lens, the voiceover reminding him of the stakes. 'As a mere mechanic his fame and notoriety would be lost. Nobody remembers yesterday's racers.'

The riders all told Wallace their fears; about keeping their eyes out for flags lest someone had left a big puddle of petrol on the road; about racing so closely on country roads with 20 other racers; 'It never used to worry me but it concerns me a lot now.' The only one who seems comfortable in his ability to out-stare fate at all times is Dunlop. 'You have to really hold on,' he mutters.

They work through the night to get ready for the Cookstown 100. Soldiers check beneath bridges for bombs; six months later an IRA car bomb will kill an RUC policeman in Armoy. Cows move from the paddock to be replaced by bikes. The soundtrack plays *sometimes it's hard to be a woman*. 'I think Cookstown is one of the best in Ireland. It's very narrow, very bumpy, very hilly.'

'There's always something to hit – concrete posts and stone walls all around the place.'

'I think the bikes are getting far too quick.'

The racers start by the side of their bikes, four adrift on a rough, country road that is barely ten feet wide. Dunlop gets two second places and then sets a lap record in the third. It is the perfect send-off before he takes the fishing boat to the Isle of Man for the 1977 TT, his second attempt at the event after an awful baptism the previous season. 'He would return a hero.'

And that is the real sadness of the film – as much as the hardship that follows, it is the sight of three friends from Armoy finding themselves on diverging paths. Dunlop goes off camera and off to sea. Big Frank breaks both his arms and thumbs and there is an almost comical scene as he wanders around with a rudimentary cage hanging out of his thumbs. It gets clipped off and he sucks in a sigh of intense pain as it is thrown into a plastic bin liner.

'You say this is the 15th time you've come off your bike, but you've only been in hospital once,' says the doctor.

'Ruptured liver.'

'What about your missus. Do you not think she might have something to say?'

'Ah, she's saying plenty.'

Then a friend is killed racing and they go to the funeral.

'There was a time a few years ago when you just accepted it was part of the sport. Now it's getting too close to home. People we know are getting killed. It makes you stop and think.' Except it does not. They suspend their fears and race on. Robinson tells Wallace that his eye has cleared up and that he will ride again. He then speaks of how nerves leave him feeling so weak beforehand that he can barely push off at the start. 'I just want the flag to drop because once you get going it's not so bad.'

With Dunlop racing on the mainland, garnering a reputation against the likes of Barry Sheene, and Big Frank condemned to the sidelines even after his cage is removed, Robinson is the only member of the Armoy Armada racing at the final race in Carrowdore. A man in jeans and a T-shirt hangs out a pit board that looks like the back of a shovel. People are brushing oil off the circuit. Seconds later Mervyn rides straight through it and gains on the leader. 'Yes Mervyn is back on form,' cries the announcer. He wins and it could be a happy ending, but Wallace captures Robinson slumped against a white wall, with his leathers unzipped as he chews on a piece of grass. He appears to be basking in relief as much as joy. There is a flicker of a smile, but maybe Robinson realised that once you get off your bike you are just counting down to the next race.

Then comes the end credit. 'Since the making of this film, Frank Kennedy and Mervyn Robinson have died after falls in the North West 200.' Robinson died at Mather's Cross, the same place that would claim Robert Dunlop's life two decades later.

I drive around Armoy and little has changed since Wallace was here to film Joey Dunlop charging down a wet road in twilight to prepare for a two-bit road race in Ireland. There is the bridge. There is the pub. And there is Big Frank Kennedy's garage. It looks the same, a small wooden building on a corner plot, the red doors now shut and the wording over them now reading 'House of Fellowship'. Finally, it seems the church approves.

For the new Dunlops this is ancient history and irrelevant, but to understand them you really need to know the place. And it is a place where life is cheap and memories are priceless. Someone who knows Michael Dunlop tells me they think he does not expect to live long. It is not a death wish, but an acceptance of the odds.

'It's the danger, it surely is,' Michael tells me. 'That's the buzz. That's the buzz.' He dominates the conversation. William has a bored, distant look. Both have ordered milkshakes. 'Some people think you're a sack of dough,' Michael continues. 'You know, when Joey ran around he was a master, but when I won it was a fluke. It was weird sometimes growing up. It made no difference to me who Joey Dunlop was. It made no difference to me who Robert Dunlop was; he was just my father who I wanted to spend time with. But people would react like a prince had walked by.

'My dad never pushed me into it and never steered me away. But when he died, my mum asked if I felt okay and that, if I did and wanted to keep going, she wasn't going to stop me. "You have to do your own thing," she said. It's not a job to me.' He is dismissive of the posh end of the paddock with its plush transporter vans embossed with sponsors' names. 'For a lot of people out there it's just wages, but I don't care much about money. All my stuff is owed to the bank. I can get by, but if I give up tomorrow, I'll be screwed because it would be impossible for me to take an intelligent man's job.'

He is where Joey was in 1977, when Wallace pitched up in Armoy and started filming. Back then Dunlop boarded the small wooden fishing boat for the Isle of Man and was a wild assortment of raw hope. He won his first TT that year and was on the path to becoming arguably Ireland's most famous sports star. Michael won his first TT in 2009 and people devalued it by saying it was wet. The implication was he could only win if his recklessness outweighed the caution of the rest. Could he do it in the dry, with a level playing field?

'I know people think, "Oh, he's never going to be as good as Joey, never going to be as good as his dad". It's just jealousy. This name can be a blessing and a curse. People think because of our name we get everything, but it actually makes it really, really hard. We have to deal with stuff other riders don't. People are jealous of us, but we race hard and we fight for everything that we get. Dad always said that when you go from racing in Ireland to the internationals you have to lift your game. We have been able to do that and some people haven't liked it. They think we have got the best bikes in the world, but we have to make them work. You have to ride them hard to win races.'

You can sense a softness underneath the bravado, but he likes to sound carefree. 'I am wild. No doubt about it. I will do anything. I will climb that lamp post naked if you want. You name it, I'll do it. I'll steal a police car. I'll rob a taxi. Anything for the craic. I ran down the street naked at the TT one year.'

Sometimes the fight can be taken too literally. That would be the case with Cameron Donald at a race in Kells in County Meath. 'When Cameron passes you he clips across your front wheel. Watch any DVD and you'll see that. He did it to me and I thought, "I'll sort you out". Then he did it again. I got my head down but William had buggered off. He won, I was second and Cameron was third. Well, he really didn't like being beaten at Kells. I went into the paddock and stopped beside William. Cameron came into the back of me. I had not really figured out what had happened, but he was giving it all that and so I punched him a couple of times. Then I gave him a couple of slaps. I felt like smashing his face in, but his mechanic pulled him away. After that he came and apologised and said whatever the problem was they would fix my bike. I thought, "Fair enough". The next thing I know they had sent a letter to the ACU to get my licence revoked. I thought, "Right, I'll take these pricks". So I took a solicitor with me to the Ulster Grand Prix and walked around the paddock together. The shit hit the fan. Didn't go down well.'

William rolls his eyeballs and looks away, like many elder brothers when witnessing a sibling's tantrum. 'I would just smash his head in and get on with things,' Michael continues as if this would be a far more sensible way of settling scores. 'But they wanted solicitors. It's getting like that now. That's how bad it's getting. You can't punch anyone.'

They are brothers, rivals, opposites from the same pod. Michael relishes the TT and is clearly excited about the prospect of returning again. William is not. He does not like the race and, after their father was killed in 2008, skipped the trip. 'Dad was never keen on us doing the TT,' he says. 'He worried about us even though he had won it five times himself.' Michael did go in 2008, though, begging the question why compete at the place where road racing's dangers were most vivid? 'It was one of those things,' he says with that McGuinness pragmatism. 'If you fall off your bicycle, the first thing you have to do is get back on. A lot of people were saying, "What the fuck is he doing?", but it was the only way for me to deal with it. It was the only way to make him proud of me. After Joey's accident, people asked my dad why he was letting his son go racing. He said, "What's your son doing on a Saturday night? I know where mine is." It's what we do. I mean, what else would I do? There isn't anything.

'Life just goes on. I remember when Joey died we were kept out of it. We were sent outside to play football. When the funeral happened it was different. I looked outside and it was just deep and black with people. They said 50,000 came. It was a family thing but that's when I realised, shit, this is a big thing.

'I was about ten and I remember going with my dad to Joey's bar every Saturday night. We would be behind the bar until about four in the morning, while my dad and about ten boys just sat there, chatting. I don't remember much about Joey; I wouldn't say I knew Joey that well.' William goes even further. 'I never spoke a word to Joey in my life.'

Yet father and uncle, brother and brother, are bound by family ties and sporting achievement. Robert did enough to be a legend in his own right, but he was always in Joey's shadow. It, perhaps, mirrors the respective standing of Michael and William. There is clearly an umbilical bond, but they still have their rifts and rows.

It bristles that Joey is the most fabled of all road racers and Robert only a domestic hero. But their uncle's status is only partly down to the record-breaking 26 wins at the TT. Some of it is also down to the blunt personality, the cigarette smoke and the one-man mercy missions to Romania and Bosnia with a van full of clothes, but then there was also the time when Joey and Robert headed for the Isle of Man TT by another fishing boat. It began to sink and disaster loomed, whereupon Joey jumped overboard and cut a dinghy free with a penknife. 'I've had many a scare on a motorbike but nothing like that,' Robert recalled. 'I was scared for my life.' His brother's action saved their lives and Joey would go on to win a hat-trick of races at the TT that year. Legend adds that, after a discussion at breakfast earlier, Joey turned to his brother as the boat sank and said, 'Have you got enough salt now?'

In 2000, aged 48, Dunlop completed another hat-trick at the TT. Shortly afterwards, his sponsor, Andy McMenemy, drove out to a field and shot himself in the head. Traumatised, Dunlop decided to escape. His manager recalled that he said he was 'pissing off for a while because he didn't want to be speaking about Andy.' Dunlop went into Joey's bar and lowered his RC45 from the ceiling. He loaded it and two more bikes into a van and set off to Estonia. A suite awaited him at the plush circuit hotel, but he spent his last night sleeping in the front seat of his van, the stove and tins of beans in the back.

Robert returned to the Pirita-Kose-Kloostrimetsa Circuit a year later for a tribute. His own career had been hampered by the serious injury he sustained at the TT in 1994, leaving him with a shortened leg and huge insurance premiums. He retired in 2004 to concentrate on the fledgling careers of William and Michael, but it did not last long and he was back winning the North West 200, his race, in 2006.

It was not long before his death two years later that he asked Stephen Davison for a favour. 'Would you mind coming up to the house?' he asked the photographer.

'Certainly,' Davison told him, his interest piqued because the Dunlops rarely invited people into their homes.

When he got there he realised Daniel, the third son, was home from duties with the Army. Soon afterwards, Daniel was due to go to Afghanistan where the war was churning out daily tragedy. The next time Davison saw Daniel was at the wake for Robert. Davison offered his condolences and Daniel shook his hand. 'You know why he wanted that picture, don't you?' he told the photographer. 'He thought it would be me.' That was the Friday.

The Saturday made Michael. 'It was just a way of dealing with it. There was no other option. We don't know anything else. Maybe, when I look back, it was a bit selfish, but my bike kept going and it was good enough. The family was grand. We came back that evening and everybody was alright.' He pauses for a moment. 'Nothing was said afterwards. I don't think it helped any. I did not think about jacking it in. But I knew that if I didn't pick myself up and go to the TT that year then I'd never race again.'

It is strange to think that these two young men, dressed in jogging bottoms, exuding scruff and sipping milkshakes, could be stars of the future. They seem like kids. William sounds like a rider who would rather the TT was not looming, whereas Michael seems desperate to prove he can win, that he is more than a postscript in an Irish family saga. The words of caution from Guy Martin linger, but Michael Dunlop is unabashed. 'People think I'm one of them arseholes,' he says. 'They're right. I am one of those arseholes.'

My teammate was killed here in '98, Mike Casey. He went in too early. A lad got killed the year before that. I can't remember his name now. He went in too late. The big problem is there is this big depression beforehand and so you're unsighted as you come over the top. You can't see your entry point and you're going 160mph. Still can't see it. Still can't. Now, see the kerb painted white. Brake on the outside and get back on the gas. Everyone slows down too much, but the fast guys are awesome through here. The top ten will be streets ahead of everyone else. They know it's the most important corner because I don't drop off the gas now for a mile and a half and it's flat out until Greeba Castle.

LAST RACE TT 2010, 11 JUNE
Senior

The practice and the other races, both the two-wheeled ones and the sidecar supports, are the preamble to the big one. The Senior TT is the finale and the most coveted prize. For McGuinness it is his last chance to save his summer. He has more TT wins than anyone alive, but the words from that earlier bike film, *The Road Racers* – 'Nobody remembers yesterday's racers' – might have echoed a warning. They would never forget McGuinness, but his status would be gradually eroded as he edged further into the past and became another old pro. And for McGuinness, with Maisie in a pram in the corner, the demands are greater. He is not a rebel racer, but a family man with growing responsibilities and thinning hair. 'There will come a stage where I can't beat them anymore,' he muses. 'Are they going to raise the bar higher than I can lift it? At that stage I'm going to have to have a good think about what I do.'

Conor Cummins' Kawasaki team are working flat out as midnight approaches on Senior eve. He has tried to keep the team happy. At times he has told them to stop, loaded the bikes into the back of a truck, and gone down onto Douglas promenade for a meal. Paparazzi is a favourite haunt, with huge multicoloured bike murals and oversized calzone.

Michael Dunlop works away too. He likes to be busy. The sounds of the bands and crowds on the promenade, a gentle rolling hill away, hum a chorus.

Morning breaks and the sun floods over cumulus clouds like egg yolk. This is the day of reckoning for all. Carl Fogarty, skin pulled tight over craggy bones, devilish eyes alive, talks to his old friend Jamie Whitham on the grid. 'If you've never taken part in a Senior TT then you've never raced a motorcycle,' he says. Fogarty has won four World Superbike titles, led a team bankrolled by Malaysian millionaires and is a copper-bottomed bike legend. But he misses the buzz of racing and life will never be quite the same again. It is the conundrum McGuinness is beginning to wrestle with as he nears the end of his career.

Guy Martin has time. 'It's hot but it's been hot before hasn't it?' he says. 'The pace will be hot anyway.' He has a second place, two fourths and a fifth from the week. It is good but it is not enough to silence the doubters. Dunlop has done better, with two seconds, a third and an eighth. He is agonisingly close. Cummins has been third, sixth, eighth and nowhere after breaking down. All have done better than McGuinness who has only a fourth, fifth and seventh to go with his breakdown.

The race is fast and hard. McGuinness is on the pace and challenging. He has never been beaten around the TT circuit on 'the big bikes', not when he has made it to the finish anyway. Ian Hutchinson has a sort of confidence rarely found on the Isle of Man with its myriad obstacles, but winning breeds a sense of invincibility. Cummins too, looks in good shape and attracts huge roars as he rides his way home to Ramsey in a purple and green haze.

And then the red flags come out and the race is stopped. The Grandstand shrinks with unease and uncertainty. Friends and relatives await news. This is how it works. People follow the timing screens and note who has come through each checkpoint. If a rider fails to do that alarm bells ring. The longer the wait for news the worse the news is likely to be. It eventually filters through that Guy Martin has crashed at Ballagarey. 'Jesus,' someone says in the press room. 'Not a good place to crash.' Not at 160mph with its big depression and unsighted entry point, not with Paul Dobbs being mourned following his horrible accident there. So they wait and pray. The riders return to the paddock. Some ride past the body lying in the road as they work their way home. Cummins is one of them. 'I'd been losing time and if I am being honest I thought, "Great, I have got another chance." I went past the crash. I could see yellow flags being waved frantically. The closer I got they were shouting at us to slow down. I was virtually at a standstill. There was debris every-where and a huge plume of black smoke. He was still in the road. He was only 20 seconds up the road. It was obvious who it was.'

Cummins knows how this sounds, but the ability to ban-ish bad thoughts is part of being a TT racer. You cannot let the outside world intrude on your personal quest. 'The selfish bit goes through you, but I can guarantee that if it had been on the other foot, then he would have been the same. I was stopped with four other riders and we were all thinking the same thing even if we weren't saying it. Just not good. It was a really downbeat mood. But even then I was trying to figure out what was going wrong with *my* bike. We were basically allowed to circulate up to the paddock. The mood there was low. You're allowed to work on your bikes and get ready for the restart.'

Eventually, they do restart the race. It is 3 p.m., almost three hours late. Martin has already been airlifted to Nobles Hospital. The word has come through that he is conscious. The word that goes around the paddock, through old sages like Clive Padgett, John McGuinness and Wilson Craig, is 'lucky'. The Senior will now be run over a shortened four laps. They count them out. Bruce Anstey is first away on the black Relentless Suzuki. McGuinness is second. All forget about Guy Martin.

'There's Conor Cummins, the local boy,' Steve Parrish says in the commentary booth. 'Came so close to winning last year.'

Time gives shape to the new race. Hutchinson catches Ian Lougher, the veteran, and Cummins overtakes Adrian Archibald. McGuinness is dredging his weary frame for the last vestiges of teenage spirit and he is only half a second down on Hutchinson. The younger man suffers a huge wobble on his Padgetts Honda, but the bike eventually straightens itself. Michael Dunlop feels his bike failing beneath him and frowns. He comes to a gentle stop at Joey's, the section of the course that bears his uncle's name. It is no consolation. His TT is over without a win. It is June but the year can only end in disappointment now. Expectation fades to a whimper along with his engine.

After one lap Hutchinson leads McGuinness by 0.6 seconds. Cummins is just 2.2 seconds further afield. But at the TT everything hinges on uncertainty and it coughs up another disappointment for McGuinness. He drifts to an apologetic halt after a tiny wire snaps. That is the difference between success and failure. Success hangs from slender strips. McGuinness dismounts and kicks the bike just before Hutchinson roars past in peak health. And Hutchinson is now in pole position. But can any man really expect fate to shine on him five times in a week, when all around there is gloom and despondency? Hutchinson might have felt blessed, not in a religious sense, but in a way that hints at the island folklore. It is, as film-maker Steve Christian says, an almost mythical place, a wanton boy to flies, flicking away the rest but somehow letting Hutchinson through the net. Maybe someone or something was looking after him. Maybe the mooinjer veggey, the fairies of Manx lore, were sharpening their axes for others.

Four

Conor

*T*he mooinjer veggey are around three feet short and wear red caps and green jackets. They carry axes and have a spiteful streak. It is perhaps this which makes both grizzled biker and cynical visitor say 'hello' when they pass over Fairy Bridge on the road into Douglas from the airport. The Isle of Man may be a lush, green idyll and a tax haven for the mega-rich, but it is not the sort of place where you want to take chances.

'Hello fairies,' says Conor Cummins as he steers his white van over the Santon Burn. It is a silly superstition, but there is a rich vein of insecurity running below this bridge and through his sport. Mervyn Robinson was wary of the No 31 plate after Big Frank was killed while bearing that number during his last race. A year on and Robinson relented, took the number and was also killed. Joey Dunlop, the undisputed captain of the Armoy Armada, never made that mistake. He shunned the No 31, wore his lucky T-shirt and then relied on his ability. He survived until his 31st year of racing.

Cummins is a product of the Manx way of life, its whims and its ways. It's winter and with the TT in the distance, the island is in its semi-dormant state, and Cummins is restless. 'When the TT finishes it's like the whole island goes into a depression,' he says. Tall and gangly with pale skin and a shock of slate black hair, he is an island hero. He parks up on Douglas seafront, with most of the shops shutting early, and we relocate to a hotel bar. He is the man on the cusp and he thinks his time is coming. Second place in the 2009 Senior suggests his faith is well-placed. Where Guy Martin is a maelstrom of eccentricities and Michael Dunlop a whirlwind of testosterone, Cummins is a polite thinker. He still lives with his parents, Carole and Billy, over the Mountain in Ramsey. They are rational and supportive parents, which did not make it any easier when he decided he wanted to race the TT.

'We had a family meeting,' Cummins says. 'It was the elephant in the room. Me and my dad were talking about it and the more it got mentioned the more my mum caught wind of it. I had to get it out to get it straight in my head. So I decided we needed to have a real good chat and thrash it out. Initially, my mum didn't take to it very well and rightly so. But I was 19 and it was purely my decision. In the end they said, "Whatever makes you happy, whatever you enjoy". That's their main concern. "Be safe, do nothing stupid and be happy". That gave me peace of mind. They accepted what I was doing. I am sure there are riders whose families struggle against it, but to do the TT you're past the age of consent anyway. You have to do what you have to do.'

His father, Billy, had one race at the TT in 1985 and was 28th, but he was a regular at the Manx Grand Prix and lesser races, bit-part cameos for the painter and decorator, and that was enough for his son to get the bug by osmosis. It was hard not to be infected. If you were a Manx boy with an interest in motorcycles then you did not have to look far for career advice.

'It was in my blood from day one,' Cummins says between sips of a coffee. 'I was born in Douglas and if you're Manx-born then you can't get away with not being involved. I watched the TT religiously. We live less than 500 yards from the track. It virtually goes past the front door. Back then they did the early morning practices, so I'd set the alarm and be out there, freezing my nads off, snot running out of my nose, four or five years old. I loved it. For a young boy it was the best. These guys were my gods and Joey Dunlop was my hero. My sister liked it too. She raced motocross when she was young and was quite good, but girls grow up.' He looks out of the enormous bay windows and out to sea, and I think of Martin sounding like a modern-day Peter Pan as he battled the expectation to grow up. 'If you're not aware of the TT here, all year round, then there is something wrong with you,' Cummins says. 'It's such a small place, not even a drop in the ocean, so for the size of it, the enormity of what goes on here is crazy.'

He speaks about his first time as others might about losing their virginity. Those making their debuts must do a newcomers' lap, with bike-bound marshals leading them around the circuit, through country lanes and high streets and over the Mountain. For Cummins it was a concentrated dose of unbridled joy. 'I distinctly remember that lap,' he says, his stoic features breaking into a half smile. Cummins is not one for exaggeration or hype, and emotional outpourings are leavened by common sense, but he is close to gushing now.

'We went out of the holding area and I thought we'd get stopped so we could get our bearings. No chance. We were straight off. I thought, "Better get tuned in quick". The marshal was shifting. Everything went dead quiet. It was the first night of practice and one of the best laps I've ever done. We came to Milntown near where I live. There's a bridge just before it. I was enjoying myself so much and thinking, "Here we go" when I hit a manhole cover. It was a slight divot and the bike twitched. I thought, "Oh wake up". I thought this is one of those places where I really don't want to mess up. Not outside my front door. I'd look a right plonker. Then we came to the Mountain climb out of Ramsey and it was just the most amazing experience I've ever had. It was still. Quiet. The ruffling of the wind going past your helmet. The sensation of being bumped up and down. I will never ever forget it. I know boys who have gone around and, when they start to climb the Mountain, they literally have a lump in their throat. It's a pure emotional experience. I don't know what causes it. I think you're just looking forward to it so much, and if you've grown up around it then more so. I was simply blown away. From that point on I thought I'm going to do this until I win it. And I still have that same burning feeling inside me now.'

Back then in 2006 Conor Cummins went almost unnoticed, apart from by his low-tier backers and parents. His mother watched him from the Grandstand, which is always an unhappy experience for relatives. They see the bikes pass around once every 20 minutes and then rely on the half-heard commentary and florid imaginations. Their worst fear is when they hear there has been a red flag which often means someone has crashed. If no names are mentioned the subtext is that it is bad. There are various timing points on the course and every family holds its collective breath until their rider passes through. The huge blackboard opposite the Grandstand, operated by local scouts, is a work of art and engineering, explaining positions and progress, but it only reveals the numbers, and the race is more often an interior monologue.

Carole Cummins sat and watched while Billy looked on from nearer to home. 'My dad was right by where we live on one of the corners,' his son tells me. 'He never told me he was there and I just cracked on. He will always be out and about. He doesn't want to distract me.

'I got back to the pits and said, "Fill her up boys". I was in love with the place. When I was working down in Douglas, I lived in Ramsey, so every morning I would come over the Mountain on the course. Then, every night, I would finish the lap on my way home. I had a Vauxhall Corsa, a peach of a car, but back then the course was a means of getting from A to B. I did not learn it. People think you have this advantage being from the island but you don't. I got on the bike and thought, "Crikey, I don't actually know lots of the course". And then it is a matter of scaring yourself a bit, scaring yourself into concentrating and learning. I could have done as many laps as I'd wanted in the Corsa and I would not have been able to replicate what I felt on the bike. I never had the lump in my throat, but I was in love.' Hopelessly and totally. 'It might sound a bit soppy, but I was right into it. From the first lap.' And like all love affairs the course of true love never did run smooth.

That 2006 TT belonged to John McGuinness. He won three of the four races and set a new lap record of 129.5mph in the Senior race. 'People had written me off in the 600 Supersport saying I was a bit of a fat boy, but that just lit my fire more,' he said. 'Everybody who doubts my ability just winds me up all the more so they're actually doing me a favour because I'll try even harder to prove them wrong.' McGuinness, like Joey Dunlop before him, said his ambition was always to win in the slowest possible time, but in 2006 he was forced to find what Michael Dunlop terms 'the pencil line'. With Cameron Donald excelling on only his second visit, McGuinness pushed the parameters and relocated the edge. 'I could hear the Manx commentator shouting I'd done 129mph. I was like, "Fuck me! Did I really do that?" I thought 128.5mph was just about possible. It took me half a lap for it to sink in. I was riding along thinking, "If I can do that why do I ever need to come back?" And then Cameron Donald does 128mph and I'm thinking, "What the hell is going on?"'

Cummins was as happy as both, even though his results were modest. He had failed to finish in the Superstock race, was 22nd in the Superbike and 17th in the Senior. He had lapped the fabled circuit at more than 118mph, but it was a battle against himself rather than the elite. For Cummins, smiling at the memories, the adrenaline of young love still on tap, it would never be thus.

Others had long fallen out of love with the TT. Barry Sheene may have been the Gauloise-chomping playboy whose first sexual encounter was on a pool table in the crypt of a London church, but he did not much care for the filthy romance of the island. Back then the TT formed part of the World Championship and so the top GP motorcycle riders were forced to take on the unique challenge in the search for points. Sheene was on the way up, a jack-the-lad who always had a fag, a girl and a comment, but his effervescence was dampened on the island, just as it had been when he visited as a child and had spent three days in an oxygen tent in Nobles Hospital with asthma. Sheene fell from his 125cc Suzuki at Quarter Bridge in 1971, a thankfully slow turn, at the start of the second lap. When he got up his opinion of the TT was formed. He broke down in the production race on a 250c Suzuki and his TT career was over. He did not race there again, but railed against the dangers, hailing it a suicide mission and turning his penchant for a soundbite to telling effect. 'Why bother?' he mused when the subject of the TT would come up. 'It's so much easier to just shoot yourself and get it all over with.'

As Sheene's star rose, all the way to the world 500cc title in 1976 so his comments bore more weight. Fans of the TT have long attempted to paint him as an agent provocateur, hiding his fears behind his headline-grabbing asides, but Sheene had a point. The TT was perilous and pernicious and to force people to ride there was a huge call.

The year after his accident he gained a heavyweight ally. Giacomo Agostini had cemented his legend since trying to entice John McGuinness' mother into his soft top Lamborghini. He got the last of his ten wins in 1972, but his mind was made up by the time he dismounted. Earlier that day he had looked into the eyes of his mechanic, Magni, and he had known. His friend, Gilberto Parlotti, had been killed that morning. Agostini had shown him round the circuit the previous night as a favour. Now his head was a mess of conflicting emotions, but like road racers do, like Michael Dunlop would do all those years on with his father still to be buried, he rode on. But when he dismounted Agostini was not in the mood for partying with willing wives. Instead, he turned his back on the island that had given him so much success. That hurt both him and the island. After all, it had been here where he had truly ingratiated himself into every greasy lock-up with bike calendar hanging in well-oiled corner. He was suave, debonair and rode for an Italian count, but he was one of them.

His iconic status had been truly cemented in 1967 when the riders wore thin black leathers and rode through morning mist. This was the golden era. Agostini, his hair immaculate but long, sat on his bike and waited. And there was Mike Hailwood, his noble jaw, mischievous eyes and air of invincibility. Together they toiled, swapped the lead and made memories. Hailwood tore into the pits at one stage in a panic. The grip on one of his handlebars was coming loose. 'Someone get me a bloody hammer!' he roared. His father, a multi-millionaire with a taste for loud bow ties, self-promotion and women, leant across and advised him to retire. Not bloody likely.

'We were black and white,' Agostini told me. 'Black leathers tinged white from touching the walls. We were over the limit, but we had to be.' The problem in the pits had given Agostini a 12-second lead, but Hailwood refused to concede. He edged across the deficit and then Agostini's chain snapped and the race was won. The Italian cried all the way back to the pits, while Hailwood sought him out and said, 'Ago, you are the real winner.' That night Hailwood taught Agostini to say, 'Fuck my old boots' and tutored him in the most inappropriate places to use the phrase. They drank vodka and jumped in the Casino's swimming pool with some girls. The security guard demanded they get out. 'Come and get me,' Hailwood grinned.

Agostini had lost but he had been accepted into the fold and from that year on he dominated the TT. Right up until 1972 and the realisation that the death toll was too much. 'We pushed for change because we thought, "Maybe I die today?" Sometimes you have to stop and think.' But unlike Sheene, Agostini did know the thrill of racing on the Isle of Man. The closeness of the walls and the proximity of danger were only part of it, but when Parlotti died so did a part of the TT. Agostini was a global superstar and when he decided the TT was no longer a valid risk, the death knell tolled. 'Racing on the Isle of Man is the best in the world,' he told me many years later in his plush villa in the hills above Milan. 'But eventually too many people you know are killed and you have to say, "Enough".'

The top riders on the Grand Prix circuit stopped coming after that. Sheene was a rising star and was not about to go there again. Agostini was now a committed absentee. Phil Read, a bloody-minded man with a habit of getting under the skin of both individuals and, then, an entire island, joined the boycott. So the following year, 1973, was the beginning of a new, diluted era.

The TT hosted the British round of the motorcycling world championship for the last time in 1976. Then it was stripped of its status. It had hung on for 27 years. Read came back in 1977 as the organisers, desperate to retain some kudos, stumped up a massive budget. As committed TT racer Tommy Robb had predicted – 'give them £500 and you would find that all those telegraph poles and concrete footpaths would suddenly become a lot softer' – the risks were evidently not so horrible as to get in the way of a windfall. The status had gone but a new Armada was coming across the grey ocean. In 1976, for the first time, a lank-haired Ulsterman got off a weather-beaten fishing boat, fag in mouth, and walked along Douglas promenade, road racing in his soul, silver lettering spelling JOE over his heart.

Conor Cummins knows the chequered history of the TT as well as most young men, but for him it remains an exquisite dream. It may well be right that it was removed from the World Championship calendar as this is not just any other race. It is unique, a festival of free spirit. But if you want to test the depths of your resolve, faith and skill then there is no better place to be.

'I know I sound like an old scrote, but I love history,' Cummins says. 'Hadrian's Wall, how it goes all the way across, how the Romans built it but how they didn't actually get into Scotland. That's interesting to me, but it must be hard for a teacher when you have 30 kids who are not that interested in being there and would really rather be outside playing with their bikes and toys.'

He did not like school, but he appreciates dedication and he quickly moves on to Jonny Wilkinson, the English rugby player. 'I admire him so much,' he says, although like many Manxmen he has a closer affinity with Ireland. 'The dedication he has, staying out there after training to kick ball after ball after ball. You have to like that. I loved rugby and I still do, but I always had bikes.'

He was a motocross champion when he was young but

then quit to play football for a few years instead. 'I was a defender.' School was a necessary evil. 'I would have done better if it had been made interesting for me. I loved the practical things, like woodwork and graphic design, but it didn't do it for me. Don't get me wrong, I could have tried harder. I wasn't an angel – still not – but I never bunked off. I was tempted every Monday morning and I wasn't the most punctual of people, but I always turned up. I passed my GCSEs, but when I walked through the door for the first day of the lower sixth I thought, "You're definitely not going to university". It just did not appeal to me. Thinking about it now I guess I already wanted to be a bike racer. The thing is I didn't want to waste any of my parents' money. At that time they had already put a lot into it, to the point where I thought they must be skint, and they probably were, even though they didn't tell me.'

Life on the mainland did not tempt him. 'I didn't want to get away from the island. It's not like I am such a die-hard Manx person that I'd be on the point of tears if I had to go, but I just couldn't see the point of leaving.' So he stayed on the hulk of rock, some 32 miles long and 14 miles wide, out in the Irish Sea. He was in the minority as most of the 85,000 population were born overseas. The island has long been seductive because of its rolling hills, old world values and 20 per cent tax cap. There is crime, but Neil Hodgson, a former World Superbike champion who relocated there, told me that people left their doors open and cars unlocked. 'I mean, where are they going to run off to?' he asked.

Cummins did not have posters of women or pop stars on his walls. 'I was too afraid of getting a slap around my head.' Instead, he had pictures of Joey Dunlop. 'Because my dad raced on the roads that was what I followed. It was all good.

I loved it at home. We all got on. There was never anything major like getting caught with porno under my pillow.'

It was bikes that did take him away from home. 'The ACU had lowered the age limit to 13 and I thought, "Brilliant, I'll have a go". There was a race school at Jurby, up the road, and I signed up for a couple of weeks, but I thought, "If I'm going to get any better I have to get away". I was allowed to race on the mainland at places like Aintree and Three Sisters. My passion changed to short-circuit racing. Switch on the TV on a Sunday afternoon and it would be British Superbikes or MotoGP. When you're a young lad you think, "I'll have a go at that". But opportunities are few and far between. Mum and dad had bought a 125 Honda – hard to believe, the size of me, I know – and we did as much as we could for a few years. Then I turned 16 during TT week, 28 May, and a local sponsor called Dessie Collins offered me the chance to go on a 600 Kawasaki at a track day in Jurby. That was my first taste of four-stroke racing and it was a massive leap. So much to take in – engine characteristics, gearboxes – and I loved it. It was totally alien to me, but I thought, "This is brilliant". Ha ha.'

Cummins was described as 'abnormally tall' in one of the first press articles to mention him and it remained the tallest of orders to break into this hugely competitive world of escalating cost and ability. 'The turning point was when my parents, and my loyal sponsors – some of them are still with me today – chipped in and bought a really good 600 Honda. It was the level down from national championship and the more I challenged myself the better I got. We had a few good results so at the end of 2003 we decided to sell everything we had and have a go at a series called the R6 Cup.'

Cummins leaves the bar for a moment to check his van

and walks with the slightly awkward gait of the overlong. He is thin, wearing jeans and a T-shirt, spider limbs slung from back pockets. He does not look like a racer and does not sound much like one either, his speech bereft of boasts and put-downs. He also seems unusually considerate of those around him.

'The first R6 meeting of 2004 we got third. We were like blown away. At the end of the day my dad had never raced in national championships; he'd never been in a national paddock before. He'd sacrificed so much just to get us over there. It was a huge commitment. Dad's a painter and decorator and mum works for Lloyds TSB. I was still at school at the time and wasn't earning anything so I couldn't put anything in. I felt terrible. You commit a massive amount of money and that covers you for crash damage. I did have a few big ones. I crashed at Oulton Park and broke my ankle, but being present in that paddock was an eye opener. I saw the top riders walking out of deluxe motorhomes, and the machinery on display was ridiculous. But as much as it was daunting being in front of this audience, I relished it. I got two podiums and was fifth overall. It was hard to get sponsorship when you come from such a small place so we stuck with what we had. That next year did not go to plan. I crashed at Mallory and broke my knuckle, tore all the skin off, little niggly injuries, yeah, it was pain.

'It's a double-edged thing being from the Isle of Man. More than people realise. It didn't help financially and we had to make the best we could of it. It was only last year that I've been able to buy my own camper van. I've worked my behind off and saved and saved. It's hard because every weekend we'd sail over to the big smoke and drive our way down to the race meetings.'

By now Cummins had left school and had followed his mum and taken a job with Lloyds TSB in Douglas. For a teenager who had already tasted the thrill of racing overseas and lived that erratic life, it was soul-sapping work. He clock-watched and realised the time was ticking on his opportunity.

'At the end of 2005 I had no money. I had a ride sorted out with a team in Manchester, in principle, to compete in the National Superstock Championship. It entailed a big financial commitment. The commitment never came. I was properly down in the dumps and thinking that it was not going to happen. I thought I'd be stuck in the bank for the rest of my life. But my mum and dad kept encouraging me. My granddad had died that year and he had left me a bit of money. It was not a massive amount but it helped and we put that together with a bit from my parents and a part exchange. We got a R1 Yamaha 1000 road bike and converted it into a race bike. I did as many races as I could. Made a positive out of every negative. And I really fancied going over and doing the North West 200. I had been over to spectate the year before, when I had a broken ankle, and I was blown away. It was quite a bizarre experience, the closeness of the racing, the excitement, it just bit me there. It was strange because even as late as the end of 2005 it had never crossed my mind to race on the roads. My parents had put so much into me and the short circuits that I didn't want to let them down. I thought I had to be 100 per cent committed or not bother. But never say never.'

And so in 2006, at the age of 19 Cummins went to the North West 200. The third race was won by Robert Dunlop. The fourth saw Cummins finish ninth. He won the fastest newcomers' award for his efforts. From then on he would be a road racer.

'The North West was my first real, pure road race,' he says now, the waitressing staff filtering through for the evening session, his face darkening as clouds dull the sea view. 'Don't get me wrong, short circuit racing is fantastic, but with road racing there is a different atmosphere. It's more relaxed but still very serious. I thought I fitted into that environment better. It's made me a better person. It's made me think out-side the box. I'm not speaking bad of the short circuits. I just liked the whole road racing environment. As of late, that's come to my mind more. It's more a family-originated community.'

You cannot help but warm to Conor Cummins. He is one of the rebel road racers but he is also both dutiful child and honest bloke. He is neither vain nor false, but a tall, gangly Manxman who would like to be a home-grown winner. He has a strength of will that is about to be tested like never before, but he does not use it to belittle others. Waiters and passers-by wish him well. They are too late.

You can make up to ten seconds by the time you get up to terminal speed. You have the downhill section as well. You can close up on people there. It will take you three years though. You can't just go in there in your first year and get it right. You would scare yourself senseless. This left-hand band is where, unfortunately, David Jefferies crashed. The big problem is it's flat out. You have to build up all week to get it. Just come up and roll it, don't go too early. That's the problem with the TT. Ninety per cent of corners are late-apex corners. You go so fast that you go too soon. Then they tighten up on you, strangle you and it's 'Oh bollocks'. That's the TT. The corners suck you in.

Last Lap TT 2010, 11 June
SENIOR

'Ian Hutchinson, he's waving to the helicopter,' Jamie Whitham cries as Hutchinson takes his hand off the grip for a second, high up on the Mountain. 'And taking a tear-off,' Steve Parrish corrects. 'Not much room for that on this course.'

Incredibly, he wins another race. Five in a week. Unprecedented. The new king of the Mountain. Better than McGuinness. Better than Dunlop. Some weeks earlier Guy Martin had pondered the meaning of the word unbelievable for Steve Christian's film crew. 'It's another word people use too much,' he said. 'Unbelievable. When a man eats his own head now that will be unbelievable because I don't believe it can be done.' But now Hutchinson gets off his bike. 'It's unbelievable,' he says. 'Luck has been on our side so much.' He goes to Colours and makes good on a promise to get pissed. 'Well, you've got to haven't you?'

This is Hutchinson, up to his neck in luck and bullets. His greatest moment contrasts with the lowest low suffered by Bridget Dobbs. It jars with the shuddering end to Martin's

TT in a fireball and then a helicopter and now a hospital bed. And then, last but not least, it mocks the fall down the Mountain of Conor Cummins, who crashes at the Verandah with only a couple of laps left, just miles from safety, miles from his home. Blacked-out memories and a green-stained cat's eye, a dark rubber scar and a dry stone wall. This is the path of his descent, retold by others and borne witness by the five broken vertebrae and ten-inch rods in his back.

Five

Conor

Father Brian had watched the Senior TT from Cruick-shanks corner in Ramsey. As the local priest he prayed more than most during the fortnight. It was a summer that brought out the best in people, a sense of community and camaraderie, but it could all be undone by a perverse form of providence. Father Brian watched the bikes fly by and perhaps felt that there was something life-affirming about these men, crystallising so much goodwill into the crouched, leathered frame of the risk-taker. Perhaps, in a fleeting moment, surrounded by the joyful faces of the TT congre-gation, he might have pondered on the religious theme of sacrificing yourself for others.

But now the race had been stopped after Guy Martin's crash. People held radios to their ears for news but it was not forthcoming. The TT was in one of its horrible infor-mation vacuums, with marshals and medics working franti-cally to stem the wounds, real and figurative. The riders were drifting back through Cruickshanks at a snail's pace, heading for the paddock and the re-run. Father Brian looked out for Conor Cummins, the tall polite son of Billy and Carole. The purple and green machine croaked into sight and that was when he felt it. Deep within himself, Father Brian suddenly felt a sense of horrible foreboding. Cummins passed in front of him and waved to the crowds yearning for a Manxman to win. Father Brian had to turn away. He walked away from the course and went to his church where he prayed for three hours.

It was not enough to stop the crash. Carole traditionally sat on the wall by the shed on the start-finish straight. But when her son did not come past she wandered back to the pits. She was not panicking at this stage. Almost always a missing rider is down to a breakdown as bikes struggle to deal with more than 200 miles of hard riding. But almost is a word of hidden depths that hides enormous import. Almost was not good enough. Carole asked what had happened but nobody knew. Conor was nowhere. Just as it might have been for relatives of those Dunlop and McGuinness boys, who fought for their country in war zones, the thought that her boy was missing in action unearthed half-buried agonies.

Minutes passed with no news. 'I walked down to the retirement office,' Carole said. 'I was thinking, "Oh yeah, he broke down again", but they couldn't tell me anything and that was distressing. It was very, very slow. Whatever system they had did not work. Fifteen minutes down the line I was still standing outside the retirement office not knowing anything. It was hard too, because my friend worked in the office and she was desperately trying to ring up and get information. I don't know why they couldn't get information, but that wait was horrible. I would not want anyone to go through it. You think, "Curtains".'

Cummins' girlfriend, Zara, and his sister, Roisin, were there too. So were Joe Grant and his partner, Claire, friends and loyal sponsors from Solway Slate and Tile. They tried to calm Carole but it was an impossible job. 'There must have been information from somewhere. From the helicopter or something. Even if they'd just said he'd crashed but he was still alive; that would have been enough. But the longer it went on the worse it got. The first we knew was when they announced it over the tannoy. By that time I was literally jumping up and down.'

As usual, Billy Cummins had been watching out on the circuit. He made it back to the pits and found Carole. His sister was with him too. 'They've taken him to Nobles,' Carole said and so all seven of them squeezed into one car and went to hospital. 'We piled in and went up an access road that I didn't even know was there,' Carole said. 'It seemed to take an eternity.'

The sheer horror of Cummins' crash would be known only to a few souls for some time. Fellow rider Jenny Tinmouth had an idea that it was bad. 'I saw Conor Cummins' scratch marks and thought, "Someone's gone off there", the blonde Liverpudlian recalled. The Verandah is a series of blindingly fast bends on the A18, high up Snaefell Mountain.

It was here where Syd Crabtree had died back in 1934 and where Gilberto Parlotti had lost his bearings and life in the rain in 1972. Tinmouth sighed and said: 'It's a huge drop. The next lap there was a marshal's bike on a stand there. You see it all fleetingly, glimpses at that speed. You never think it's going to be one of the top riders. You always think it will be someone, well, someone like me. After Guy Martin's crash, we got pulled up on the Mountain and someone said where he'd crashed, and we all went, "Ohhhh", because well, potentially, you're dead really.'

Tinmouth, though, was in her bubble. The race had been a personal triumph and she was exhilarated. She had just lapped the course at an average speed of 119.945mph. She was the fastest woman in history. Adrenaline coursed through her. 'It's two weeks of pure concentration and stress,' she said. 'So I went out that night and got really drunk. I guess it's in the back of your mind. I guess Guy would be there somewhere. The first year I came I saw a couple of big crashes. I didn't look at them. Someone else did. I said you shouldn't look. It will affect you. So in your mind you think, "I hope they are alright", but we knew before the restart that Guy was okay. Well, maybe not okay, but alive.'

The staff at Nobles Hospital know all about motorbike injuries. For some it is a tedious scenario, especially the yearly crashes involving punters who treat the roads as a race track. These are the ones who are truly mad. The racers take calculated risks, but the amateurs are often mired in rank stupidity. I think about what McGuinness had told me about Mad Sunday, the day when the roads are cleared for any motorcyclist to tear around the Mountain section. 'I might take a flask of tea, sit on a bank and watch the one-day heroes,' he said. 'They had a big bike in 1979 and so they think they're it. It's like a football crowd – there'll be some fucking idiots in there.'

Crashes to the elite were different. The TT was a huge boost to the Manx economy and, though some residents chose to clear off during the annual invasion, their home was a better place for the biking Valhalla. The majority cared for the racers.

'When we find out anything we will let you know,' a nurse said to the Cummins' clan as they flooded out of the car and into the entrance hall at Nobles. 'We were there for maybe an hour before he even arrived,' Carole said. 'He'd gone quite a way down the bank and so it took them a long time to get to him. Then it emerged that they were treating him at the scene. They had problems getting him into the helicopter because of his size. It wasn't just a matter of getting him onto a stretcher. There was a big German doctor at the scene and he realised that Conor's knee had been totally dislocated and there was no pulse in the foot. He managed to put Conor's knee back in. If he had not noticed that then he could have lost his foot.'

Michael Clague had seen the crash. He spent each TT on the Verandah. Some thought he was mad. It could be bleak and cold and wet up there. Fog banks often drifted up from the mines like dragon's breath. When the skies clouded over and the day turned pewter, it was a hellish, isolated spot. Yet it could also be beautiful and Clague, a Manxman in his sixties, was happy there and had been a marshal since he was a teenager. 'It's a job to get people to go up there,' he said. 'Younger people don't want any inconvenience. They just want to get away. You can't do that up there. It's a godforsaken place up there when the wind is blowing.'

It was blowing that day. Clague was the flag marshal for the middle section of the Verandah. He had already been impressed by Cummins that week. 'He's an extremely talented guy,' he said. 'The best I'd ever seen through that section. He was fractionally faster every lap and perfectly in control of the bike.' Clague had a habit of counting when he saw a helmet come into view at the Black Hut, so called because that is literally what it had been. Now the original building, also known as the Stonebreaker's Hut, had been replaced by a concrete building to give the marshals some shelter.

'One, two, three.'

At four the best were past him. He counted Cummins and was impressed. 'He was exceptionally good that day. I think that lap would have been the record if he had finished it.' But, of course, he did not finish it. 'At such speed it's difficult to say what happened,' Clague said. 'He came into my view and took a slightly different line to the others. They all go wider than they used to nowadays. I was in my box, freezing cold, crouched back. I remember saying a hurricane was coming and the people down in Ramsey couldn't understand it, but up there it was extremely windy. He just passed me and the wheels went together. He went off at terrific speed with the bike shooting ahead of him. He slid on his back until he reached a little lay-by area. There was a certain amount of smoke from sliding on his leathers. I'd seen crashes there before but never as fast. The lay-by had a tapered kerb and when he hit that he just went up into the air. He did a very big cartwheel. I thought, "He's directly in line for the dry stone wall down below us in the field". Then he went out of my view.'

Clague called the helicopter, but the wind was so strong that he could barely hear the other end. He breathed a little sigh of relief when he heard the chug of the chopper fighting against the howl of the wind.

'Most people who crash do a couple of little bounces and come to rest on the grass bank. But Conor went up into the air. Eventually, when I saw the footage, I was staggered. The last guy who had crashed there, a guy called Spooner if I remember rightly, had bounced along and not made the wall. Conor spiralled into the air at terrific speed and went straight over the wall. It shows how fast he was going.'

A spectator Clague had seen on the inside of the course had disappeared and he wondered fleetingly where he had gone. 'I don't know what happened to him, but I was more worried about the marshals up the road. Some of them are very experienced, but I'd not had a lot to do with the guys who turned up that day and I was worried about them getting hit as they crossed the road. It's so damn fast around there.

'I've been there a long time. Too long I think. It's a place nobody wants to go. Not a lot happens, but I like it because when you come off there are no walls. In the aftermath I go round the corner and the guys were saying they had got him in the helicopter. They were telling me he was partly conscious. The travelling marshal parked his bike so he was not in the racing line and went down to help. I didn't do anything. I'm nothing special. I've got a long service award but there are loads of friends doing exactly the same up there. I like it because you feel you can contribute in some way.'

There are 35,000 people on the marshals database. Six weeks earlier they had all been emailed. Through the fortnight 1,400 were used. On any given day there would be between 500 and 650 marshals on the course. 'Unless we have 500 where they are supposed to be then we can't start practice,' Terry Holmes, the chief marshal, told me. Travelling marshals are mounted on motorbikes so that they can access trouble spots quickly. They can play a vital role in areas where fans fear to tread. Des Evans was one such marshal. He explained to journalist Mick Duckworth: 'At the end of a race or practice a sweeper goes round to check all's well. I was doing that once and I noticed something funny about the straw bags at Ballaspur. I stopped to check and found a passenger who'd fallen out of a sidecar lying on them.'

There was no confusion this time. Cummins was in a bad way. Clague had two mobile phones with him and they rang a lot after the crash. 'People were after a story, but I was not interested. I didn't want to talk about it. My cousin came over for TT week and everybody in the pub had a version of what had happened. I never said a word. I'd seen the crash but I didn't want to gossip. I think it was probably caused by extremely strong wind, but it doesn't matter. The main thing is he survived.'

Indeed, he had, but it had been a close-run thing. The damage was huge. Cummins had broken his back in five places, fractured his pelvis and had severe bruising to his lungs. His left side was carnage, his upper arm broken in four places, his leg dislocated, his knee joint shattered. There was a broken collarbone and nerve damage and there was also the unseen trauma to the bruised mind of a TT dreamer. Yet he had survived. Perhaps the power of prayer had worked. Maybe it was the fairies. The first question, though, was whether Conor Cummins would ever walk again. He had fallen down the Mountain and into the abyss.

Coming to the Crosby jump here and for me this is the place. See the crest of the road. Get as close to the kerb as possible. If you're in the right place you don't have to shut the throttle off. If you're not you're, 'Aahhhh', out of control. You have to use your head. People used to go on about Bray Hill being steep, but this is the one that always scared me, like I was gliding out into outer space. You are doing 190mph here. It launches you.

Six

Guy

You don't think at 190mph. You try to remember to breathe. Your eyes are starched open with air and concentration. But somewhere, deep in his subconscious, Guy Martin thought this might be it. All the knockers and the jealous snipes silenced by winning the Senior TT. The big one. The greatest prize. And then he came to Ballagarey. *Ballascary.*

'There was an incident involving No 8, Guy Martin,' Charlie Lambert, the voice of Radio TT and so also the voice of doom, said. 'The bike was in the hedge and on fire. A red flag was shown to allow a fire engine on the course. No word was given regarding the rider's condition. More to follow.'

It had been a horrible crash. Wilson Craig's bike had a tank full of petrol and so it exploded. Martin leapt clear and emerged through the wall of fire in blackened leathers. Debbie Barron, a marshal with spiky peroxide hair, rushed over and cradled his head. Another marshal spoke calmly to the stricken figure. For once, all that natural ebullience and spirit and life had been scraped out of him and left down the road with the detritus of a crash.

Yet, whereas Conor Cummins was a broken man, Martin had enjoyed miraculous good fortune. Before long he was wired up to a drip in Nobles Hospital and on the mend. He raised his eyebrows and laughed at his luck. He shook his head when he mentioned Cummins, down the corridor, down and out. 'This bit of an accident caused a massive load of get-well cards,' he said. There were more than a thousand emails wishing him well. There were books and Lego and iTunes vouchers. There was 'enough chocolate to feed the 5,000'. There were Meccano kits and tea bags and teapots and model bikes. People even sent him money.

He went home to Kirmington and made light of his near-death thing. 'I've not been at work for a week and so that's put a fair bit of strain on my mum and Mr and Mrs Lancaster, as well as the farmer's daughter, but none of them have told me to piss off yet. It'll be right next week. I'm off back to work. I'm not sure how you can find the will to live watching daytime TV, so whether it kills me or not, I'm off back to work.'

This was typical Martin. He revelled in his ability to make light of things. He had a mania about being practical and so he would refuse to be dragged into emotional soul-searching. He was okay and that was enough. 'A crash is a crash.' But what happened? Later, he told me.

'Aye, it did look spectacular, I'll give you that, and I can remember all of it. I was never knocked out. No, no, no. I was a bit dazy, but I remember hitting the wall. I was coming into the corner. I was going no harder than I had been on the previous lap, but because of the pit stop I had a full tank of petrol. I hit the corner and lost the front end. Now if you get a rear-end slide then nine times out of ten you catch them, but no one catches a front-end slide. I say no one, I had a few in previous races at the TT and saved them, more by luck than judgement, but you could pick any corner and the one that most riders would say they don't want to crash at is that one. It's just a blind crest. You get to the apex and it's just furniture on both sides of the road. Walls, telegraph poles, the lot. I lost the front. I thought, "I've got it, I've got it", but I hadn't. It comes with experience. When you start racing and you lose the front then you jump off. As you get older you realise that you might be able to save it. So I hung on and hung on until the very last second and that's when I thought, "No, I haven't got this". That's when I jumped.'

How Martin emerged from crashing at one of the TT's most cursed corners was, as he put it, more luck than judgement. 'If I'd jumped off as soon as I lost the front end then I would have gone into the wall at 90 degrees and it would have been game over.' He says this without any ghosts in his eyes, just a nuts and bolts approach to the past. 'But because I was a little bit further round I glanced off the wall and went into the next one. I think I hit it with my feet. I certainly remember just sliding off the wall and then just rolling and rolling and trying to get up. I was thinking, "What's wrong with you?" Then I thought, "My back's not right". I was out of breath because I'd punctured a lung, but luckily the other one was alright. There was a marshal there. He was talking to me dead calm, like a waiter might when you are ordering your Sunday dinner. He sent me an email or two afterwards. He even came to see me. He put me in the right place.'

They wanted to cut off his leathers, but Martin told them not to. They were retro black and cool. He did not want them ruining. It evinces the seam of common sense running through men who appear bereft of the stuff. Martin knew that he was fortunate. Conor Cummins was in desperate straits in the same hospital. Paul Dobbs had suffered the ultimate fall. Yet Martin was in a buoyant mood as he lay in that hospital bed, his only reminder of his frailty when he forget himself and tried to move too suddenly.

Martin clearly does not dwell in the past, but he remains grateful for that kindness. 'I wasn't in a lot of pain. Maybe the one thing was my back. I could feel everything. I thought I've not hurt my back like that before. It took a matter of minutes. Neck brace on. Winning never crossed my mind. The race was gone. I was just thinking, "Oh shit".'

Six days later he had left hospital and the Isle of Man had reverted to a sleepy backwater. The trucks and transporters had left muddy shadows on the grassy paddock. Cars and lorries and buses crawled down Bray Hill. Douglas was in the early stages of its post-TT depression. The diesel chug was a peal of ordinary, low-gear living.

For Bridget Dobbs life would never be the same again. A petite woman with a bohemian air, she issued a statement that would touch all who read it. The statement also cut to the heart of what the TT was all about, its fatal attraction and its enduring mythology. She wrote:

> While we are all devastated by Dobsy's death during the 2nd Supersport race at the Isle of Man TT on Thursday 10 June 2010, I feel that we are lucky in so many ways. Dobsy died doing what he most loved, in a place he loved and felt at home and surrounded by people he loved and admired. He died instantly and felt no pain. He had no knowledge of his end but was fully focused on the bike and the race.
>
> After making a hard decision and missing the TT last year, I am thankful that I was here at this tragic time. We have been

wholeheartedly supported by the whole racing community in both a professional and personal way. We held nothing back in pursuing Dobsy's racing and so I need regret nothing. Our lives have been immeasurably enriched by the TT and the Isle of Man. I would like to thank Bruce Anstey who had Dobsy in his thoughts even in his moment of glory after the Senior TT. I would especially like to thank Paul Owen. Paul was perhaps Dobsy's greatest rival and friend at the TT. They were very evenly matched and Dobsy measured his performance against Paul's. They invariably got together soon after a practice or race to share their experiences. Paul's selfless and big-hearted action on Thursday moves me beyond words. Without hesitation, he did everything in his power to try to help Dobsy. Paul truly embodies the spirit of the TT.

This is a difficult time for Dobsy's mother, Dawn. I hope that she can overcome and put aside her hurting. She helped to make Dobsy what he was and she should be very proud. Dobsy's daughters, Eadlin and Hillberry, are two very special people. They have lived an honest and unsheltered life and I know they both understand exactly what this means. They will miss their dad terribly and there will be some hard times over the coming weeks, months and years. But I also know that they have been shaped by having Dobsy in their lives and they are all the stronger, smarter and braver for that.

He really spoilt my week but he has brought infinite joy, adventure and fun to our lives. He has energised and inspired. He will live forever in our esteem, our thoughts and our hearts.

It was a message from the heart that provided a window to the soul of a sport. Four days after being sent an email by Steve Christian, Bridget Dobbs would reply and allow his cameras to attend the funeral for his film. 'I'll do it but on the condition that you're not going to hide anything,' she said. She wanted to get the funeral right and so she issued a practical notice in tandem with her statement. It read: 'Dobsy will start his final lap around 2.30 p.m. and bikes particularly will be welcome to join him. There will be no formal order, overtaking is fine but legal speed limits will be observed.'

Death is always close at the TT, literally by way of the wall of plaques in the finish-line cemetery and figuratively on the 37.73 miles of roads. It does not stalk thoughts, but it is a horrible reality nevertheless. For many this has proved too much and they have left the island to its peculiar ways. They get what GP and TT racing legend Ron Haslam termed 'the Knock', a sudden awakening of the real dangers when fear takes over from the fun. 'The sport is based on self-belief,' Haslam told me. 'If that goes then you're on a fast track to the scrap heap. Most riders get the Knock at some point in their career, and for a period it will completely destroy them. When you're in the throes of a downer it's the hardest thing in the world to claw yourself back. Belief ebbs away, and that depression can last for a week or a year. For others it never ends.'

But for most the TT remained a glorious test of spirit that is remarkable, in part, because of the proximity of disaster. Some have suggested there is a macabre voyeurism in watching the TT, but the fans do not come to see tragedy. They come to see gilt-edged sport, and the lurking 'what ifs' merely magnify the heroes. It is something many of us might like to do, as Christian says, but we never will. We will not because we do not have the talent or the nerve or the ability to balance risk and reward in the way they do.

Back in Kirmington Guy Martin was scratching his head. 'I broke my back in three places, broke six ribs and punctured a lung in two places.' Yet his injuries had all but healed. He was doomed in terms of his results but charmed in life. Others had been crushed and killed, but Martin had emerged from a horrible crash at one of the TT's most unforgiving corners, and looked almost unscathed. The fractures had been minor. He singed his eyebrows but they were restored to their bushy norm. Martin had been inordinately lucky. Nevertheless, to his great disappointment, he was not passed fit to ride in the Southern 100, but he had plenty on his plate anyway. He was due to start filming for his new BBC One show, *The Boat That Guy Built*. The premise of the show was simple. Martin would be introduced as a world-famous motorcycle racer and would then don a blue boiler suit as he and a friend, Mave, would take a canal boat called *Reckless*, with the expressed intention of renovating it with methods honed from the Industrial Revolution. In truth it was an excuse to show off Martin's oddities to a new audience, and making a tin can, a Wedgewood pot and a rudimentary shower were means to that end. Narrated by Liza Tarbuck, it was shown at the coveted 7.30 p.m. slot and would receive warm reviews. The flipside was that Martin was already contending with the mounting criticism from those who struggled to ally his lack of a TT win with his spiralling profile.

One such critic was Simon Buckmaster from PTR, the company that had tuned his engines at the TT. Buckmaster lauded Wilson Craig's professionalism and had claimed his Supersport bike was the best in the world before launching a damning attack on Martin's approach and talent. The statement issued to a website would have some nodding in agreement, but prompted a deep sense of grievance from Martin's huge fan base, not least because Buckmaster did not wait for the injuries to heal before he weighed in.

'Guy is a quick rider who is immensely popular but he is flawed,' Buckmaster started. 'He needs to listen to some advice if he wants to win at the TT as he says he does. I had numerous conversations with him and he listened, but then completely ignored everything we agreed on. He ignored and didn't win; unless he changes his attitude he never will. First thing Guy needs to learn is that the rules apply to him as much as anyone else. He may cultivate a "just another one of the boys" image and have legions of admirers but it is not true and distracts him from the racing. How many of the boys have Aston Martins for a start? Not many. How many race at the TT and have credible chances to win? Again not many. It's all a facade. He needs to stop being distracted and lift his professionalism. Instead of being a TV star and courting publicity 24/7, he should be concentrating on racing and what's needed to win. Get his focus and concentration into racing, not promoting his name and money-spinning deals. He needs to drop the "I am only interested in racing my bikes and sleeping in the van" act and actually show that winning is the most important thing to him; as they say actions speak louder than words.'

By any standards this was a meaty attack with all guns blazing. It was clearly heartfelt and Buckmaster also took issue with Martin for using bad language and for criticising PTR when they were tried and tested at elite level, whereas Martin 'still has it all to prove.'

It went on in the same vein with Buckmaster condemning Martin for his hissy fit following his time penalty in the Superbike race at the TT. 'He is not approaching it seriously or with a professional attitude, instead spending far too much time promoting this image of what type of person he is. If he keeps up his unprofessional approach then he may never win a TT. Not only will his own preparations be flawed but there will be very few teams, capable of fielding a winning bike, that will want to deal with him. Mind you, that might be the best thing for him because then he would have to buy and run his own team by himself and then he can do what he likes. The one thing he is unlikely to do in that situation is win.'

The attack hinted at a growing sense of resentment towards Martin. He would laugh it off and did not seem deeply hurt by such remarks, but such animosity grated and he felt people were increasingly beginning to misunderstand him. If he was a showboating attention-seeker then why go for the dull leathers and retro design? 'Everyone else was trying to stand out like a sore thumb, but we didn't. Less is more. Now Wilson [Craig] was good and is a proper bloke. What a bloke. Proper. But he put his confidence in the wrong people.

'Simon Buckmaster. He's not a bad person and has done well at world championship level, but he hasn't built bikes for the TT before, so don't start telling me how to do it. I said to Wilson, "The way to go for 2011 is give me the bikes and let me get them ready. Give me more control". I thought riding for Wilson meant I was getting my own way, but he had this other guy and that upset the apple cart before it even started.'

It had been a testing few months for Martin, but he was soon back on his bike and shaking away the ring rust at pace. He was on the way back, but as he prepared to start work with the BBC, he knew that the critics were going to mount.

'The thing is Simon Buckmaster said all of that while I was still lying in hospital. I don't know why. Like I said, he's not a bad person but maybe he thinks it gets to me more than it does. It obviously bothered him that I pointed out all the bits and pieces that were wrong and said, "Would you ride that at the TT?" It bothered him that I took pictures of everything. That really got his goat. I'm not a flash bastard at all, but yes I do have an Aston Martin. He's really into his cars and so that really niggles him. The car's in my mate's garage and I hardly use it and that niggles him too. But I have got a 53 red Astra too and he doesn't mention that. I'm not toeing the corporate line here but I'm not doing that on purpose. Simon Buckmaster wants me to slag him off, but he isn't a bad person; he's just got a massive chip on his shoulder.'

The row would simmer in the background as Martin got back to his best and started to turn his thoughts towards 2011. In the end he signed to ride for TAS Suzuki, a team run by Hector and Philip Neill, a father and son combo, off the back of a salvage business down a long windswept road in County Londonderry.

Martin would explain to me that he could have made the break-up more amicable. 'There were a lot of cross words,' he says. 'I had done the deal with TAS before I told Wilson. I was over in Ireland and it was coming out on the BBC. I rang him up five minutes before.' He sighs and shakes his head. His father has annoyed him too. A cock-and-bull story he had said to describe his excuse for missing the TT, and he repeats the phrase again. 'He did not come over and he should have. I go about things in a strange way and the old boy is the same. We don't sing off the same hymn sheet, though, and I hold that against him. He'd never missed the

TT before. It's not his fault what happened. I would never say that. I would never try to pass the buck to anyone. I'll hold my own hands up. Okay, we had a few upsets with the team, but I'll hold my own hands up. The only thing that let the side down was me. But he should have been there.'

He still had not got the win he needed for himself and others. He was still the outsider seeking the majestic, life-altering win. In the meantime he would live the solitary life of the man owned by others. And he would keep going back to take on the challenge and risk all.

'I've had mates killed,' he muses. 'I was working for Martin Finnegan.' This was the same Martin Finnegan who warned the errant novice that his style would catch up with him. 'He was my best mate in racing. I went to his wedding in November 2007. No one else from the racing world was invited apart from me and my girlfriend. The funeral was the following May. That was a bit near. I don't go to racers' funerals. When it came to that one, I should have been there to support his missus, but I'm selfish. I knew that would affect my racing. There are bits you have to put out of your mind.' Like a suspension of disbelief. He raises his eyes at that and emits a high-pitched squeak of doubt. 'Ruddy hell. Takes a lot of knocks on the head to come up with something deep and meaningful like that.'

But surely he thought about his mortality now, after the summer he had endured, with the fireball and Conor Cummins and Paul Dobbs? 'You need to live, though, don't you? I could never fit into that 9 to 5 thing. That is why I am getting more into my cross-country cycling. Like a sadist. It's not like downhill mountain biking which is about skill and balls and being hurt; it's about getting your head to deal with pain, when your body is screaming at the head to stop but the head ignores it. That's what I like about it. The pain. I need it.'

Need?

'Yes. I do get off on the pain. I look back on my crash and yes it hurt.'

He knew this sounded strange but I felt pretty sure it went beyond bragging machismo. Martin was a complicated figure who seemed to enjoy the highs and lows with equanimity. People talked of the camaraderie but the TT was also an isolating world.

'I've always said marriage ain't my thing.' It was not quite a non-sequitur and he was drifting back to thoughts of Martin Finnegan. 'Lots of racers are married with kids and have all these commitments with mortgages, and some of that must be going through your mind when you are on the start line. I don't want that. It affects people in different ways but I think it would affect me. You wouldn't go in like a bull in a china shop. I have no commitments. I've nothing to worry about. What have I got?' He pauses and thinks long and hard. 'I don't owe anything to anyone, I'm not married, I haven't got any kids, I've got my mum and dad and brothers and sisters, but we're not a close family, we get on, they're all lovely people, but I'm an outcast.'

And without a TT win he remained so, the outsider looking in, nose to the sweet shop window, condemned to coming back and trying again and again until he could sate the craving.

I've been flat out since Ballagarey, head, elbows, ankles and toes tucked in to try to get out of the wind, running up to Greeba Castle. These big trees on the left are the braking point. So come off the gas, fifth gear, close the throttle, use the chest as a brake and then I'm back on the gas for these three left-hand bends. One, two, three. Now hard on the brakes, down two gears, onto the right of kerb, but don't get on the gas too early. Why not? Because there's a trap. The camber goes from left to right, see how it drops away, so as the back wheel comes over the crest it's very easy to high-side. Rob Barker crashed here. Did exactly that. Bit too anxious. Now short shift back to fourth gear, wheelie, elbow on the kerb on the right side of the road. Have to close the throttle to get the bike to turn otherwise it understeers and I'm into that hedge. On towards those two dogs on the left, back right and click another gear on the exit. Gorgeous. You're not doing anything with the bike now and the whole road is rooting for you.

Seven

Conor

Conor Cummins spent several anxious days in Nobles Hospital, where he compared notes with Guy Martin, and was then flown to the Royal Liverpool Hospital. For a man who once baulked at the idea of leaving the island for the mainland it was an unhappy departure.

The damage was as severe as the drop had been. Carole Cummins had already driven past the crash scene on her way to visit her son in Nobles. This was what the island was like, a long and winding road of stories, both happy and sad. Now Cummins was heading to Merseyside, where expert doctors had a long history of mending TT racers.

His grandmother visited him before he left. 'Are you going to go back and work in the bank now?' she asked. Cummins did not miss a beat. 'Not flipping likely. I'd rather go off the Verandah again.' He later said that that was just the drugs talking, but there was no doubt in his mind about his primary concern. Having survived falling down the Mountain, he now wanted to scale it again. Carole had already resigned herself to that. They had both worked in the offshore department at Lloyds, but she knew his spirit could not be contained among the figures and ledgers and other people's worth.

'Pretty much straight away he said, "I'll be back", she said. 'I think that was the adrenaline, but it was always there at the back of his mind. That was the point. That was what kept him going. I would have been perfectly happy if he had turned around and said it wasn't for him, but I also knew there was no point trying to talk him out of it. I knew that was not going to happen.'

Cummins, though, had been transformed from the man who had so impressed Michael Clague on the Verandah, threatening the lead of the Senior TT, to a brittle shell of a rebel racer. 'One of those things,' he says, echoing Martin's 'crash is a crash' mantra. 'I didn't think it would have me off. All I can remember is getting my last pit board on the Mountain. I saw somebody waving me on. That's all I can remember. That and the side of a mountain, like a bad dream, falling. I must have totally blanked out because the next thing I knew I was waking up in hospital.'

A huge lump had been beaten out of his helmet. He would send it back to Shark, the manufacturers, but not before he had taken a picture of it on his mobile phone. 'I was in a bad way,' he says with characteristic understatement. 'They x-rayed me and got my leathers off. I had really broken my upper arm badly. I had four fractures to my humerus and I remember grabbing my arm as I heard this crunching. I wasn't in a lot of pain but I was heavily sedated. I wasn't fit for anything. I was in a bad way. Guy was down the corridor. The next thing I knew he was barrelling up and we were in the same ward. We talked about a lot of stuff. Nothing deep.'

It was after leaving Martin to go to Liverpool that the

extent of Cummins' injuries were laid bare. His sponsor, Joe, and Joe's girlfriend Claire, were with him. Carole and Zara flew out as soon as they could. He would need major surgery on his back and arm and knee. Fractures in the lumbar region, L1, L2, L3 and L4, were diagnosed. Ligaments would need to be rebuilt by transferring some that were still working in other parts of his body. 'It was time to assess the whole job,' he says. 'It was all down to me. That was hard. We had a big discussion about it. My family didn't overload my brain with rubbish. They didn't say I should be jacking it in. They didn't say I should seriously be considering doing something else. It was just, "Let's get fixed and take each step as it comes". The trouble is they were bleeding painful steps.'

He spent much of those early days being scanned. 'I was flat on my back and they kept taking me down. Every time the results seemed to come back worse and the x-rays threw up something else – broken back, fractured pelvis, scapula, arm bust big time, nerve pulls inside the hand. At that stage it had still not sunk in, which I think was down to the drugs.'

It had already been a hellish ordeal but it was only just beginning. The Sunday after the crash the sector marshal had gone to the hospital to give Cummins his version of the events. Was it the wind, as Michael Clague suspected, or a mechanical failure or a bump in the bumpiest of roads? It did not matter. What mattered was the German medic who had attended him beyond the drystone wall and noticed that there was no pulse in his foot.

The German medic was just another of those faceless heroes giving his time for others, but it was during these bleak days that Cummins met Marcus de Matas, a young surgeon whose no-nonsense approach was offset by encouraging optimism and who would come to play a lasting role in the racer's life. Yet De Matas was not about to fool Cummins into any false sense of security. 'It was a maturing experience alright. The worst moment was when they came around with the consent forms. Jesus. Consent forms are such frightening things. They said they could fix me up, but there were obviously no guarantees.'

'Now let me tell you the risks,' De Matas said.

'I thought, "Brace yourself." And then they said there is a risk of paralysis, there is a risk of blindness and there is a risk of mortality. I thought, "For crying out loud". I was speech-less. As if the wind could not get taken out of me anymore.' He slumped into the doldrums, sails slashed, adrift across the Irish Sea. 'I don't know what to do,' he said to the sur-geon. 'I don't know what to do,' he said to Joe and Claire. 'I really don't know what to do.'

The offer was a mammoth operation to fix his back and knee. Two metal rods would need to be put in his back. 'My knee tendons had all been ripped away too. I needed two pins here and two pins there. Another risk was nipping an artery. The magnitude of it slowly filtered through. It helped that I had my family as my first port of call. I discussed it with them. I spoke to the surgeons. I weighed it all up, but at the end of the day the buck stopped with me and that was hard. I had to make that decision and I'd never had to go through anything like that before in my life.'

It was a tough call. Cummins remembers the surgeons telling him to have a few days to think about it.

'We can stick you in a body cast and hope it heals', said De Matas.

'What do you mean "hope"?'

'Or we can go in and operate and sort it out, but obviously that comes with risks.' De Matas gave Cummins the odds, adding, 'I've only ever seen injuries like yours in a text book.'

'Oh, for crying out loud.'

In a way it was in keeping with the family history. Carole had met Billy when she visited the Isle of Man for TT week. 'Billy was always into his bikes,' she remembered. 'He was already racing when I came on the scene.' Not long after that TT she would come back on holiday. She stayed. 'Billy was racing at 16 and it was not like I didn't like bikes. My dad had one so it was not alien to me. It was just the way it was. You worry about things. Of course you do. Billy had a bad crash at Greeba Castle one year in the Manx Grand Prix. Broke his leg in three places. Then we found out we were having Conor. He had the accident in September and Conor was born in practice week for the TT the following May. There is no set way of dealing with it. You just get on with it. You just find a way to cope.'

Conor was not blasé about his injuries. He knew the gravity of the situation, but was hit with such a welter of information that he struggled to comprehend the future. 'I was dosed up on morphine and had pills coming out of my ears. I liked Marcus de Matas. He was the coolest fella I had ever met and he just oozed confidence. That was reassuring, but I was struggling with these decisions.'

'Either way you have to get it fixed,' Carole said. 'If you're happy to lie around in the plaster cast then fine or you can have the operation done and out of the way. Then it's a quicker road to recovery.'

The operation on his back and knee took around ten hours. Another one followed within days on his arm. In the end he had four surgeries. There were brief reports in the bike press and in the Isle of Man media, but they all dealt in the black and white of physical problems. His back was broken and so they had inserted metal roads to mend it and stop the spinal chord being damaged and thus leaving him paralysed. That was the fact, but the fissures spread to the mind and the dark clouds forming there.

'Four operations,' he recalls. 'The first was to fix my back. Five broken vertebrae, one unstable. It was described as they had to 'fix' me. I felt the only option was to have the operation, but knowing it was the sensible option did not make it any less scary. What people could do to themselves in a lifetime I'd done in one blow. It's not a sob story, just the truth. I felt emotionally dead.'

Cummins would have dreams for a considerable length of time. Some of them were about the accident and he recalled how he came to, counting fairies. Others would be a sort of wish-fulfillment with his body folded into a fetal position, his limbs flexed and supple and perfect. He tried not to think about concepts such as fate, but there was a theme of ruptured flesh running through his story, from being born in TT week, just months after his father broke his leg, to being named after Conor McGinn, a much-loved Ulster racer for whom goodwill was no barrier to crashing in the 1981 TT. Now McGinn was wheelchair-bound although his affection for the TT remained and he often visited on holidays, staying in the Hotel RIO on Loch Promenade.

Even the path of Cummins' descent had been foretold. Just before he had ridden off the Mountain, he might have seen the subliminal marker with the cross and Italian flag, marking the spot where Agostini's great friend, Gilberto Parlotti, had crashed in 1972. Parlotti was the 99th victim of the course, which peaked at almost 1,400 feet closer to heaven, and was bound by those 264 corners. It was a place where fears had been vented every year since a teenager named Victor Surridge crashed at Glen Helen and became the first fatality. That was 1911, a century ago, and even then the *Isle of Man Examiner* had asked 'whether this dangerous form of sport is to be permitted in the future.'

The operations were just the start. 'Psychologically, it got much, much worse after that. The decision had been hard but I later realised that that was the easy bit. I'd never experienced it before, but I now know what it is to be depressed. I tried not to show it, but I was on that many different drugs that I couldn't sleep. I was on morphine up to my ears. It was incredibly difficult to adapt. Although I was only a few miles over the water in Liverpool, it felt like a million miles.'

It was barely a fortnight since he had so impressed Michael Clague with his line and speed. Barely a fortnight since all that consumed the young Manxman was winning the TT. Now all that had quickly faded to sepia and into irrelevance.

'I was on an emotional roller coaster instead. The operations came thick and fast. One after the other. The nurse had to come in at night and roll me. I couldn't sleep and had to get them to prescribe me a tablet so I could get a few hours.' With the surgery completed, it was time to free up the bed and transfer him back to Nobles Hospital on the island. They strapped him onto a stretcher and carried him onto a tiny plane. 'As soon as the plane left the ground it all came rushing out of me and I bawled my eyes out,' he says. 'I don't care how that comes across. It's the way it was.' Unbeknown to Cummins, he was in the grip of the black fug of depression.

Your head's behind the bubble and it's effortless. The road throws you out towards the telegraph pole on the left. Back down to third and there are two traps on this corner, Greeba Bridge. Watch your shoulder on this wall. Feel that bump, very easy to highside. I've crashed just there. Been through that hedge. That's what broke this finger. You have to be a bit patient before getting the power on. Coming up to Gorse Lea now and it's back up through the gears, third, fourth, fifth, sixth. It's a real big-boy corner.

Eight

John

John McGuinness was worried as he backed his enormous motorhome into his drive. There was no margin for error on either side, a garden with a child's trampoline and manicured lawn out of one door, a curtain-twitcher with bottles in her front window out the other. The TT was over for another year and, with that, came the depressive lull in which unsatisfied riders did a lot of soul-searching. For McGuinness, the doyen of modern riders, it had been a terrible fortnight. For the first time in nine visits, he had failed to win a single race.

Rumours began to circulate after that. There were knee-jerk responses from fans who decided he was washed up and finished. That segued into gossip that he was considering retiring. As a rider who had grown up with the TT, McGuinness knew that there would come a time when he had to bow to the taunt of time and leave. 'I'm waiting for the day I get that demon in my head,' he says. 'I'm waiting for it to say to me, "Forget it John, it's time to pack in". I know it will come. It comes to everyone in the end.'

He was 38 and had made enough money to move comfortably into the life of an ex-pro. His house was no mansion and not lavish, but it was enough. 'In the early days you would always put the money back in,' he says to me. 'The last few years have been okay, though. When you see some people have to save up to take the kids to Frankie & Benny's, we don't have to do that; we can order whatever we want and have a few nice things on the side, but my feet have never left the ground. It's always been the same since I was out in Morecambe Bay. I look at a rider like Keith Amor. He earns five grand and spends six and I think, "What an idiot." But is he an idiot? I could be dead tomorrow – that's his attitude. And the thing about him is he will give you his last tenner.'

TT racers do not do it for the money. They do it for love and to sate some inner need. But it rankles with McGuinness that riders are, to his mind, undervalued. 'I get £20,000 for winning a race,' he says. 'There are all sorts of add-ons too, but what everybody forgets is that the Government takes 40 per cent of everything I earn. I'm paying for people who live in flats. It's a vicious circle and it's not fair. The TT track is nearly 40 miles long and I have to pay 40 per cent tax. I say to the taxman, "You sit on the back and for every mile you can hold on you hit me on the back and tell me I deserve to pay 40 per cent tax." They would be fucking fed up by five miles I can tell you. That's how hard we have to earn our money.'

The prize money at the TT is small but complicated. If you won the two big races, the Senior and the Superbike, the most you could pocket would be £20,000 for each. If you led after the first lap you got £200; after four it rose to £1,000; after the sixth and last lap you got £16,000. The total prize fund was £62,000 for those races. For the Super-sport race it was £30,000 and the winner could go home with a maximum of £10,000. There is a limit of 70 bikes allowed in a race. The last position to earn prize money is 20th. In the Senior that would net you £350; in the Super-sport a paltry £100. The costs are bigger. Wilson Craig needed to find around £250,000 to run his team for a season. A brand new Superbike costs around £100,000. Insurance is £500 for each rider for each start. The organisers would then provide cover to the tune of £10,000 for 'death or per-manent total disablement' and £20,000 for the 'loss of or loss of the use of, one or more limbs or eyes.' The good news is the organisers will give you up to £400 to help with travel if you can demonstrate that you will provide good media coverage and have a decent track record.

McGuinness is not mercenary but he has a sense of self-worth. 'Why should we give it all in? Some people stumble into some business on the Internet and make £10 million, and they are sat on their arse and paying the same tax as me. But that's what we have to do. That's what we are. I have to wipe my mouth and get on with it. I don't think about money when I'm on the bike. It's when I get off and then it's, "Right, let's get it sorted". I still love getting on the bike. Every year there is something different, the track, the tyres, the start numbers. People go on about my weight and the rest of it, but I'm professional. In the old days maybe you'd get drunk after the Formula One race but that takes the edge off you. Now I keep my head down at the TT and get on with the job. The winning is more important than anything. You can always have a drink, but you can't always race. I want to give myself the best possible chance of winning. When I retire I will have half a dozen cans in a hedge, watching the race.

'What you need at the TT is good people around you. You have to respect them because then you listen to them.' I think about Guy Martin's run-in with Simon Buckmaster, the barbs and counter-barbs alongside the empty wins column. 'The thing is, at the TT, you often think you're doing it right, but in fact you're doing it wrong,' McGuinness says. 'You listen to some of the younger ones now and it's all what they are going to do and what they deserve to earn, but it's just not happening. They rock star it up. That's why I had so much time for Hutchy when he was coming through. He was dedicated and doing it for the right reasons – he was passionate about motorbikes. The money thing is an added bonus really. Jim Moodie always told me that you need to have a value, but the value we have is an insult. No disrespect to the man, but I saw some tennis player on the box pick up a cheque for $2 million. It doesn't seem quite right. Know what I mean?'

The talk of Moodie takes McGuinness back into the past. He is wondering whether he is now destined to reside there, one of the TT greats who climbed the Mountain but is now over the hill. His confidence was taking a hammering after a barren summer on the island and he moped around the house. It was a year until his next attempt and those months stretched ahead of him like a jail sentence. Days and months would be crossed off as he morphed from the thrill of charging down Bray Hill, with runaway hope assuaging any fear, to the sleepy half-life of Morecambe and its absence of risk.

Jim Moodie was a gritty Glaswegian who did not suffer fools. He carved out a successful career on both the short circuits and the roads, but ultimately joined the ever-increasing list of TT stay-aways. He has seven TT wins but knew when his time was up. 'Jim Moodie did it for me,'

McGuinness says. 'I was sacked at the end of 2002. I finished second to DJ [David Jefferies] in the TT and they let me go. That was hard. You think, "What have I got to do?" It's hard to go on. There's nowt you can do if nobody wants you. I half-expected it, to be honest. I was in the World Supersport Championships at the same time. I was living the dream. Except the dream was not all it was cracked up to be – I struggled like mad, got pneumonia, broke my collar bone at a press day at Croft. You fall off the wagon. When you're on a crest of a wave and then it all comes down on you, it's the worst thing. High to low. I struggled. But Jim helped. He has always been pretty inspirational in my racing career. He was very professional. He taught me fitness even though he could never quite drill it into me. Jim steered me and kept me out of the pub, got me to bed early, made me eat decent food. I half-expected someone to come in for me, but they didn't and I thought I'd better dig deep and find something else. So I went away and did things with Yamaha. I came back stronger. In 2003 I rode the Triumph at the TT. I had a big Union Jack down my front and won the manufacturers' award. That was special.'

Moodie's influence on McGuinness stemmed all the way back to 2000. With the time ticking down to the start of the Singles race at the TT, he sought out his friend for help. 'I was running late, fucking last minute and was not the best organised person,' he recalled. 'I knocked on his door and said, "Jim, I need some knee-sliders". Well, he stitched me up didn't he and gave me the Saltire ones. I've worn them ever since. But Jim always had a value. He always thought riders should have a value. He was right too. Riders do have a value. He always taught me, "Don't do owt for nowt". This is the way it is. You're providing a service and there's money out there.'

But now, in the summer of 2010, with the dust barely settled on another TT and with no trophies to show for a fortnight of hard riding, the value of McGuinness was up for debate. It was talked of in the pubs and paddocks and in the interior monologue. 'I had a lot of self-doubt,' he says. 'The bike broke down twice and I thought, "Is it trying to tell me something here? Is it time to do something else?" It was a let-down for the fans and the people who were paying money to go to the island and watch me. Nobody was seeing anything. It was a waste of money. Maybe it does not make a lot of difference to people, but it does to me – wages, prize-money, accolades. I lost it all. I did not know what was happening with my job. I did not know which direction Honda was going in. I was lacking a lot of confidence.'

It felt like a turning point, but the past was littered with them. It had been now or never before, back in 1999, when he had done his apprentice years and was riding the 250cc Vimto Honda. It was one of those rare bikes that he felt he merged into, like a centaur, and he would win the British Championship on it that year. 'I was on by far the best bike,' he says, a smile flicking his lips at the memory. 'TSR frame, full A-kit, I set off as No 4, I went through the bottom of Bray Hill and thought, "If I don't win on this thing I'm never going to". There was not much pressure. I was younger, I was leading the British Championship, I'd won at Daytona, I'd won at Scarborough. I just felt good going into practice. And I loved that bike. I felt part of it.'

McGuinness would walk up to the bike and feel an inviolable sense of conviction. 'It was a bit like that with my 2007 HM Plant bike, but that 1999 250 was part of the furniture. It is very rare in racing when you walk up to a motorbike, look around and think, "I'm going to beat them all". You can't say it because it sounds cocky, but I felt it inside. I finished on the podium in every single race I ever did on that bike. I qualified on the front row of the British Championship every time I got on it. It sounds crap and corny, but it was easy. I didn't feel like I was trying.' He pauses. 'Maybe that's the secret of the TT.'

The secret was eluding him now. He was trying hard but success was going elsewhere, to younger men with a '99 swagger. The riders would give their knowledge and help to others they liked, a generational pass-the-parcel, and times changed. Moodie had helped McGuinness and McGuinness had helped Hutchinson. 'You can't put 2,000 people in a car park and expect them all to get on,' McGuinness explains. 'That's the nature of the beast, innit? David Jefferies was a good friend of mine. When my son Ewan was born DJ was there at the hospital within an hour. Nobody did that. You don't have many friends in the paddock. Don't have too many people you trust. But I'd seen Hutchy come from nothing to be a successful TT rider. Now he's won five in a week and people say I taught him too much. I wouldn't say that. I didn't teach Hutchy at all. I remember him coming on the scene and DJ gave him a bike. He had won TTs and got bonuses with bikes. He gave one to Hutchy and looked after him a bit. He was working in a bike shop, working and riding, and he reminded me a bit of myself, beg, borrow and stealing. He crashed at the North West and I helped him put the bike in the van. I said, "Keep going". He's done a fantastic job. To win five in a week was incredible. If Guy Martin won five TTs then they would have a national holiday. Hutchy's won five and it's gone a bit under the radar.' But at least he had raked in around £50,000 from the summer of 2010 with Clive Padgett getting the other half of the winnings.

McGuinness kept going after being sacked in 2002 and bounced back with a win, but 2003 would, for many people, be the nadir of the TT. It was the week when he won and yet was left devastated. It was Thursday 26 May 2003 when the death knell sounded long and loud.

Jefferies had won a hat-trick of TT races at each of the past three festivals, the 2001 event being cancelled due to the foot and mouth crisis. He was a big man, a hulk of beef dripping, and the shining star. But in practice that Thursday, he slipped on oil left by Daniel Jansen's blown Suzuki, and crashed into the garden wall of No 29, Woodlea Villas in the normally sedate village of Crosby. He was hurled back into the road and killed. McGuinness was following and knew instantly that he had lost a friend. He pulled up. A telegraph pole was severed and fell, leaving wire strung across the road. McGuinness watched as Jim Moodie arrived at pace and was almost garroted by the wire. His speed saved him as it snapped the wire, leaving Moodie with a lacerated neck. 'I thought, "This is it", he would say afterwards. 'If the cable hadn't snapped then I was on the verge of blacking out. I'm amazed I'm in one piece. It's a miracle. My time obviously wasn't up.' His time at the TT was, though, and he would quit with a diatribe.

In the paddock McGuinness was surrounded by people wanting to know what had happened. 'One of my closest friends in racing has just paid the ultimate price,' he said. 'It was a like a war zone, a bomb site, horrendous.'

Jefferies' father, Tony, a doyen of motorcycle racing, and his sister, Louise, were at a BMW conference in London when the call came. Louise would remember seeing her father on the phone and tears running down his face. That was when she knew. She grew hysterical. All those years spent fearing phone calls during the TT had given way to the one that counted, the horrible premonition she had suffered in silence before her brother departed for the island now raw and real.

The accident was shocking and the aftermath controversial. Many people had been killed at the TT in almost a century of racing, but never had the leading protagonist been the unlucky victim. And it was luck, rather than weakness, that caused the crash. Jefferies had never crashed at the TT, had won nine races in three visits and was simply peerless. Yet not even he could ride through an oil slick at around 170mph.

Tony Jefferies wrote a detailed, heartfelt and magnanimous appraisal of issues arising from the crash. Rather than being hell bent on legal revenge, Jefferies, a road racer who had won at the TT but was now in a wheelchair, questioned the lack of oil flags waved and the training given to marshals. 'It is totally unacceptable for there not to be an oil flag on the corner at Crosby, or at any point on the circuit,' he said, noting that more than three minutes had passed between Jansen's bike spreading oil on the circuit and Jefferies' ill-fated arrival. 'It is totally unacceptable to leave one lady in charge of one of the most devastating crashes in the TT, where a 180mph stretch of circuit was destroyed by the remains of a rider, smashed up bike, half a ton of rubble, a telegraph pole felled with wires across the track, and only one flag being intermittently waved on the actual corner. It was in fact a spectator waving a red jacket that stopped some of the riders.'

Father and son had argued against silencers being used on Production bikes, feeling silence was deadly, but the Tourist Board and ACU had ignored them. Jefferies senior was also incredulous that the sector marshal at the inquest admitted she did not know what to do in the event of a fatality. Jefferies said he was unlikely to pursue a claim for negligence, even though it had been advised he had a case, but the damage done to the organisers was irreparable.

At that time many predicted the TT would also die. Yet for McGuinness, dealing with the death of a friend would be the making of him as a rider. It enabled him to return time and time again to win on the same roads. It enabled him to surpass Jefferies' tally of nine wins and stand squarely in the light rather than the shade of the TT. He would never forget but he would find a way to ration his memories.

'The DJ thing was the most powerful thing I'd ever seen in terms of annihilation of bikes and scenery,' he says. 'To me Dave was a hero and there was a lot of fucking rubbish afterwards – people said bits flew off, this was off, legs and arms were hanging all over the shop, but it wasn't like that. I told Tony and I think it comforted him a bit. The truth is he was just lying there like he was asleep. Perfectly straight. It was, "Bang", he's gone. That's it. He was a good mate of mine. He was Ewan's godfather. I'd seen him crying when we'd asked him to be that. I've been through a lot with him, stuff with his women and bits and pieces. I came into the pits and that was it – I was going home. His mum, Pauline, was there. A strong woman. She's passed away too now. She said, "What are you talking about? You have to carry on racing." I thought about what. "What else was I going to do?" She was right. I would only go home and be grumpy, kick the dustbin around the house. It's our choice. It's 100 years old. I have articles from the 1980s saying, "It's too fast, ban it". It's going to carry on isn't it?'

It did not look like it in 2003, though. 'The TT was

completely on its arse after DJ died,' McGuinness says. 'There was a lot of dead wood there. I never sat there pointing fingers, but I felt I'd done my bit, now they needed to do theirs.'

The effects of Jefferies' death would be manifold. Early morning practice sessions were abandoned. A state-of-the-art radio system was introduced to improve communication between marshals. More marshals were used so that no section of the road was blind. Better fencing was introduced. Most importantly, there was a freshness of thought brought in by the likes of Paul Phillips, the Isle of Man Government's Motorsport Development Manager. Yet, at its heart, it remained dangerous and no amount of improvements would dull the personal pain felt by friends and relatives. They were part of the TT's horrible collateral damage.

'I have my memories of Dave and they are great ones,' McGuinness says. 'I had a lot of respect for him as a rider. He would always give you room. Hard but fair. You have people like that and you think, "Why do they get taken away?" Why is a smackhead who sells a cut and shut car to your grandma still walking around the world, and someone like Dave, who gave a bit back, isn't? You think that. Then you start getting emotional and religious and I don't get it. Why does it happen? It's not right. Bad people in the world should not be here. Good people should be.

'But DJ's death made them realise the safety of marshalling needed a big review. I think there should have been an oil flag out. A bike had blown up. The verdict was misadventure, but to this day I believe he crashed on oil. Other people might say it was mechanical failure; other people might say he was trying too hard; for my part, whether it's for my own comfort or whatever, I think he crashed on oil, because Dave could do no wrong. It pisses me off. It could have been me. Because Dave is bigger than me, he roughed me out of the way and was ten seconds ahead of me on the road. If I'd out-roughed him at the start then it would have been me. If and but – the biggest words in the dictionary.

'It's a bad thing to say, but if No 58 had crashed then things would be no different today. The truth is No 58's life is worth just as much as No 1, but this was David Jefferies crashing and dying. It caused a storm. No 58 would have caused a press release and that would have been it.'

No 58 at the 2011 TT would be Lee Vernon, who worked in a motorcycle shop in Manchester. He had gone to the first major meeting when he was 18 and, hence, legally old enough. That was the Ulster Grand Prix in 2006. 'We entered that thinking it was a holiday and the bikes were a bit of a sideline,' he said. 'My dad, my stepmum and a few friends went. If I didn't like it I'd stick it in the back of the van and we'd come home. Turned out I loved it.' So much so that he was fourth. 'I remember sitting on the start line,' said Vernon. 'My dad said, "This is mint isn't it". I ended up leading, but then got a bit lost.' Of course, the TT could never truly be a holiday, as McGuinness knew from the foulest, bitterest experience.

'Dave's mum and dad, his sister, they are strong people who have been around the sport a long time. Tony's in a wheelchair because of an accident at Mallory Park. They have lost friends and they know how to deal with it. It was one of the worst days of my life, but the next day I got up for 5 a.m. practice and it was just normal. Life goes on.'

Now the man who had been taught by Jim Moodie to know his value was doubting his self-worth. And when that happens a rider may not be too far from the Knock and the naked realisation that, for all the buzz and drama and life-giving risks, there comes a time in every TT racer's life when it is just not worth it anymore.

You are here in two and a half minutes from the Grand-stand. That big tree is the braking point and that's Bal-lacraine. Seventh gear down to second, lash the anchors on. By this time the newcomers are into it, their minds starts to wander, they scratch their balls and want a cup of tea. Glen Helen is in the trees. Like a tunnel effect in the middle of June with all the trees low. Like strobe lighting. The next two or three miles look the same and a lot of newcomers struggle. This left is where I had my big accident. Uphill, very steep. Can't afford to shut the throttle off. I just got through and caught my shoulder and bang, I flew into that wall, and that threw me back into this wall here. They have boards on it now. That was the best thing about my crash. I was the guinea pig. I saved a few people. It was pretty bad. Broke my left shoulder, all my ribs down my left side, punctured my lung, sprained a kidney, lost my spleen, broke my right ankle, intensive care for a week, that was about it really.

Nine

Conor

'You know before they even shake your hand that the question they want to ask is, "Can you fix me?"' Marcus de Matas is sipping on a Diet Coke in a London hotel opposite the American embassy. Protestors against the US blockade of Cuba are camped outside in the rain-dashed square. Inside the bar is a phalanx of internationally renowned surgeons. 'I'm not at that level yet,' he says, looking around and sounding like the medical version of the wannabe racer climbing the greasy pole. 'The shoulder surgeon at Liverpool is globally recognised; I'm not. Nobody knows who little old me is.'

De Matas, the surgeon who saw Conor Cummins when he arrived at the Royal Liverpool Hospital, is a modest man. He has glasses, a ready grin and a pinstripe suit. He says people only remember him because he has an exotic name, and is keen to stress that fixing Conor Cummins was a team effort. The back-room teams would be manifold, the comforters and cheerleaders at home in Ramsey, the crew and sponsors in mud-flecked awnings, the back-room band of scientific minds in an anodyne hospital ward.

De Matas assessed Cummins. He was a mess, but trauma teams were used to that. For De Matas, Cummins was just another problem, the same as the 80-year-old cancer sufferer. As usual, there was a trauma meeting at 8 a.m. where he consulted three wise radiologists. 'The older generation of surgeons would have seen his injuries as self-inflicted, no different to smoking,' De Matas says. 'I didn't see it like that. If you're a window cleaner and you fall off a ladder, then that's your chosen profession. There is no moral judgement. If someone chooses to do the TT and they have a licence to ride at that level, then who am I to argue? This guy was not an amateur rider. He knew exactly what the risks were and he had the skill to carry that risk. They don't let anybody go and ride on that track, and the modern surgeon would not make a moral judgement – or at least he shouldn't.'

De Matas met two other surgeons whom he worked closely with in Liverpool, Jo Banks and Matt Smith, and they drew up a plan of action. The first issue was Cummins' back. 'If you imagine taking a breadstick and twisting it then you get the idea. It would crack along one set of lines, but if you looked at it from another angle, the lines would be different. It's quite easy to misinterpret something and so that's why we work as a team. His [Cummins'] recall is absolutely right – paralysis, death, blindness. Those were the salient points. I said my operation would give him the platform to rehabilitate, in terms of moving him about and getting him sitting up, while the other operations were performed. What's scary about fixing the back of a patient who is neurologically normal is that I can make it worse. That's why my job is a bit like his.'

Cummins had already told me how he consulted his

mother over whether to go through with the back operation. De Matas was more phlegmatic, divorced from the
emotion of the choice. 'His fracture could have been treated
non-operatively,' he says of the back injury. 'Just stay in bed
for six weeks and see what happens. The problem with that
was his limited mobility, the risk of pressure sores, and the
fact he still needed complex knee and elbow surgery. I
gave him the option, but I knew what he was going to say.
I gave him 48 hours. You can't say, "You've got 20 minutes to
decide your whole life". He was basically trusting me to tell
him the truth and then trusting that I had the capability to
put him on the table and avoid those risks. Essentially, it
was just like him riding around that track. But he was still in
that period of shock. He was 23, still thinking, "Oh my God",
still wondering how he was alive rather than about the spe-
cific injuries.'

The ordeal started with Jo Banks stabilising Cummins'
damaged knee. An external fixator, effectively a cage, was
attached. For all the risks, De Matas says it was a relatively
routine spinal operation. Ten inches long and six millimetres
wide, the metal rods were inserted to hold the vertebrae
rigid. 'Prevent movement and allow healing,' De Matas says.
'Spines generally break when a mobile segment meets a fixed
segment.' The operation was a success, but was merely the
preamble to more medical miracles.

'Conor's fracture was a wolf in sheep's clothing,' says De
Matas. 'His humerus fracture was quite horrific. For want of
a better word, it was rogered. If it was an isolated injury
then you'd be doing well to recover from that, but his worst
injury of all was his knee. Why? Every ligamented structure
in his knee was ruptured so that the only thing holding it
together was some of the muscles and his neurovascular

pedicles.' Like most medics, De Matas can blind with science, but he reduces it to layman terms. 'There was a 20 per cent risk of amputation. He could have been in trouble.'

Another member of the team, Matt Smith, fixed the arm and Cummins remained in Liverpool for three weeks. De Matas was pleased with the progress, but knew the biggest test would come further down the line when he had surgery on his knee. Not until the knee was rebuilt could the trauma team begin to rest on their laurels. 'I didn't know that he was feeling low but a change in mood is very common,' De Matas says. 'I don't want to de-motivate someone who is 23 years old, but nor do I want to over-inflate expectations.'

As Cummins disappeared out of sight and, fleetingly, out of mind, the man in the glasses and the pinstripe suit could scarcely have known that his patient was consumed by tears in a small plane being buffeted by winds on his way back to the accident. Cummins was young and full of life, but he had been rendered a cadaverous relic of his former self. The youthful spirit had been stolen and now he was returning to the crime scene. His last lap had been on Friday, 11 June.

He would remain in Nobles well into August. His family tried to relive the boredom by taking him out and shepherding him around. 'I had the cage on my leg and could barely fit in the car. I had to sit across the backseat with my legs stretched out. I was totally demoralised. I was a wreck.' He tried to put on a brave face for the press and public. So when a TV crew turned up to Nobles to film a pre-arranged interview, Cummins gave a phlegmatic self-assessment. It was 30 July, seven weeks on. 'I'm getting more movement every day but it's never going to be what it was,' he said of his back. 'The next operation was for my arm. I broke the humerus in four places and I'm waiting on the nerve to wake up. Two plates and 20 screws later I'm on the road to recovery. I think it's a good thing I did not remember it. One of those things. Take it on the chin.'

He had been out to the Southern 100, the post-TT meeting in Castletown, where his father was racing, but for all those who had wished him well, there were more who were struck by just how withered and white he looked. Wearing old tracksuit bottoms to cover his cage, slippers and an old coat, he was pushed around in a wheelchair. Most people who saw him felt sad. All wanted to know about the future. 'I'm just waiting for the surgeon to give me the green light,' he told the camera in Nobles. 'The season was going fantastic. It was gutting I did not get my first TT win on the Saturday, but I'm a big boy now and should be able to take that on the chin. Unfortunately, I've had a little blip. Dr de Matas and Dr Banks have done an astonishing job on me. The support has been astonishing. My mother especially has had a crash course in the whole racing scene. Dad raced for years before I came along. I think that's helped in coping.'

Looking back at that film now it is easy to see how depressed Cummins was. He drags up a smile but it is hollow and brief. There is that fraudulent look in his eye, flitting back to the past and to the future. The present was probably just too horrible. 'I could not get out of bed at first,' he told me. 'I could not stand for more than ten seconds without feeling really sick and dizzy. I could not go to the toilet; I had to do it in the bed. Dignity went out of the window. I felt helpless, awkward. It sounds awful but when I was able to go to the toilet I was straining and blood started gushing out of one of the pins. That was day one.'

But the Southern 100 did light some spark deep inside him and made him realise he truly wanted to get back.

Michael Dunlop won the Senior race but crashed in the finale and was taken to Nobles, himself. The checks were precautionary, the fortunes jarring. Dunlop flew home, fit and well, with a hat-trick of wins, a feat matched by his brother William. Both men were on the cusp, but the message boards were filled with remarks about his wildness and the inevitability of Michael's crash. Meanwhile, Billy Cummins competed in two races in the packed programme. He was 16th out of 17 finishers in one and 18th out of 19 in the other. It was curious to think he was rubbing shoulders with some of his son's rivals, but he felt he wanted to do something. He admitted he had gone outside the house and cried after his son's accident. He blamed himself for getting him involved in the sport. What had he done? The self-flagellation was harsh because the truth was Conor was always going to go racing. Short of moving from the Isle of Man, he was never going to be able to live a sheltered life. Now Billy hoped that riding might inspire his son again and give him some motivation.

It was around this time when Cummins decided to go back to the Verandah. 'It was mid-July when the doctors deemed me fit to come home and visit my grandparents. I had to be back in hospital that night.' Carole was in the car too. There was only one way from Ramsey back to the hospital and it went past the accident scene.

'Do you want a look?' Carole asked.

'No, you're alright,' said the backseat rider. 'I can't be bothered.' Then he reconsidered. Would it be so bad? And he had to admit he did have a slither of curiosity. So they pulled the car to the side of the road and he got out. He limped to the edge on crutches and looked down into the valley below. 'I just thought, "Yeah, I'll have a look and see where it all went wrong." There was a big black mark across the road. I saw where I'd hit the grass and cleared the wall. I was amazed. The distance from leaving the track to the wall was well over 200 yards. I'd crashed in maybe under four seconds. There was a hint of green off my leathers. I looked down and thought, "Christ, no wonder." '

He was allowed home from hospital in August, but he was far from well as he made his way to the physiotherapy clinic in Peel. The place was run by two women, Isla Scott and Cath Davis. It was Scott's business and several years earlier she had taken the decision to target motorsport. It was a slow process, but now the top riders all used them. Davis' father had a Triumph and so she was not immune to the lure of bikes. The pair offered physio at the TT but there was no money exchanged. 'For two weeks we do it for free so effectively that's a loss,' Davis said. 'But we don't go for the money; we go because it's exciting.'

When Cummins struggled into the clinic she was dumbfounded. 'I have to be honest, I scratched my head. I didn't know where to start. Everything was broken and he looked very unwell. He had lost a lot of weight and most of his muscles had shrunk to nothing. His scapula was broken and was flopping around in space; he had already had the repair work done to his spine and that was pretty extensive as far as we saw; he had raging sciatica down his left side; he was wearing a brace on his leg to restrict his range of movement because the ligaments had all snapped and needed to be repaired.' He was a mess of shattered bones and hope, a spine of lattice work behind him, an uncertain future ahead. But the thing that really worried Davis as she examined the ashen victim in front of her was the arm. 'He had broken his humerus badly and my main concern was that the radial nerve had just switched off completely. There was nothing going on in that upper limb at all. That was the one that concerned me as a physio. When it comes to bones, if you've got a good orthopedic consultant, then they will get better, but you never know with nerves. They are very temperamental.'

'What are your goals?' she asked.

'TT 2011,' he said.

If that sounded bullish it belied the sense of fragility that was dismantling his stated ambition. Davis knew that it would take hundreds of hours of repetitive exercises to give Cummins a chance of ever riding again, let alone in 2011. Unless the nerve could wake up then all the surgery and pep talks and demon-dashing on the Verandah would be useless. Cummins was also depressed at the thought that he had gained a reputation as a crasher. 'I hated that idea. It's why I put off watching the footage for so long. I didn't want people to think that that somehow represented what I was. I still had that feeling of total helplessness. I relied on other people for everything. For my parents and Zara it was incredibly taxing. They carted me everywhere. I wasn't my normal self. Eventually, I'd be grateful and consider what I had in life, but not then. As soon as I left hospital my leg began to feel better, but mentally it was a lot slower.'

That really hit home in August. Cummins found himself at home with his sister, watching television, when the depths of his depression hit home again. 'I'll give you an instance,' he says. 'It sounds really sad. I was sat at home watching the Women's Rugby World Cup, when I was suddenly overcome with emotion. I had no idea why, but I was absolutely all over the show. I started crying my eyes out. Irrational. I can't explain how it felt, but there have been a few occasions like that.'

Guy Martin. 'I'm different.'

That Near-Death Thing. The sprawling cemetery behind the start-finish straight.

(*above*) The old stager. John McGuinness in his TT Legends livery.

(*left*) 'I'm so proud of him.' Carole Cummins with her son, Conor, before.

The Verandah.
Conor Cummins heads
for his fall, 2010.

'He spiralled up in the
air.' Conor Cummins
before the descent
down the Mountain.

The eyes have it.
Michael Dunlop
focuses.

Happier days. Guy Martin and the deceptive idyll of the Isle of Man, 2009.

'I'm not scared of dying.' Guy Martin's bike erupts in flames, 2010.

The luckiest – fate, luck, providence? Martin survives.

The sorcerer and the apprentice. A young John McGuinness with his hero, the peerless Joey Dunlop.

Brass tacks. Tea, sarnie and legend. A younger Joey.

He kept up the physio and mixed it with sessions in the island's one hyperbaric chamber behind the old fire station. Davis was convinced those sessions helped. The chamber is a cell where patients sit and receive oxygen at a higher level than atmospheric pressure. The benefits are believed to help conditions ranging from thermal burns to broken bones to cerebral palsy. 'There is not an evidence base for the hyperbaric chamber, but I am 100 per cent convinced it helped,' she said. 'That and the fact Conor was fortunate to have physio four or five times a week. I kept seeing him and seeing him. A lady sports psychologist attached to the Sports Institute gave us access to their pool, which was very cold, more like cryotherapy. That kept us private and that was good because there was a lot of attention. We did loads of soft tissue work. Loads and loads of boring routines to try to get the brain to remember. We went over and over it, for hours and hours, him lying there on his back. But the problem was always the same. That damned nerve.'

Davis explained it to Cummins as best she could. 'Look, Conor, the nerves are like telephone wires,' she said.

He nodded.

'We have conductive material wrapped in an insulating sheath and this is the message centre. The trouble is the wires are broken so we need to remind the telephone wires what type of information they are meant to be taking back to the message centre.'

That was why his left hand would not work. It flopped and whatever he did he could not get it to flex and move and grip. Without the hand he was finished. 'He couldn't think those nerves better,' Davis said. 'It wasn't the message centre that was damaged. It wasn't his emotions that were damaged. Someone had stepped on the telephone wires. He wasn't imagining it and he wasn't making it up. He just could not physically make that hand work.' The wires were down, just as they had been when Jim Moodie had torn into them and nearly decapitated himself seven years earlier.

Unlike Moodie's post-DJ exit from the TT, Cummins was not blaming anyone and safety had improved enormously, but his future was also a case for serious consideration. Davis, like De Matas, did not want to give him any false hope and so the goals were rooted in realism. 'The first goal was to get him to put his shoe on with his foot, because there was no way he could use his hands with the limited range of movement.' Was she fooling herself and him? 'I didn't think it was a pipe dream,' she said. 'If he wanted to make the TT in 2011 then that was the goal. That's what we were aiming for.' But she did have a caveat.

'You need a Plan B.'

So Cummins went to his local college. 'I thought about doing carpentry and joinery. I needed something to do for the next 40 years, but it turned out I was too late with my entry. It was probably just as well. I was on crutches and couldn't use my left hand so god knows how I thought I'd be sawing up great lumps of wood.'

He went back to the drawing board and to Plan A. There was no option now, but he was a broken man with an uncertain future. The crash was barely three months ago, and so he was hobbling towards the next TT, nine months away, with a lopsided gait, searing pain, well-worn crutches and withered limbs.

This bend is very bumpy and very fast, fourth gear on the exit as you want to be on the right-hand side down to Laurel Bank. Bang, bang, bang through the gearbox. Re-surfaced this bit, like a mini Daytona. Now go into the wall and then when you get there come off the gas and close the throttle into Glen Helen. Into the kerb now and I am shallow breathing. I have been working so hard to get here. I am exhausted. I need some air in my lungs. My brain is lacking oxygen. I move my fingers to get some circulation back so I don't get arm pump. You can't relax, though. It only takes a gnat's second.

Ten

Guy

Guy Martin's path to another stab at the TT seemed smoother, but still included rows, rifts and appearances in court. At least his back healed quickly. 'I'm a 100 per cent,' he had said into another camera while still in his hospital bed in Nobles in June 2010, cup of tea in hand, elfish eyes darting round his head like a glitterball. 'Well, maybe not quite 100 per cent, but I'll be back racing soon.'

He went home and kept himself busy with his toys. He bought a Martek turbo monster bike and would work on it in his front room for months. 'If you want scaring this is the tool,' he said. His friend, Yim, had got hold of a 'nitrous system to put on her'. Martin said his goal was to get to 500 bhp. 'It'll end in tears I'm sure.' He worked on his Martek and watched his favourite films – *Pulp Fiction, Dumb and Dumber, Jackie Brown* – but all he really wanted to do was get back to racing.

So he went to the Southern 100 too, just like Conor Cummins did. One man was a tormented figure there as he watched his father try to induce some optimism, the other watched from Stadium Corner and supped from a beer can. Martin went to see Cath Davis' colleague, Isla Scott, while he was on the island to get the all-clear. He did his best to convince her that he was ready for a return and so she passed him fit. Martin pencilled in the Ulster Grand Prix.

In the meantime he and 'the farmer's daughter' took the van and went to Fort William for a six-hour bicycle race. It was downhill and downright dangerous. Martin crept into the top ten after three hours, but faded away after a puncture, still finishing inside the top 20 after a quarter of a day in the saddle. He said it was 'hardcore', his favourite phrase for anything that truly tested the limits of his self-belief.

In August he travelled to County Antrim for the Ulster Grand Prix. There were six races. Martin entered five. They were all on the same day. He had feared that he would be unable to wrestle the huge 1000cc Wilson Craig Honda around the circuit in Dundrod, but he lapped at an average speed of 127mph in the opening race and the case was closed. He finished in the top six every time. The third race was the feature one, the Ulster GP Superbike race, and Martin was embroiled in a five-man battle for supremacy with the likes of Ian Hutchinson and Michael Dunlop. In the end, Martin, emboldened by his six-hour downhill ordeal in Fort William, was just 1.2 seconds off a win. The back was clearly healed. A last lap with an average speed of 133.5mph proved the bottle was still there. The fireball and the aftermath were ancient history, the Knock some way off, perhaps never to be encountered.

'My lack of race fitness began to take its toll as the day wore on,' he admitted. 'I wasn't intimidated or scared to be back out there racing at 190mph and I gave it my all in every race, but I'm man enough to admit I just didn't have that last little bit to give.' He felt fit, but would not be working out in the gym. 'I saw a picture of a gym once,' he mused when I asked how he trained. 'That's as near as I've got.'

He thanked his team, his old pals, Danny, Cammy and Alastair, and he thanked Wilson Craig and even someone from PTR. The writing was on the wall, though. Martin was charging towards what he felt was almost an inevitability, a first TT win, and the team would soon become a severed alliance as he left no stone unturned.

Meanwhile, a footnote to the Ulster Grand Prix saw Paul Owen return to action with a ninth place, another rider who had managed to put personal doom behind him, his friend Paul Dobbs gone but never forgotten. Owen was another of the TT's journeymen, sleeping in the second paddock and working from a converted prison van. He ran something called the 98 Club to fund his passion. For £98 punters could become one of the 98 members. In return they would get a membership card, a mug and some advertising on his bike. He had been a lifeguard in Wales in his previous life, but now he wanted to be a racer. So he struggled along with an old bike and loose change, gaining a bit more sponsorship from a company who made hangover cures. He said his income was less than £30,000 and that his heroes were Elvis and anyone who rode the TT. For many, he was also a hero. He had been awarded the Spirit of the TT award for his actions that summer. He recounted what had happened. 'Paul (Dobbs) was just ahead of me and went round a blind bend. Very quickly afterwards the marshals started to wave flags, indicating danger. I braked hard and when I got around the corner I saw Paul had crashed.' He did not regard himself as a hero, but he had dismounted and told the marshal to attend to Dobsy while he waved a flag to warn other riders. He had no thought about winning or his position or the money that would make his life-choice work. He just wanted to help. 'When I was told about receiving the Spirit of the TT, initially I didn't want it,' he would say. 'But on reflection I decided to take it in honour of Paul and as a tribute to him, a wonderful man and rider. He is very sadly missed by his family and friends. He will also be greatly missed by the sport, but this was something he loved doing and we all know the risks that are involved.'

Dobbs and Martin had crashed at the same place. One was doomed, the other charmed. Nobody knew why, but Martin's progress continued. He went to Oliver's Mount, Scarborough, the place where poor Phil Haslam had died when he was still a rising star, and won the International Gold Cup Trophy for the seventh consecutive year. He was back to his mercurial best.

His season was over, but Martin was a maelstrom of energy that contrasted sharply with the crumpled form of Conor Cummins. So he went back to Scarborough for a downhill mountain bike race, with a course formed of 400 descending steps. The farmer's daughter was with him, along with his friend Mave, his accomplice in *The Boat That Guy Built*. Their relationship was key to the success of the programme, a buddy boat trip in a blue boilersuit. 'From the word go it was carnage,' Martin gushed about the bike trip. 'I reckon by the time they called it off at about 10 p.m., there had been six ambulances full of broken legs, wrists, noses, knees, collarbones and ankles. It made the Isle of Man TT look like a nice gay day out.' The bad weather meant the race was called off, but the damage had been done in qualifying. Martin's sense of invincibility had been restored thanks to hurtling over the handlebars in qualifying and being spread-eagled, cartoon-style, against a wall. He picked himself up and promised the organisers he would return the following year.

Martin had other problems that would linger into the following year. The first was the BBC show. It would not be screened until 2011, but Martin knew he was leaving himself open to more criticism and the likes of Buckmaster would use it to question his commitment. 'They came to me and asked me to do it,' he says in his front room one night. 'I didn't go looking for it. They came to interview me in my tea break. I weighed it all up and took it into account and said, "No thanks, I'd rather not". I don't want to be rich and I don't want to be famous. At the time I still built engines and still worked for my dad full-time, as well as working nights at the farm for a few months from the back end of June.' But the BBC ideas people would not be placated. They returned and pleaded with Martin to do the show. 'I don't think they could believe that anyone had turned them down. They offered me twice as much. I thought it would be mental to turn that down. I didn't want to get ten years down the line and think, "If only I'd done that then life would have been so much easier". It can cause me trouble, I know, because of the attention that comes with it. I don't really want that. I did it for one reason only; I want to grow old regretting what I have done, not what I haven't. I don't care if people think it's fantastic or if people think it's shit. I'm quite happy with my life as it is.' He drifts off as he sometimes does. 'We don't like change do we?'

Perhaps not, but he would soon be drowning under the stuff. He split from the farmer's daughter and began seeing a new girl called Steph. 'I'm really into her,' he enthuses. 'She's got her own business, her own house, her own car.

She's a very independent woman. The further on I get in life the more I enjoy my own company. The amount of driving I do means I've grown to actually like myself. So me and myself talk a lot. I'm the only one who makes sense sometimes. But Steph is different. If I am ever to marry a girl then it will be her, but I'm not ready for that yet. There's been too many crossroads in my life lately. Too many and, like I say, we don't like change.'

One thing that did not change was his fractious relationship with the police. This stemmed back to the previous year when his pushbike had been stolen from a meeting at Oulton Park. 'I don't own much,' he had said back then. 'A toolbox and four pushbikes. So when someone goes and nicks something I've worked fucking hard for it makes my blood boil. I got stuck in, told the coppers what I thought. I didn't hold back. I was telling them how I pay their wages, I went off the rev limiter at them.' Two hours later the police called and said they had found Martin's bike. Cue contrition and fulsome apology for his language to the law. 'There she was. Not a mark on her besides the dust from the fingerprinting squad. And they got the little bastard – a one-armed Scouser.'

Martin was back in trouble with the police in 2010. He got caught speeding but ignored the ensuing letters. He reasoned that he had nine points already so a ban was coming. He got a call while at the North West 200. 'The woman from the farm said the coppers have come down to arrest you. I thought, "Fucking hell, it's caught up with us". I rang up and said sorry and they said that if I didn't come to the station by Monday morning then they would come out and arrest me. I went to Scunthorpe Magistrates and they put me in a cell. Dead sociable, like. Then I went in front of the judge. I was in my overalls and had two letters, one from my dad and one from my boss at the farm saying I needed my licence. Well, that swung it. He took pity and said he would give me another six points. He told me I could only use my job as an excuse once in my lifetime. I was on probation for three years.'

He lasted a few months. He was wrapping up filming with the BBC and Mave, when he slipped and ended up doused in his own blood. 'I fell off the end of the dock and smashed my gob on the end of the bleeding boat. I shattered my jaw and smashed my teeth,' he says. 'I got in the van and was driving to hospital when I got pulled over by a copper. I was pissing blood and could not speak, a right bloody mess, but he did me for speeding and for having two bald tyres. I would have been off the rev limiter again if I could have spoken properly, but the copper was an arsehole.'

He was sent a form and ticked a box for the matter to be dealt with in his absence. 'I thought there's no way out this time. It was due to be heard in court on a Monday morning. I thought, "I'll hear about it soon". I was still driving about as normal. It got to Friday and still nothing. I was out driving the tipper and I got pulled for being overweight.' The load was only marginally over the limit so Martin climbed on top and starred shovelling some of the load out. Then he sat in the cab and counted the minutes. An hour passed. He leant out the door.

'Is it going to take long? I've got to get back to work. I'm on a job.'

'Just stay there,' said the policeman. 'Five minutes. We're just waiting for details and checks.'

Martin muttered to himself and waited to be sent on his way, but then a police van pulled up.

'Get in the back there. You're under arrest.'

'You what? I've just been done for being overweight, that's all.'

'There's a warrant out for your arrest.'

'You what?'

Martin shakes his head as he recalls the episode, guilt and incredulity forming a potent mix. 'I got stuck in the back of the van. I went to court. I thought I'm going to get done here so there's no point having a duty solicitor. But it turned out they had sent me the wrong form. They should not have let me say I wanted the case dealt with in my absence. They were in the wrong. He gave me another six points and let me keep my licence.'

But it was, he says, the straw that broke the camel's back. Martin lost his job, even though his father owned the business, and left under a cloud after ten years. Father and son fell out. It is something he says little about. For a man who did not like change, Martin was dealing with a new home, new girlfriend, new job and newly-amended driving licence. And then there was the change that he hoped would bring him that elusive TT win so he could tick the box and move on to the next near-death thing.

There's nowhere to relax. Across to the right-hand side of the road and I have to make a conscious effort to pull the bike straight because of these bumps. Going into the 11th milestone. Sixth to fourth and out towards the orange sign, now back into the milestone itself. Then let the bike run out to the kerb on the right side of the road and back into this left. Can't rest though because now it's Handley's Corner – a complete slut-bag.

Eleven

Michael

Robert Dunlop is taking a cameraman around his stately pile. He explains that it was built in 1861 and, hence, the high ceilings. The plan is to turn it into a guest house with a restaurant. A chubby-faced boy in a yellow jumper and Wellington boots is making nonsense noises in the background. 'My first allegiance is to my wife and sons,' Robert says. Michael kicks his boots out and grins.

Dunlop sits down and the interview is filmed for *Between the Hedges*, another seminal film about road racing. He has jet black hair and piercing eyes. His voice is gentle Irish and his good looks are enhanced by natural warmth. 'It's a fact of life that people like winners,' he says. 'It's why I'm employed by Norton. I'm more in the public eye now too.' Then he sighs deeply, tips his head and, for a brief moment, looks almost close to tears. 'It's different now. It's not as funny anymore. Not as good a, er, I was going to say craic.'

This is Robert Dunlop in 1992. He is a star of the Irish road racing scene. He will never match his brother's feats, but he is riding for Norton in the iconic black livery and he is paying the price for success. A teenager sticks a camera through the loose flap of his awning at a race meeting and clicks. People accost him for autographs. He is a lively figure, the antithesis of Joey, but the sigh, tip and near-tear paint a vivid picture.

The film follows the path trodden by *The Road Racers* in following three riders into the madness. Dunlop is the star turn. Then there is Gary Walker, a nervous man with a Madonna calendar and part-time acting career. 'I am an actor,' he says after pumping a car full of bullets. 'Most of my time is spent unemployed.' The last of the trio is Brian Gardiner, a thoughtful man with a permanent smile, a devout Christian with wife, child and faith. 'Not the image the public has of bikers,' he admits. 'But it's a close-knit community. It's a fast and dangerous sport that pulls us that much closer again.' Walker tells the camera that he will never be any sort of champion, because he lacks the sponsors and the ability, but he says that 'in my head, I have done what I wanted to do.' He is where Robert Dunlop might, perversely, prefer to be, a journeyman doing it for kicks rather than a pay cheque.

Dunlop is a more gregarious figure than Joey, but viewed with the benefit of hindsight, the film exposes the common frailties of the racers. Walker ends up on a bed, with a Batman T-shirt and a hand injury, talking about losing limbs. 'I have never really thought about losing any part of my body,' he says. He makes a joke. It rings hollow. He talks of how he has come to realise his racing affects his family and friends too.

The film cuts to a church where Brian Gardiner is in the congregation. 'We remember different individuals who, through injury involved in motorcycle racing, cannot be here with us,' says the priest. The church is winter brown, the flock a typical mix of blue rinse and dark suits. The average age looks around 60 and yet they are united in prayer for bikers. It is a scenario unique to Northern Ireland. 'We ask you Father to lay healing hands upon them and build them up with hope and courage and faith.' He adds the postscript: 'We especially remember the bereaved in this sport.'

The congregation stands to sing a hymn and it echoes over footage of Dunlop racing in the 1992 season. He straps a toe. 'Why does that one always get skinned?' asks Louise, his wife. 'Gear change foot,' says Robert. He talks of hope and courage and faith. 'At the beginning of a road race I would think more about God,' he says. 'Because I believe in God whereas at short circuit racing I would not be as conscious about knowing something very serious could happen. At road circuits I get more nervous and itchy. I certainly do.'

Dunlop had already carved out a name for himself in 1992. He had won the Manx Grand Prix way back in 1983 and took a hat-trick of TT titles in the ultra-lightweight class from 1989–1991. He was the master of the small bikes and was the British 125cc champion in 1989, proving he was one of the road racers who could ride and win on the tracks too. Yet, just as his son Michael would tell me, the sense of pure enjoyment seemed to be ebbing away in tandem with his rising status. 'In the beginning, first or last, it was all the same,' he says in that gentle voice. 'We went down the pub and either celebrated or drowned our sorrows.'

He said he felt the bikes were getting too fast for the Northern Ireland roads. The Isle of Man was far safer, by comparison. He conceded that 'danger is excitement' but said that he felt he would keep going between the hedges for another five years or so. Then it would be time to build up the business and leave something for his sons. In the end he kept going for another 16 years.

Dunlop's career was pockmarked by periodic injuries. At 17 he crashed his van into a tree outside Ballymoney and broke his neck. Then, in 1994, came the big one, the one that the old-timers would have termed the 'Big Slide'. It happened at the Isle of Man when the back wheel of his Medd Honda disintegrated at Ballaugh Bridge. Dunlop sued Medd. The court case was long and occasionally bitter. Fellow riders Steve Parrish and Roger Burnett spoke on behalf of the insurance company. Parrish said he did not think Dunlop would have been good enough to compete in the World Superbike Championship, a remark that went down like a lead balloon with the family. Dunlop was seeking a million pounds because he said he had never been able to reach his potential. His right-hand was badly damaged and one leg was shorter than the other. In 2002, eight years later, he received £750,000 in damages. By then the mansion had been sold to pay off debts. It would get worse in 2008 when he gave £465,000 to a man to invest on behalf of his family. The man, Darren Johnston, would end up getting seven years for stealing more than £1.3 million from various clients. Johnston, a Presbyterian church elder, was reported to have a lavish lifestyle funded by his victims. For Dunlop, who admitted he needed to claw back the money shortly before his fatal accident, it was an added, unnecessary burden.

He was always resilient. Even with his injuries and reduced ambition, Dunlop achieved much. The highlight came when the two sides of the racer, the charmed and doomed, merged to telling effect in 1998. It started in hospital. Dunlop, the king of the North West 200, crashed at his beloved race, struck from behind by a rider called Davy Lemon and thrust into a telegraph pole. He broke his collarbone and his right leg. A metal rod in his leg, a relic from the 1994 crash at the TT, was bent. The TT was fast approaching and it seemed, as it often does, impossible. Dunlop sat at home, working his way through bills, crutches laid by the side of his armchair. He picked up each bill and tossed it in the fire. Finally, he came across the letter he had been searching for. It was his form to get a pre-TT medical. He got an old friend, a journalist named Willis Marshall, to sign his name in three places. When he got to the island Dunlop blagged his way through his medical. A generation before Cath Davis would work with Conor Cummins on his rescue mission, a pretty woman with a brown bob named Fiona Gilliland gave Dunlop the physiotherapy he needed.

The rain was bad that year, with one race even being cancelled, and the ultra lightweight TT was also reduced from four laps to three. Ian Lougher clocked an average of 107.53mph on the final lap, but he could not catch Dunlop. It was one of those emotional road racing triumphs, where the back story dripped into the foreground, much like the time his son would win in the wake of his own death some ten years hence.

This was Robert Dunlop the racer. A popular hero but a man destined to stay in his brother's shadow. Even that year, in 1998, when Robert strode to the top of the podium in his white leathers, Joey surpassed him by doing a 100mph lap in the rain to win the lightweight race; John McGuinness was third.

The brothers were chalk and cheese, friends and rivals. When Joey died, Robert went to his mother's house in Union Street in Ballymoney to break the news. His four sisters were with him. He would write about it in *The Joey I Knew*: 'Mum was just coming home with her little dog after a walk when I met her outside the front door. I couldn't tell mum – how could I? I just said, "I've a bit of bad news" and mum replied heartily, "What's wrong with you now?" But it became devastatingly clear what was up as we entered the living room and saw the looks on the faces of her family. I will never forget my mother's weeping at the loss of her son. I wept for my mother that day for I was chilled to the bone.'

A eulogy like that made it hard for some outsiders to comprehend the row that engulfed the family in late 2010. Their mother, May, supported a move by the council to link the brother's separate memorial gardens with a pathway. However, Joey's side of the family said they were disappointed the work would be going ahead without their blessing. It would cause too much disruption. Robert's side said they were delighted with the plans. It was a bitter disagreement that would cut slashing wounds. The local media picked up on the story and it spread. May told reporters: 'They were so good when they were together at 11 so I don't think that it's right that they should be separated in death when they weren't separated in life.' Before long Michael too, was standing in front of a camera in the memorial gardens. 'People don't understand how close they were,' he said. 'They shared a bath together so I think they would enjoy sharing a garden. Whatever rifts there are between families should stay behind closed doors. Sadly, somebody's brought it up and now the whole world is speaking about it.' The reporter said the issue had 'exposed a rift' in the Dunlop family and, for once, the media was not overplaying its hand.

It was hard to fathom. The Mayor of Ballymoney, Bill

Kennedy, called for calm. 'The council has invested thousands of pounds in a memorial, first for Joey and then for Robert, to honour the Dunlop name and the contribution they made to their sport, Ballymoney and Northern Ireland as a whole.' He then explained the timeline of the row. Joey's garden had been there for a decade. Robert's was erected and opened in May 2010. 'After Robert's garden was erected, May Dunlop put a letter into the council to request a linking path, but Linda Dunlop [Joey's widow] felt this was very much something she was against. She was very determined that she didn't want the two gardens joined.'

The brothers were buried next to each other in their local church. However, a mile or so away in the gardens in Ballymoney, barriers remained. Joey's family were so incensed when the council planners voted to install the path that they removed his memorabilia from the town museum. A statement from the family said they were 'disappointed' that Ballymoney council had decided to proceed with work on the memorial garden 'without the endorsement of Joey's wife and children'. It went on: 'The garden has played a very important part in our lives for the past ten years and we are deeply upset that there will be so much unnecessary upheaval in this place of remembrance.' Kennedy, sounding dumbfounded, said he had spoken to Linda and hoped she might come to view the path as a good thing.

It did not seem that way. Months later, the cabinet in the museum remained half empty to the bemusement of pilgrims. Next to it was a synopsis of Robert's career, along with his North West 200 trophy from 2006 and his leathers.

The new brothers were just as complicated. They could irritate each other and they had had their own fallings-out, but they were as close as anyone in the paddock. So if the rest of the world would occasionally criticise Michael's riding, his brother had no such problems. 'He's the one I enjoy riding against most,' William told me when we met in Ballymoney. 'People say he is rash but I've never had any problems.' They looked out for each other too. 'If there's a crash then I always want to make sure that it's not William,' Michael said. 'On the bike I take no prisoners, but when I race against William I enjoy it. I know there's not going to be any hassle. People do stupid things, but me and William can ride close and know there's never going to be any issues. Some riders get up the front and, if they are not normally up there, they get a bit excited.' He then mentioned Ryan Farquhar, one of Ireland's top riders from Dungannon. 'He goes from being inside you at one corner and not the next,' Michael said. 'That gets frustrating. People think I'm one of those rash ones, but I don't think I'm too bad. I do the odd stupid thing, but not too much. When I was starting out I was keen as mustard. I was a bit wild and, though I didn't think it at the time, I might have been a bit reckless. But to make the jump to being a real good road racer, you have to take a couple of tumbles. I took mine and got away with it.'

It is hard not to be moved by his strength of purpose when he recounts how he sat at home as a newly bereaved son, listening to the radio reports from the TT practice in 2008, growing more depressed. Eventually, he says his mother hinted that she did not want him to go to the TT, not with the funeral so raw and their lives in flux. He started to unload his van, which had remained unpacked since the emotional North West triumph. He looked for a sign. He said he wanted his father to knock a spanner from the garage wall. He wanted his mother's blessing. In the end he got a phone call from Paul Phillips at the TT, telling him that

Wednesday's practice had been cancelled. It was the respite he needed. 'That's when I decided I was no longer a little boy and made the decision I was a man and should make my own move. I was off to the TT.'

The rest of 2010 had tested that inner strength further. The results were good and backed up John McGuinness' belief that the Dunlops were the coming force. Michael won the Post Classic Senior at the Manx Grand Prix on a 1981 Suzuki. The margin was a massive two-and-a-half minutes, a record time. William took a second and third at the Ulster Grand Prix. Yet it had been difficult. Road racing in Ireland was struggling to survive. A lack of sponsors, rising insurance premiums and a number of fatalities were tempered only by a nostalgic affection and visceral thrills. Even the Ulster Grand Prix had looked in doubt for a long period, while the Dunlops found themselves in the midst of another row when they pulled out of the Mid-Antrim 150 races.

The problem was money. The Mid-Antrim Club was so broke that it could no longer cover the top riders' entry fees. The previous year had cost the club £3,000, a paltry sum in global sporting terms, but make or break in the hand-to-mouth world of national road racing. Michael was elected spokesman. 'William and myself have had enough of this,' he said. 'We have won races the length and breadth of Ireland and beyond and we draw spectators to their events, yet when we ask the Mid-Antrim Club what they can do for us they appeared not too bothered as to whether we rode at their meeting or not.' It seemed much ado about very little. Jack Agnew, the Mid-Antrim Club's spokesman, said the entry fee would have cost the Dunlops a mere £140 each. Yet they were not prepared to pay up. Much later, Michael looked weary as he tried to explain to me why he had taken such a tough stance. 'The thing is we can't have full-time jobs during the racing season because of all the time off we need,' he said. 'Other people are not out testing and doing PR. They cannot understand why we get into races for free, but we're the ones who bring in the fans and we're the ones paying to wreck our bikes. If it costs us then what's the point? We have to make this work. People are saying we're whingeing about the entry fees, but it's our main income. It's our job. It pays our bills. And the fact is the people whingeing don't ride bikes at 200mph.'

Several months later, in the spring of 2011, Robert Dunlop is standing in his memorial garden again. A statue has been commissioned, paid for by backers and erected on his side of the hedge. The brothers are now linked by a pathway. Michael and his uncle Jim unveil the bronze. 'For some people they are to motorcycling what George Best was to football,' Michael says to a journalist. 'That makes us very proud.'

It was sad that the cabinet up the road at the museum remained a tribute to a family row. They had overcome so much but overcoming a hedge was too much. Some time on I visited the gardens with Michael and William for a photo shoot. Michael checked the statue to make sure it had not been vandalised. We were a stone's throw from Joey's bar, a short drive from the dentist who had fixed Robert and William's teeth before becoming Ballymoney's most infamous resident. As we spoke, Colin Howell was just beginning a life sentence for gassing his wife and his lover's husband. A former lay preacher, Howell lived with his crimes for almost 20 years before confessing to church elders.

It was a sleepy town with stories on every corner. This particular one, in the gardens, had stories yet to be told. Michael and William would continue to ride on the roads in

Ireland, but it was the Isle of Man that was going to make these Dunlop brothers and enhance the family odyssey.

The deals were being done. William would sign first, for Wilson Craig's established team in 2011, and Michael would hold out and cut a deal to ride for Kawasaki, with help from Paul Bird's World Superbike team, but riding under his own banner. They were excited but not brimming over. 'It's getting shit,' Michael says. 'Too corporate. If you tell someone to go suck their bag they go bananas. You need one or two of mes to keep it lively. I don't regret anything I've ever done or anything I've ever said. I like to race hard. I like a bit of craic. I say what I think.'

William laughs. 'What do I think? I think he's so stupid. He does not help himself.'

'I get away with murder,' Michael retorts. He had just seen the final version of *TT3D*, Steve Christian's excellent documentary, and while the critics line up to laud it, he gave his damning assessment. Admittedly, this was largely formed from spending days filming and then realising he was only in the film for a matter of seconds. Meanwhile, Guy Martin, the man who has never won a TT, took the central role and gave his thoughts on everything from mastering the track to masturbation. 'I done five days,' Michael spits. 'And then it's all about someone talking about wanking. It did not show much road racing really. It was more the Guy Martin film. That's what it was. That's what we seen.'

They are not convinced by the accuracy of their father's statue either. 'I don't think it looks like him,' Michael says. 'But it's good they did something for him,' William adds. 'It's all Joey, Joey, Joey, but my dad did a lot.'

'Yeah, to come back from the crash in '94 ...'

'I want to make him proud.'

'When you needed a slap you got one,' says Michael. 'That was the worst thing. He used to hate us lying and I would lie all the time. I used to do stuff and blame William or Daniel. He would beat all three of us until someone owned up. Sometimes William would even though it was not him.'

'I thought we'd all get a slap anyway so I might as well take it. I think my dad knew who it was, but he wanted us to admit it.'

They edge away from the statue of their father, with his list of achievements etched in white on black stone – 15 wins at the North West 200, nine at the Ulster Grand Prix, five at the TT, the freedom of Ballymoney, the Joey Dunlop Trophy – and leave the Mighty Micro with his champagne forever raised in celebration and Joey astride his bike with a wreath around his neck.

'I'm the sensible one,' William insists. 'I don't hang around with Mickey's crowd. The guys he hangs around with couldn't get a ride in a whore house.'

'Life is good,' Michael retorts, suddenly uplifted. 'A lot of boys take it very seriously, but it's good to get out and enjoy yourself. William takes two beers and that's good. He does his own thing and I do mine. I'm a thrill-seeker. I get done for speeding and the sad thing is that most of the time it's in the van. I got done at the Ulster Grand Prix and the bloke said, "Just because you're Michael Dunlop doesn't mean you're getting away with it". I said I'd never expected to get away with it, but he went on, "My mate's Eddie Irvine so I'll not be scared of you". I don't know why he said that but it's the jealousy thing again. The Dunlop name can be a good thing and a bad thing. I told him, "I suppose you haven't had a shag in a while have you?"'

The return of the bluster was never far away, but these brothers have been through so much and are deeper than they let on. 'I go there now and again and have a think,' Michael says of the gardens. He thought about his father as any bereaved son would, but separated by the dichotomy of trying to emulate his feats while avoiding his horrors. He told me of the woman at the TT whose job it was to break the news to families. 'The grim reaper we call her. If she comes towards you then run.' I remembered what Louise Dunlop had said, about how Robert lost himself in a fog of depression after Joey's death and so could never have gone and ridden two days on from a tragedy, as Michael had in 2008.

I remembered reading a remarkably candid interview with his brother, Daniel, in *Road Racing Ireland*. The soldier son spoke of his tour in Afghanistan. 'I spent six months in an outpost with eight of our regiment and 15 local recruits,' he said. 'It was simply a hot, fly-infested, smelly mud hut where we all ate, slept and fought together. We were attacked every day and had roadside bombs all around us wherever we moved. It was exciting, scary and fun at times, but everything depends on your own state of mind. I have seen some locals killed and have been brought some casualties that you instantly knew by looking at their bodies they were beyond help.' He also spoke of the day he heard of his father's death. 'There was no signal on my mobile phone until I left the barracks with my girlfriend. The phone then went mad with all these bleeping messages – people were just saying they were sorry to hear of my tragic news. I listened to them and knew something wasn't right, but somehow I didn't think it was either William or Michael so I knew straight away something must have had happened to dad.'

He rang his mother and she told him the truth. 'Even when I woke up the next morning and took a shower, it still hadn't sunk in. It was a strange feeling as I had expected to lose people close to me in the Army, but not my dad. It wasn't until I arrived home and saw all the cars in the yard on that Friday that I realised what was really happening. I found it hard to come into the house, but I had to try and keep it together.' And then he gave his siblings his blessing too. 'It was up to them to race again as I am in no position to judge on what they want to do or how they go about it. Their relationship will be strained at times as they are doing the same things and are still living under the same roof. I am sure people will always want to compare them to dad and Joey so they will always be under pressure. But dad encouraged us to be our own men and that's what we now have to be.'

Michael is bounding up the High Street, a long way from Afghanistan but always close to the North West of 2008. 'I want to win the Senior at the TT,' he says with a conviction so strong the words are almost embossed on the air. 'I want to win them all but I *need* to win the Senior.'

It's a complete slut-bag purely for the fact there is such a big wall. As it comes towards you it's like a giant stone face. I used to slow down far too much for it, but one night a lad passed me in practice. I was braking as late as I could and I thought he was never going to make it. But he did. I was hanging off the bike too much for the left, so by the time I tried to get the bike over I'd run out of room. I missed the apex and was running wide, scaring myself, saying 'Fuck, I've gone too fast'. This lad sat up in the middle of the bike and just dipped into the left and pulled it onto the right. After that it was mega.

Twelve

Guy

*H*ector and Philip Neill are a father and son team bonded by blood and passion. Hector has bloody cobwebs framing his warm eyes and an ossified face with lines as deep as mountain passes. Philip has long grey hair and a mind that has bridged the gap from grass roots racing down a windy road in Moneymore to the increasingly corporate world of TT racing. Hector is the life and soul of the team, Philip the brains. And now they have signed the most eccentric man the sport has seen in decades.

'Guy is a unique person both in general life and as a racer,' Philip says. He is sipping coffee from a mug in the upstairs office of Temple Auto Salvage, a business that deals with cast-offs, waste and the detritus of speed. It is the family business that put its name to TAS Racing, the company that was now partnered by Relentless Suzuki, with its Coca-Cola big buck fizz. 'He has always intrigued me. I've always been interested in him. I've always found myself wanting to read what he has said, even if I don't agree with it. The thing about Guy is people have to understand, and this is not meant to be disrespectful, but Guy is the first person I have ever met who really does not care what people think.'

It was more complicated than that, as Neill knew. Martin was not some force of nature, selfishly set on a path from which he could not diverge. He cared about people's feelings and had already told me that he had been disappointed with how his switch to TAS had become public knowledge. The partnership with Wilson Craig had ultimately splintered and failed, but Martin deemed Craig worthy of respect and a better farewell. But that was racing. It was tough.

'There is no front with Guy,' Neill continues. 'Well, I don't think so. He's a bit eccentric, but in a nice way. And he's very deep and very detailed in what he does. He actually has really high moral standards and he won't lower them for anyone. Me and him have butted heads on a few occasions, but you have to admire someone for standing up for their beliefs. I am trying to help him become, shall we say, more diplomatic. We talk about humility a lot. Sometimes you can't be as up front as you might like. There is more than one way to skin a cat. Yeah, we talk about humility a lot.'

The TAS story is rooted in Northern Irish road racing legend. Hector was involved in almost all disciplines of motorcycle racing, from speedway to endurance, but his love lay on the roads. Philip was a motocross man. 'He helped me as much as he could,' he says of the nascent father-and-son hobby. 'I never opted for a road racing career. It never occurred to me, but secretly I always believed he didn't want me to do it. It's ironic, I guess, but it's different when it's your own son. I have a six-year-old son myself and he's started motocross, but in truth I'd have loved him to do another sport.' Philip said he could see the light go on in his father's eyes whenever talk turned to the TT. It was

Father and son. An injured Robert Dunlop with son and picture of innocence, Michael.

Sibling rivalry I. Joey and Robert.

Sibling rivalry II. William and Michael.

'It was black with people.' The final journey of Joey Dunlop, 2000.

'I'm not a flash bastard.' Guy Martin in his comfort zone, 2009.

The pencil line. John McGuinness finds it.

The broken man. Conor Cummins withers away.

Tea. Guy Martin enjoys a cuppa.

& Sympathy. Ian Hutchinson chats to the injured Conor Cummins, but will soon be in the same sinking boat.

A family odyssey.
William, Robert and
Michael Dunlop, 2011.

Go for laughs. Guy Martin passes The Raven, Ballaugh.

One year on. Conor Cummins, back in the saddle, approaches the same pub, 2011.

'Crazy.' GP legend Valentino Rossi gives his assessment, 2009.

Breaking down barriers. William Dunlop comes close to taking things literally.

Craggy Island. John McGuinness buries his doubts in the Superbike race, 2011.

Woman's world. Jenny Tinmouth prepares for more history, 2011.

Back to the drawing board. Guy Martin ponders another barren year.

The most dangerous race in the world. Alan Connor heads towards concrete walls, 2009.

(*above*) 'The place was on its arse after DJ'. David Jefferies.

(*right*) Back to his best. John McGuinness, the king of the Mountain, departs.

like thinking of an old flame, the thrill and excitement somehow enhanced by the bittersweet taste.

'I'd been to the North West 200 and Ulster Grand Prix and I was fascinated and frightened by it – the big bikes, the noise, Roger Marshall, Mick Grant, Joey Dunlop. Tom Herron would have been regularly round our house and in the garage. I was heavily affected at the time. The Norman Brown era was taking place with my dad. This young lad from County Down was doing tremendously well and taking the road racing world by storm. He was the man everyone was talking about. Joey, himself, said he was going to be the next big thing.'

Brown won at the TT in 1982. He raised the lap record to 116mph in 1983. A few weeks later he rode in the British Grand Prix at Silverstone. There was a crash. The BBC cameras found Barry Sheene in the pits. As the interviewer posed questions, Sheene lit up a fag. 'There's been an accident and it's pretty nasty,' he said. 'The flags were out. What the bloody hell the others are doing going round I don't know. I saw the flags and stopped. That's what they're for isn't it?' It would be worse than Sheene and the rest feared. Brown and Peter Huber, a Swiss rider, were both killed, and the aftermath hit Hector Neill hard. 'I remember seeing the effect Norman's unfortunate accident had on my family,' Philip says. 'It was the last straw for my father. That pretty much finished him. He still owned a bike and Neil Robinson still ran at GP level under Sunflower Products banner, but my dad did not want to be seen to be involved. He was out of it for a long time.'

Until one day in 1999.

'I'd like to put a bike out at the TT,' he told his son.

And so Philip plotted to do the TT with a messed-up

bike, but quickly got more ambitious as he worked away and ended up building a machine that was far superior to the standard Superstock that had been the original plan. They had no rider at the time. Brian Reid had connections with the family, but then the name Ian Lougher came up. He had hitherto been associated with two-stroke bikes, but they decided to give him a chance. 'We had a good year,' Philip says. 'We were fourth in the Formula One TT race and were running third in the Senior until the thing broke up in the pits. But that was it. Hector was bitten again and that was that. And I had the passion too.'

Philip suggested they try to get a manufacturer on board for the following year. Yamaha and Honda were already sorted and Kawasaki was steering clear of road racing. Hector contacted an old friend, Rex White, and asked what the situation was at Suzuki. That led to a meeting with the racing director, Nick Barnes, who felt they could not offer a good enough support package for the Neills to do the job properly. 'But anything was better than nothing for us and so, six weeks later, some boxes arrived at Temple Auto Salvage office here. We'd only just started the business so there was a lot going on. We got lucky. We had no idea how good those bikes in the boxes were going to be. We kept Ian Lougher and agreed to take Iain Duffus. We had a low-key launch. The riders had no idea what we had either. Duffus got cold feet and he was poached away from us. That was my first experience of realising that a gentleman's agreement was not enough. It was ironic really because he had a miserable year and we beat him every time we went up against him. That left us with one rider.'

Philip continues: 'I was just married and living in Cookstown. We built the first bike in my garage. Then we built some in a wooden shed in a barn where we stored some cars from TAS. It was fine. But then we got the deal with Suzuki and they started asking questions about how serious we were. Well, we had nothing. We weren't even run as a company. The 2001 TT was cancelled because of foot and mouth and that was a real shame when we found out how bloody good the bikes were. Lougher went to the Ulster Grand Prix and totally dominated. He won four out of five races. The buzz was crazy. We had a rider not renowned for racing four-strokes, a brand new bike, no expectations and, within the space of one meeting, people resigned themselves that this was the bike to have and we could not be beaten. With one lap to go of the Superstock race, one of the Honda bosses shook hands with my father.'

David Jefferies had also noted how fast Lougher had been moving. He had already had huge success on the roads with V&M Yamahas, but nothing was forever in road racing. Father and son spoke about signing DJ to partner Lougher for 2002, but they were still a new team with little financial clout. 'There's no better way to find out than asking him,' Hector said as they attended a bike show. So Philip did. 'I could see he was interested right away. But one of the most annoying things about this job is you never have your commercial agreements in place when you want to sign a rider. The amount of times I've had to put the cart before the horse and signed riders before I have any money is incredible. I told David we wanted him but we didn't have the finance.'

Jefferies was a resourceful figure, though, and as well as being the best TT rider of the time, he was well versed in the wheeling and dealing needed to fuel the passion. He had a deal with an oil company.

'Do you have an oil deal?' he asked Neill.

'No we don't.'

'Give me 20 minutes.'

He went away with a mobile phone attached to his ear. They reconvened in the Hard Rock Café in Belfast. 'He tucked into a big rack of ribs and had barbecue sauce all over his face,' Neill recalls. 'He said, "You're using Putoline oil; I'm riding your bikes". We shook hands.'

He had wanted a £20,000 retainer to ride for Yamaha. It was chicken feed, a desultory sum that underscored why riders like Jim Moodie and John McGuinness demanded their value be recognised. Hector Neill tells the story that the deal for Jefferies to ride for TAS Suzuki was struck five minutes before the team were due to announce their rider line-up. Even then, with the best rider of all signed, sealed and delivered, Suzuki, fearing failure, wanted minimal publicity. Nick Barnes told them not to use the words Suzuki GB on the side of the truck. It was scarcely proud, unequivocal support. Success changed everything. In practice at the Isle of Man, Jefferies set the fastest ever lap on a production bike from a standing start. In the opening race, he became the first man to break the 18-minute barrier for a lap of the 37.75-mile circuit. John McGuinness was riding as hard as he had ever done, dipping his toe into unknown risk. He ended up taking 27 seconds of his best lap time, but still struggled to stay in touch. At that time McGuinness, humbled by Jefferies' omnipotence, could not have believed that he would surpass all his achievements. Back then Jefferies' veneer of invincibility was polished by the fact he had hit trouble on the last lap. Realising there was a gear selector problem, Jefferies decided to stay in third gear lest he exacerbate the fault. He spoke of almost losing control of his bodily functions. Hector would explain that each of the engines had a tiny gear selector fault and Jefferies' engine had been fitted to the bike without anyone fixing it. So the race was unravelling and for 13 miles he struggled on in third gear, the best road racers in the world behind him with all the gears but no idea how to stop him.

It was the start of something big. Everyone was sure of that. He won the production race too and Suzuki's Nick Barnes flew to the Isle of Man and told Hector to put 'Suzuki GB' on the side of their truck at once. Jefferies set a new lap record of 127.29mph in the Senior TT. Giacomo Agostini presented him with his trophy. The Neills sent the Japanese hierarchy a piece of Manx slate as a present. TAS had arrived.

Jefferies' death at the 2003 TT was a personal tragedy for a family, a seismic blow to a sport, and a depressing attack on the senses for Philip Neill. 'My father had seen it before, but I hadn't. I didn't know how to react. There were a lot of negatives and a few positives. One of the positives was the motorcycle community is very tight-knit and everybody pulls together. I felt a huge sense of camaraderie. The Jefferies family are fantastic people and they gave us their blessing to carry on racing that year. That was good because we had Adrian Archibald too and he had put six months of his year into it.' Neill's glassy eyes flick to the window as if it were a porthole to the past. 'David and I were friendly and we talked about a lot of things. He talked openly about the dangers and was fully aware that, if something went wrong, then he might not be coming home. That does not give you strength; it's just the reality. I'm sure my feelings do not come close to those of the family, but we had a sense of involvement. It was a tremendously stressful time hoping nothing had gone wrong with the bike. It was horrendous. I'm not going to hide behind a door; the organisation at that time was diabolical. The riders confirmed that there was oil on the road. They tested it with their feet. But we never got an unconditional admittance that there had been oil from a blown engine approaching the Crosby section. The implications were huge but we weren't seeking legal damages and we weren't seeking to damage the reputation of the TT. We wanted to make it conclusive public knowledge that nothing had happened to the motorbike and we wanted to make it clear that David had not made a mistake. The big man was just too good for that.'

In the space of three years, the father and son team had suffered the elation and devastation that are the twin emotions of the TT. That short time span served to prove the ultimate wisdom of the TT in its message to live and enjoy the moment. Yet the past always looms large over the event, even as new blood such as Paul Phillips came in, the 'dead wood' was stripped and the festival became a modern-day sporting event.

'I would have to be honest and say it never ever really crossed our mind to stop,' Neill admits. 'But it was hard and, more so, when we went away, when the absolute, raw emotion around the whole thing had died down. It was then, in that winter, when I sat down and asked, "Is this really worth the potential outcome?" And I had to drag myself to the TT for the next five years. I realised we had made a commitment to the sport and had built a good team with sponsors and with employees. It was bigger than just me. But, personally, I dragged myself there and I made a point of never being there on the Thursday of practice week. My philosophy is that these guys are going to race bikes and so I might as well make them as safe as they can be. I would hate to see the day arrive when the sport continues, but it's a black market job run underground.'

It was a dilemma. Neill was sometimes mocked for being too corporate, but he saw the attraction of the road racing scene and its deep sense of community. He also saw danger at every turn and was a strident voice for improving safety and improving the odds. No longer were we in the era where a rider would simply hope to emerge from the equation of six deaths and three crashes with his health intact. 'It's fine having that gladiatorial aspect,' Neill says. 'But there used to be far too many fatalities. That's not sustainable; that's not even sport.'

Now Neill was working with Martin, who had reacted to signing for one of the top teams with characteristic colour. 'Winning a bleeding TT is taking a bit longer than expected so if it means I have to do a bit more PR then that's okay. These boys have won more TTs than you can shake a stick at and they are dead sound. Hector and Philip get me. I think.' He then segued into an aside about his new set of entirely false teeth which he was proud of. 'They are waiting for my jawbone to grow back before they screw in some real ones,' he explained.

There were hidden depths as Neill had identified. Indeed, Martin said one of his heroes was Von Dutch, an American artist famed for customising cars. Von Dutch was out of kilter with much of 1950s America and he struggled with success. So he shunned the corporate clients, took to shooting at people and, when his health worsened and he was diagnosed with a stomach abscess, took to shunning doctors too. 'I make a point of staying right at the edge of poverty,' he said by way of boast. 'I don't have a pair of pants without a hole in them, and the only pair of boots I have are on my feet. I don't mess around with unnecessary stuff. There's a struggle you have to go through, and if you make a lot of money it doesn't make the struggle go away. It just makes it more complicated.'

Martin said he could empathise. 'I'm confident of the person I am. I'm not trying to model myself on some corporate dummy, saying the right things to the camera. I'll stick with the truth; it's easier.' He took a job on an industrial estate but it did not meet the Von Dutch ideals. 'It's a good job but it's all civil engineering. I'm a truck mechanic and I love working with my spanners. This is all diggers and cement mixers and tarmacking shovels. I'm not getting my fix.'

He wanted Von Dutch-like simplicity, but he was being pulled every which way. He was like a bird flying into the Mountain wind. Philip Neill insisted that he knew what he was getting himself into. He said Martin would make the occasional concession and that the humility talks continued apace, but his new rider would never bite his tongue for long. His aim was to cut through what he believed to be the bullshit of modern life. So he said of politics: 'Conservative, Labour, I don't want any of it. I think it's a load of shit. I don't envy them boys. There are a lot of oxygen thieves in that business. I listen to them talk about it on Radio 4. Double-dip recession. I don't care as long as they keep out of the Euro. But you ask who won the war and it seems the only ones pulling the oar now are the Germans. Spain's nearly a third world country again. Greece is fucked. But I listen to Radio 4 for *The Archers* omnibus and *Woman's Hour*. I love that. Not bothered about the rest of it.'

The 2011 TT was approaching fast. With TAS Suzuki's

bikes, experience and understanding, it was going to be Guy Martin's best ever-chance to win. It was the final piece in the jigsaw. Neill was certainly excited after signing him. 'People think that because he is at TAS he will have to become very PC and say this and thank them. But Guy Martin has created his own brand without even trying. We would not want to change him in a million years. He brings a huge amount of commercial coverage from just being natural. He is what he is, but I tell you this – when the visor goes down he's a racer, 100 per cent.'

Had a slide here once, nothing too much, back to sixth gear, thinking about coming to the top of Barregarrow. It's a nightmare because it has two big entries. Look for the little cottage here on the left, drift over. As soon as you pass the cottage, go straight to the right and kiss the kerb. That opens the corner. Run down to the bottom of Barregarrow and the problem is the depression there and the left-hand bend. You have to jump it diagonally but make sure you're on the gas. If the bike doesn't jump it will spit you off. This section is where you feel the lumps for the first time. It really bothers me. Head for the 13th milestone. Unlucky for some.

PART TWO
LIVING

Thirteen

LAUNCH

In an ideal world Jenny Tinmouth would be winning races rather than the battle of the sexes. As it is, she is a debunker of macho stereotypes, twirling blonde locks around a calloused finger as she prepares to make motorcycling history. 'It irritates me to be honest,' the reluctant hero says of her landmark status.

Tinmouth is the first woman to gain a seat in the cut-throat bear pit of the British Superbike Championship. The first race is coming up at Brands Hatch and Tinmouth is at pains to point out that she is neither token nor trailblazer. 'I just want to be known as a racer,' she says in the bike work-shop she co-runs on an industrial estate near Ellesmere Port. The irony is that, while she scythes through prejudice in the pursuit of equality, it is her sex that makes her stand out. Motorsport is a man's world that thrives on testoster-one and PVC grid girls so her mere presence is a welcome anomaly.

'I was never a girly girl,' she concedes and the soft Scouse accent and penchant for giggling fails to mask a bellicose core. 'I was a proper tomboy, climbing trees and making mud pies. I had a poster of Ayrton Senna on my bedroom wall. I still do. Why? He was just so focused on everything he was doing; he had every detail worked out. I was thinking of art college but then something just went "bing" in my head and bikes took over.'

She had scrimped and saved her bloody, bruised way to BSB level, ignoring the danger and also taming the infamous TT course. 'I remember when I was at college and I was practising how fast I could go in the wet. I crashed and got a scar from that, but I got back on and went to a lesson. I was only wearing jeans and a T-shirt and the blood was seeping through. Not good. My tutor said, "I think you should go to hospital". There have been a few other crashes and it should probably put me off, but it's kind of fun; it's an adrenaline rush.'

Tinmouth was 32 when we met but still lived with her parents, ploughing all her money into racing. It was a pure love of her sport that was at odds with the pampered elite in other fields. The nadir came as she and a friend tried to set up their Two Wheels garage business in a back room rented off her father. 'I had no job and the promise of a ride on a 600 Supersport collapsed. I felt like quitting, but thought if I could just get through that season, by hook or by crook, then it would be an achievement in itself. It was scary. I could not buy myself lunch and I pilfered everything that year. I went to a lot of scrapyards.'

Tinmouth became the first woman to enter the British 125cc Championships in 2003, but was involved in a 'four-man crash at Cadwell Park' and broke an arm, an ankle and collarbone.

It had been a slow-burning dose of trailblazing, but a

decade of toiling paid off when Tinmouth was third in the British Supersport Cup and lapped the TT circuit at 119.9mph in 2010, a record for a woman. It was the latter feat, racing along the wall-lined lanes, that put paid to any lingering notions that motorcycling was a men-only affair. 'The TT is the ultimate,' she says. 'I'd done no road racing but watched a lot of videos beforehand. When I first went up the Mountain in 2009 I had a massive grin on my face. The danger is the attraction, but it is hard to deal with when someone you know dies. I'd experienced it before on the short circuits and it's a massive shock to the system. You're just getting to know guys and then they're gone. That has to make you think.'

In 2010 Tinmouth had been in the Senior that had ended so badly for Conor Cummins and Guy Martin. Her assessment of Martin's crash had been brutally honest – 'potentially dead' – but they survived and she got drunk. 'I planned to stay on a couple of days, but the paddock had emptied by the next morning, tumbleweed, Billy No-mates.'

She was planning to juggle work and pleasure in this 2011 season, still seemingly unsure of her worth in a sport where money talks as well as results. 'I'm completely ignorant,' she says. 'I don't have a manager and don't know if I should be asking for a wage. I'm a bit of an idiot regarding the business side of racing.'

Sex was irrelevant for her and her speed proved that she was no mere nod to equality. She was the real deal. All she wanted to do was compete. 'It's been hard but what else was I going to do,' she says. 'I never liked ballet.'

Tinmouth did not make it to the launch of the TT in April 2011. The star turn was Martin. He had loaned a lock-up on an industrial estate on the outskirts of Douglas for the TT and was intent on keeping his head down. *The Boat That Guy Built* had just finished its six-week run on BBC One. It had been a hit. However, it had also plucked Martin from the middle of the road racing cult and planted him firmly into the mainstream. The attention was bothering him. Now it was even worse as he and the other TT riders crammed into the Palace Cinema on Douglas promenade for the *TT3D* film premiere. Cath Davis sat inside and felt uneasy, knowing Conor Cummins was sitting at the back with his family. Billy Cummins would see the film twice, but he would never watch the crash scene. Martin was the undisputed star and it was obvious that some of the others were not impressed. Indeed, that had been clear from earlier that afternoon when they had gathered for a lunch at The Claremont Hotel. Ian Hutchinson griped about how long he had been filmed for. Michael Dunlop griped about the plane ride he had just taken. There were other moans about money. Hutchinson gave an interview to the *Daily Express* and held his leg. There were six weeks to go to the TT and his leg was still in its cage. That night the riders left the cinema and went to Colours, with its garish interior and tinted windows. Some drank heartily. Cummins sipped on an orange juice. Martin got on his bike, wearing his everpresent green and grey shorts, and pushed off.

The next day the riders and team officials gather down on the southern tip of the island, looking out to the Calf of Man, a 250-hectare island that was once a refuge for monks and hermits, and was now a nature reserve. It is a lustrous day with an aching sun and pure blue sky. After an interminable wait, the riders drift into the restaurant with its perfect view of the Sound. The water held its own secrets. There were three shipwrecks out there, the first a ship laden with gunpowder that ran aground on rocks in December, 1852. The captain, carpenter and five others crew members were washed away. Yet the worst was still to come. Days later, during the salvage operation, an axe struck a gunpowder barrel and the ship exploded, killing 29 people. The noise was heard 20 miles away. There was one survivor.

Tim Glover, a presenter with Manx Radio, makes a brief introduction and hands over to Simon Crellin, the PR chief. He says 75 countries will be taking footage from the TT, making it the biggest ever. There will be clearer on-board images, thermal imaging and 50 cameras in total. The sponsors are now big companies – Monster Energy, Yamaha, Poker Stars. He hands back to Glover who introduced the riders one by one.

'Has last year sunk in?' he asks Hutchinson.

'It was a relief after the injury to go away and have some silver ladies in the house.'

'You're having to deal with the injury.'

'I've still got the frame on. The amount of training I'm doing to get myself ready means it's just not worth the risk. It's Yamaha's 50th anniversary and so I hope we can put on a show. I am doing all I can to make it right on my side.'

Michael Dunlop is next and is told he has a fantastic deal because he has kept his loyal sponsors but has some factory backing. Talk of mere podiums is dismissed. 'Podiums are a waste of time.'

Cummins hobbles up. He too, has a Blackhorse Kawasaki shirt. 'It was only January when things started to change round. We'll see how it goes.'

John McGuinness is late after filming up on the Mountain. He stripped in the car park and got his team gear on. A bus trip with a blue rinse legion looked on. After wondering whether he might be nearing the end of the road, McGuinness had signed to ride for the new Honda TT Legends team. The Legends team was a new innovation from Honda Europe and would see McGuinness and Keith Amor competing in world endurance events such as the Bol d'Or and the Suzuka Eight Hours, as well as the TT. McGuinness would ride for the Legends in the Superbike and Senior races at the TT and for Clive Padgett's team in the Supersport and Superstock. The Superbike and Senior were the big ones, reflected by the cost of up to £100,000 for a state-of-the-art machine and the engine size of up to 1000cc for four-cylinder bikes. The Superstock bikes could be as big but were not as highly-tuned. The Supersport engines could be no bigger than 600cc for four cylinder machines. The combination of Legends and Padgett's had rekindled McGuinness' passion.

'It's real nice weather up the Mountain. Just upset a few locals by passing a few trucks. I must have won my licence in a pub because I don't deserve one.'

'You had to leave the island last year with nothing,' says Glover.

'Yeah, at the time I felt all the things that could have gone wrong did. But when you see what happened to Guy and Conor, well, they had a worse time than me.'

Others are introduced and come and go with their sound bites. There is Cameron Donald, the Aussie who would be partnering William Dunlop for Wilson Craig's team. There is also the terminally sleepy Kiwi Bruce Anstey, who still pumped himself full of drugs after suffering from cancer. He had come to the TT in 1978, the year of Hailwood's comeback, with his Manx mother. It was a fabulous year, but Anstey was a kid and uninterested. 'I was too young to know who anybody was or what they had done,' he told me. 'I was just watching motorbikes. As time went on I always wanted to come here and do it, but I couldn't afford it. There was not a lot of racing down in New Zealand so I did a lot of BMX riding. I did that until I was 21. I was working and saving money. I'm a glazier by trade.'

For the last two years he had managed to put the day job to one side. He said that had helped his fitness and that was important for a man who was ravaged by cancer 15 years earlier. 'That's part of why I sleep a lot,' he says. 'The drugs they gave me made me tired, more tired, sleep anywhere, like a dormouse. They gave me the same drugs they gave Lance Armstrong; they made him stronger and they made me sleepy. It still affects me now. All that chemotherapy. My immune system is really bad. That's why I get cold. Every time I come here it's freezing and I get cold. The cancer did change my life. How? I don't know, it just made it nice to get up and take one step at a time. I'm a similar age to Armstrong and it happened at a similar time, but no, I've never read his book. I don't read books or papers. Reading's bad at the best of times.'

There is Donald and Anstey and Klaus Klaffenbock, the long-haired Austrian sidecar champion who was once sponsored by a porn star named Dolly Buster and had lost a passenger because the authorities took his passport away after a drug bust. They are all here, all except Martin. Philip Neill is forced to apologise. 'I'm not quite sure where he is at the moment,' he mumbles. 'Yes, he's quite a character.'

Martin revealed to me that he deliberately snubbed the launch because of his ill-feeling over a BBC interview that never happened. 'I was due to go to London to do *BBC Breakfast*,' he explained to me. 'I said, "Okay, no bother".

They wanted to send a car but I said I was at work. I finished at 1 a.m. and so would get up at 3 a.m. to drive to London. The thing is I woke up at 5 a.m. I didn't make it. I had to ring them and say sorry. The BBC had a bit of whinge, as they had a right to do, and the next thing I know I have Philip Neill ringing me and telling me the TT organisers had told him to give me a bollocking. That's what pissed me off.' Then he said the photo shoot on the morning of the launch had further soured his mood. 'Stephen Davison, the photographer, is spot on. He tells you to turn up at 8.30 a.m. and he won't take long. I got up at 6 a.m., took the pushbike to the top of the Mountain and got there for 8.30 a.m. But none of the other riders were there because they've all been out on the piss the night before. That got me. I just thought, "Fuck you, fuck you" and that's all. I can be awkward too.'

I leave Neill to his apologies and walk down to the grassy cliff-top looking across to the Calf of Man and sit down with Hutchinson. He was still telling himself that he would be ready and was happy to look back at his historic success of the previous year. 'I did not expect to win all five but I knew it was a possibility. I never felt it was unbelievable because everything felt good. I built a bit of pressure on myself with each win because how many chances are you going to get to win four or five TTs in a week? The week kind of flew by. You are physically and mentally tired by the end. Straight after the final podium someone gave me a pint of Guinness and I quickly felt light-headed. I can't pretend that I know what went on in the past here. I watch some old DVDs and respect what everyone's done, but time moves on. Everyone will forget about me soon enough.'

He talks about his past, growing up in Yorkshire and having to battle against unwilling parents. 'I was never allowed a road bike. I was never allowed to come to the Isle of Man. I had no money and would struggle to borrow 20 quid off my mum. I think my dad thought that would get me, the fact I could not afford it. But somehow I got myself into the Manx Grand Prix and so I told them. To be fair, they have been real good supporters of my racing ever since. They are always there; they come here to watch; they have their own motorhome; they go to all the short circuits; they know the risks; my mum is petrified of the TT.'

Hutchinson speaks with an air of resignation. The bluff truism spoken by Michael Dunlop at the previous year's TT resonates – 'crap happens'. 'I had a close battle with Conor and John after the restart,' Hutchinson says as he regressed to the Senior race from 2010. 'I was 0.6 seconds up on John and saw him by the side of the road. The next board was plus three to Conor. Then I came into the pit and the board said plus 24 to me. I stopped and said, "What's happened to Conor?" They said, "He's out". I never knew what happened. I just carried on and it got better and better. When I came back I had my fingers crossed for both. It is what it is.'

Martin was the other half of that 'both', but he and Hutchinson did not get along. Some of it stemmed from Hutchinson once dating Martin's sister and the natural protectiveness that arose; some from their jarring personalities. 'There's a bond between most of us,' Hutchinson says. 'There's a bit of respect. Come the start line, me and John will always give each other a wink or a pat on the back. Then we get on with the job and, whatever the outcome, hopefully we stay mates.'

And what of Guy and his leading role in the film that was taking the TT to a wider audience? 'Oh, I'm not really bothered,' he says with a lack of conviction. 'I have no problem. It does not make any difference to me what he does. I think it's just a shame the way he perceives Isle of Man TT racing to be. It's a professional level of motorcycle racing, a world class level. I have massive respect for everyone behind the scenes, from the organisers to the people making cups of tea and the people looking after my bike. They are all here for a reason. I'm not anything special. Our bit is just the end bit. You need to respect the guys working for you. Without any part of the link it just won't happen.'

Like Cummins, Hutchinson needed his team like never before following his crash at Silverstone. 'It's funny really.' He pauses and looks at the seal that is bobbing in the Sound. 'Wrong word – strange. I knew something was coming. You don't end up in the middle of the track and have 30 bikes coming towards you and expect to get away with it. I was just expecting a big bang at any time and was praying it was not my head. It came just as I was expecting a massive thud. I got spun round and saw my leg dangling off. It was snapped in the middle – 90 degrees. I was absolutely gutted. I grabbed it and put it back in line, thinking if it looked alright then it would be alright, but then the pain kicked in. Jesus, it was some pain. You know it's hard to judge pain because your body takes over a little bit and allows you to have the most ridiculous pain in the world. You know, you can go through horrible pain pulling a plaster off your leg. It's not that different. The only thing is with one the pain goes away quickly and with the other it doesn't.

'As soon as I got airlifted to Coventry the surgeons said my leg would have to be amputated. I thought, "Absolutely no chance". I love racing, only racing. They said if they tried to save it and it got infected they would have to take it off above the knee; so they were going to take it off just below the knee. I said, "What the fuck, it doesn't matter, if any part of my leg's missing I can't race." They could get me a fantastic prosthetic leg, but however good it was I wouldn't be able to race motorbikes again. "Get that leg sewn on", I said. "If it goes wrong I'll take it on the chin. I need that leg to work, not just look like a foot".'

He went through 16 operations in Coventry and Bradford and said it should have taken him two years to get to where he was in nine months. I asked about his parents. 'My sister told them. They were in Spain. It was a 48-hour drive in a camper van to Coventry. My mum has been through some bad times.' He grins and shrugs his eyebrows. 'And now she's going to have to go through it all again. There's guilt and it's selfish, but they have had lots of good times from my racing; there are pictures all over the house, they love what I've achieved. You can't have all that and not have the risks.'

I leave Hutchinson to his awkward walk back to the car park and find Cummins. He is still far from right, but his hand had slowly come back. The yin and yang of racing had been in action on the day Hutchinson's leg was mangled. Cummins had been to that race with a friend, in an ill-fated attempt to lift his mood. Then, on the way back home, he felt his hand pulse for the first time. Maybe he was imagining it. Maybe it was another head-wrecking trick. But maybe it was the start of a revival. Cummins afforded himself a grin in the backseat of the car as he left Silverstone; Hutchinson left in an ambulance, the reversal of fortune as jarring as the impact.

He had been given the all-clear by his surgeon as we sat in Paparazzi one night in early spring and the bike test in Cartagena, Spain had been a success. Cummins was now hopeful he could at least make the start line of the TT. 'I was a bit on edge. I expected to go out on the plane thinking,

"Oh no, this is going to be a tricky one", but it was a surreal experience. I seemed more mentally prepared than I'd thought. I just wanted to get back on it. I was doing 100 laps a day, every day. I had a bit of knee swell, but that was it. I stuck a bit of ice on it. That first lap of the first session was immense. I felt, "That's it – over and done with".'

Jo Banks, his surgeon, rang while he was in Spain. She got the foreign dial tone and deduced that he was riding again. Cummins was unavailable to speak because things were going better than he could have hoped for. 'It was a bit, "Bloody hell, get round", but it worked out peachy, I was really, really chuffed. All the British Championship teams were there. I got a very good reception. Everyone was very pleased to see me.'

It was not over, though, and not everyone was support-ive. There had been criticism of Cummins on various web-sites with people suggesting he was mad for even trying to get back and that he should bow out gracefully. 'It didn't bother me, but Zara saw it and it did her head in,' he says. 'People have no idea what you are going through or how fit you are, but they are happy to write you off. It's ridiculous. Some of it was pretty nasty.'

The next few weeks would determine whether the inter-net trolls were right and whether Cummins, Hutchinson and the rest would make it. The first test came at the British Superbike meeting at Brands Hatch where Cummins slung a leg over his bike and rode in the National Superstock 1000cc race. He did not think of the Verandah, Cartagena and the Women's Rugby World Cup, the blood, sweat and tears that had brought him this far. He knew he could bounce back, literally, and that was a pressure valve. 'I've already had a crash,' he confides. 'I was testing at Snetterton and someone took me out. I know I can tumble. I came into a left going into right, committed on my right knee and this thing appeared out of my peripheral vision and cleaned me out. I went down on my back. There were a few choice words, but it was a fairly simple crash and it put a bit of doubt to rest. I came up smiling.' At Brands Hatch he was a distant 18th.

The only thing left was the North West 200, the traditional road racing warm-up for the TT. It would prove disastrous for the organisers. Torrential rain jeopardised the event and only one race from the packed programme was completed before rain, a bomb scare and an oil spill saw it cancelled. Mervyn White, the organiser who had been there when the Dunlop family had suffered its horrendous loss in 2008, was beside himself.

The second race of the day did start, but Guy Martin had already ruled himself out. The oil spill from the railway line to the Juniper chicane left the event on a slippery slope whence it could not recover. In the aftermath, Philip Neill was painted as a villain and the riders as pampered. 'It was heavily documented that me and the Honda team manager influenced the decision to cancel,' Neill told me. 'That's ridiculous. We were just invited to inspect the circuit with the clerk of the course. We were not asked for an opinion on whether the race should be run. But there are massive implications that the public don't realise. Tyre technology is good but they are not made to cope with everything. It's okay people slagging us off, but nobody would have been doing that if there had been fatalities or, God forbid, a spectator killed.'

Michael Dunlop said he was ready to have a crack in the awful conditions, but Cummins, at least, sympathised. 'It was bad when they started the first Superbike race. I thought, "This is a bloody nightmare, this is". I pulled in because you could not see where you were going. I'm as prepared to go in rain as the next man, but it was bad. And the bomb scare too. I thought that Fred Clarke, the announcer, was joking, but then I saw there wasn't a smile on his face. Everyone got evacuated from the paddock. I thought, "I'm here to race motorbikes, not abandon ship because of a bomb".'

Yet Cummins had come tenth in that first race. It was far shorter and less demanding than anything he would have to do at the TT, but it was a start. It was easy to sense a change in his mental state, something he admitted. 'The more I thought about getting back on the bike, the more I thought I need to deal with this mental thing. It was the elephant in the room again. I was putting it off because I didn't want to have to face it, but I had to suss it out.' So he watched the film of his crash with a racer friend. 'I wanted to watch it with someone who would not pussy foot around. Someone who knows what it's all about. I watched it and thought, "I can't believe that's just happened." It did not look like me. It looked like I was riding normally, which I was. Then bang. I had to do it. I didn't want to have to come up to that corner on the last lap in the TT and with a small margin and have to shut off because I had not dealt with it. Racing is cut and thrust and, although it would be perfectly reasonable to think that way, you can't afford to do it. Now I've done it. I've watched it maybe 200 times.'

He was also now a committed regular at his yoga class. 'It's about more than bending,' he says. 'It's about psychology. It's about breathing out at the right time. If I tried to touch my toes now I'd be, "Oh shit", but he teaches you to go into a relaxed mode so it comes naturally. In one lesson he reckoned I gained two inches of flexibility in my hamstring. I'm still having brutal physio too, bending my knee, getting to the end of my range and going that bit more, trying to force it, bloody aahhhh.'

He was up and running where others were falling. With barely three weeks to go until the TT, Hutchinson put out a statement saying that he had not recovered in time and would not be riding. With one week to go Tinmouth split from her Splitlath Motorsport team and so would not be racing at the TT that she so loved. Yet Cummins would be there and now faced the biggest test of his life. 'I can't put this to bed until I've been around the Verandah,' he says. 'Time to pull the pin and see what happens.'

This is dangerous. Late apex. Stay late. Be patient. Pull the bike up really hard. Fourth gear. It's so difficult. Another three years to learn that, but it's where the fast boys make up time. Into sixth before the little jump and the 30mph sign. Douglas Road corner. Sixth to third, easy to get scared rabbit syndrome here. Unfortunately, we lost a newcomer here because he went straight into that lamp post. Probably only going about 40mph, but rather than let the brakes off and go round, he froze and bang. He got a little bit lost and missed the braking point. As a newcomer you have to know what's coming next. You can't ride it freestyle.

Fourteen
Pulling the Pin
30 May 2011

And so, after a year of waiting, working and wringing hands and bodies for the last vestiges of hope and strength, the TT arrived. The format was five nights of practice, with the public roads shut to all but racers, followed by five races the following week. These would commence with the Superbike race on Saturday. After a rest day, which was a euphemism for round-the-clock dissection of engines, there would be two races on Monday, the first Supersport race in the morning and then the Superstock event later that afternoon. Another day off would be followed by the second Supersport race on the Wednesday and then, after a brief respite, the TT would climax with the Senior on Friday at 1.30 p.m. They were also support events, two sidecar races, concerts by Imelda May and the Pigeon Detectives, a funfair and the Red Arrows. This was the TT. Twelve days that would make or break years, careers, bodies and more.

Lee Vernon, No 58, had got there early. This was no holiday, but he had been forced to take it as such from work in that Manchester motorcycle shop. 'It's a bit of tough shit to be honest,' he said. 'I just told them.' He had borrowed the bike from a man called Jonathan Milner. 'I'm lucky. Without that you're talking £10,000 for a bike before you've turned a wheel.' He had got hold of an old R-reg Mercedes van and converted it. There was a settee and a bed in the front, where Vernon slept, and what he called the workshop in the back, an empty space for dismembering bikes. 'Dad bought a caravan for £250 and we got an awning.' A friend called Laura was helping with the cooking. 'We got here and we thought they'd be dead strict like, moaning about how dirty the van was, but the blokes on the gate just said, "This is where you are and this is how much room you've got". We set up. It's dead friendly. People wander around and dip into each other's awnings, watch a DVD and have a joke and a beer.' Vernon had been into town on the Friday to celebrate his birthday. 'We had a few,' he grinned.

The riders assembled under black clouds and impending rain. A special flight was put on so those who had been competing in the British Superbike Championship at Thruxton on the mainland that day could make it. This was the real stuff. Road racing was sport stripped to the bone and maw, whereas short circuit racing was, in the view of Guy Martin, all about ego and surface fluff. Martin was more into spit than polish and, with his black Relentless Suzuki leathers and livery, felt this could finally be the year. In the paddock I met three Australians who were debating why Martin had not yet won. One of the men was missing most of his teeth, had five-day stubble and a black leather jacket faded to grey. He said it was bad luck, simple as that. His friend was a McGuinness man and took issue. He said Martin was simply not good enough. 'Great bloke and all that, but he's had his chances.' The third member of this band, all on an once-in-a-lifetime trip to the TT, missed his mouth with a hotdog and rolled off the back of a bench. The drinking had started early.

Conor Cummins sucked in a deep breath as he swung his leg over the bike. This was it. Pull the pin and see what happens. It was the same mindset that was driving Martin, the urge to regret what he had done rather than what he had not. There were murmurs of discontent that the organisers had changed the traditional schedule to let the sidecars out onto the 37-mile circuit first. So the wait went on. Then Milky Quayle took the newcomers out for their first taste of the mythical Mountain. Cummins could easily imagine their smiles and gulps and out-of-body rushes as they climbed higher and higher. 'What's the thrill? It's a hundred things that come together.' Now it was 101 things, his crash adding poignancy to his efforts.

Then, at 7.50 p.m. on that Monday night, Martin and Michael Dunlop led the cast list down Bray Hill. A form of macho alchemy had transformed the country lanes and village roads into a world class race track. Martin was the first to complete a lap, clocking an average speed of 121.380mph. That was mind-numbingly quick to watch, but tardy by TT standards and a reflection of the damp conditions. The riders had got two laps in and were only just acclimatising when the heavens opened on the Mountain and the session was red flagged. By the time they stopped, John McGuinness was the fastest man on the course, nudging the average lap speed up to 122.84mph. That was on his Superbike. Others had elected to go out on their Superstock machines to open up with. Bruce Anstey, who nurtured a modicum of ill will after being let go by TAS to make way for Martin, was fastest of the supposedly standard machines, with William and Michael Dunlop third and fourth. A little down the timesheets was Cummins in eighth. He dismounted and hugged his mum. He texted Marcus de Matas with his times. De Matas had already decided to visit the TT a few days later during race week. 'My father-in-law went to the TT 20 years ago. He said, "Now you're a famous surgeon you should go and watch". I said, "Okay, I'll talk to Conor". He said, "Anytime. Just let me know when".'

Lee Vernon had found it tough. He was no slouch. He had once coined the bizarre nickname 'The Flying Oatcake' when he had beaten McGuinness at Scarborough, but he was on the old man's patch now and it was confusing. 'I'd been round the circuit with Milky Quayle, but you can't pick things up in a car. He says, "Watch out for this tree" and all that. I watched DVDs of laps, but somehow your attention is not on it until you're on a bike. I went down Bray Hill, turned right at Quarter Bridge and thought, "This looks completely different".'

His dad, who had thought the Ulster Grand Prix to be mint, was also having to deal with the TT's unique assault on the emotions. They had already been through much. Vernon had raced at Silverstone during the last TT and had heard the news about Paul Dobbs. 'That was gutting,' he said. 'We knew him well.' Now Vernon got off the bike and talked to his dad. 'One lap feels like five minutes,' he said. 'His dad looked at him and replied: 'Feels like an hour to me.'

Cummins was delighted. One ghost had been buried in two laps. 'That was my aim,' he said. 'The first lap of practice was always going to be my TT. It had not looked likely when my arm was all shrunken away like a bone, and when I was lying in that bed and thinking about the risks of surgery.

I'd like to have gone quicker, but I'm here. There's a hell of a long way to go, but I made it.'

For Carole, it was just as exhilarating. They were not the sort of family to live in the past – 'if you do that you'd never do anything' – but it inevitably informed the present. 'He was so happy with that first lap. I could not turn round and say, "For Christ's sake, stop it". I was proud.' She used to sit and watch the TT on the wall by the shed where the riders came in to slow down. 'I wasn't going to do that after last year. I went to the start line and then I went to the Hailwood Centre to see the different sector times to make sure he was going through places. Then, when he was due to come past the Grandstand, I'd run from the Hailwood Centre and watch from behind the pit wall.' All she saw was a flash of purple and green, passing the wall of plaques in the cemetery, passing the finish line, passing St Ninian's Church and disappearing down Bray Hill and pushing 200mph. 'It was nerve-racking.'

Kirk Michael and the biggest sense of speed on the whole circuit. Through the centre of the village now, people hanging out the windows, everyone screaming for Conor as the local lad. People sat in gardens and in the church. It's amazing how narrow and constricted it is. Your exhaust is echoing off the houses and you're convinced there's something wrong. It's frenetic. Smell the burgers. The entry's not the problem, it's the exit. Now get on the gas and the whole front of the bike is clattering and understeering. I need to be as close to that wall as possible, the camber's going away, this left-hander's tightening. Run down to Bishopscourt. This is where Pat Hennen crashed and effectively ended his career, clipped the kerb on the left. See it sticks out. Have to get close to it. Head almost in the bank and the bike drifts over to the centre of the road. Sixth gear now, 180mph, and the bike is moving all over, you're constantly fighting. It's not an easy ride.

Fifteen

Pitch Black

31 May 2011

'Things are going good but I'm getting tense and nervous being around the paddock. However many years you come, you still get it. I came across early on Thursday to get parked up. It's funny really, but I have to try to get into the Manx way of life.' John McGuinness is sitting in a leather seat of his plush Honda Legends transporter. The red, white and blue bike is proving popular. The days of endurance racing had got McGuinness fitter than he had been for years. Yet he was fidgety and anxious and counting down the days.

'It's quiet here at first,' he says as he sips a cup of tea. 'Then the trucks arrive and they were all stuck in the mud. Then we lost the Saturday practice for some reason, but now it's getting there – the bikes, the Grandstand, people from around the world. I still love it. It's different when you want to win it, and sometimes you have to move over and let someone else get ahead, but I love it. Oh yes. I want to get my bike now and get on with it. There's more pressure on me now than last year. I did not put my body through six laps last year; I don't know if I can. We'll have to see whether it holds out. I don't know what's going to happen on Saturday. Someone might go ballistic and clear off.'

McGuinness needed a win and was fed up with waiting. Six months had dwindled to this moment and he was now in the waiting room. He had enjoyed the endurance races, but they were not the same. The team had finished fifth in the Bol d'Or, a 24-hour race in France in which three riders did shifts on the bike. It had not gone so well at a similar event in Albacete, Spain. 'I kicked off after seven hours ten minutes and that was it,' McGuinness says. 'The bike was too badly damaged to carry on. It's tough. You can't kip so you're always on edge. It was good, but the truth is you can't practice for the TT until you get here.'

At 39 he was not thinking about retiring now, but he was acutely aware of his mortality and time frame. Last year – fourth, fifth and seventh place finishes – had been humbling and he needed success now to silence his inner doubts. 'I do think about it. Definitely. I know there's a bloody big hole to fill when I pack it in, a massive void. I would have to do something with people I like; I could not work with someone I didn't just for the money, that's not what I'm about.

'Breaking down twice last year I thought is someone trying to tell me something? Is it time to get out? I was in limbo. I was not in a good position or a good frame of mind. Then Neil Tuxworth came to me and said Honda wanted to do world endurance. Did I fancy it?'

If he was counting down to the races, and ultimately to the endgame, then he wanted to do it the right way. He had met numerous celebrities over the years. Some, like MotoGP star Valentino Rossi and Formula One driver Mark Webber, he admired. Webber's helmet was in his trophy cabinet in Morecambe. Others had been less impressive. 'When I come here and go to the schools I feel like David Beckham. It's weird. I hear people muttering under their breath, "That's John McGuinness". I don't want to be an arsehole for them. If I came back in the afterlife and heard people muttering, "He was a right arsehole", then I'd be gutted. I don't think I've got any enemies. I don't think I've ever stuffed anyone.'

Even now he still harked back to the day at the TT in 2000 when he had done the dirty on Joey Dunlop, his idol who would be killed within weeks. 'I was the British champion,' he recalls. 'I was the lap record holder and I had the No 1 plate. Watch me go. I passed him, got a bit close and roughed him up a little bit in practice. As soon as I did it I had that horrible sinking feeling in my body. You should never fuck the good guys. He didn't say anything, but it was definitely noted. I set off behind him in the race and thought, "Phew, catch Joey and I'm the champion. Watch me go". I never saw him. He hammered me.'

It is a revealing anecdote and segues into the time Guy Martin did the same to him. 'He roughed me up at the North West 200. He sent me up a slip road and then started saying that he was a mechanic and was going back to work at five in the morning. "What's McGuinness doing?" he said. "He's going to polish his motorhome". If I ever needed any drive that was it. There was no chance. He was having a portion. He knows that now. He learnt a lesson. Course he did.' Martin would confirm that he had regretted the 'roughing' but not the barb. Spit rather than polish, indeed.

McGuinness had told me that he slept a lot and sometimes had trouble getting up. Clive Padgett, whose bikes he would be riding in the Supersport and Superstock races, often sent him a text or went to his motorhome to bang on the door. Whatever the reason, McGuinness was running late for the second practice session on Tuesday night. The weather was better this time, with sun warming the large crowd. There were people all over the course, in gardens and churchyards, and in the paddock, where the burger van and beer tent and Red Torpedo stall selling Guy Martin T-shirts were all inundated. Further along, behind the Grandstand, past scrutineering and over the road that led out of the paddock were the top teams. Honda Legends had the best spot and a resplendent truck. Next to them were TAS Relentless Suzuki, with their uber-cool black design and iconic logo. Clive Padgett's awning was a far more basic affair, but attracted plenty of attention because their mechanics always seemed to be working longer hours than the rest. Across the little dirt path, which would grow increasingly congested whenever Martin was in the Suzuki HQ, was the McAdoo Kawasaki home of Conor Cummins. A couple of T-shirts bearing the slogan 'The Comeback Kid' were hung up for sale. Further along from him, towards the perimeter wire fence, police station and makeshift helipad, was Wilson Craig's bijoux awning housing the bikes of William Dunlop and Cameron Donald. And then, round the back, away from the deluge of fans, was the shabby tent of Michael Dunlop. Corporate mores and fancy sponsorship had little appeal for him.

He and Martin were the first away at Tuesday's practice session. The riders were released in pairs. They could choose which bikes they liked. Again the island's normal day ended, the cars and buses and lorries removed and replaced by high-speed motorcycles. At the back of the field, Guillaume Dietrich, the French rookie partnering Martin, started alone. He had fallen on his very first time around the circuit.

It was supposed to be an acclimatisation lap and he had certainly got to know how hard this stuff was from the off. Most of the riders were able to get in five laps, or 188 miles, before the end of the session. McGuinness complained that his leathers were too tight, but he posted the fastest lap of the week so far when he clocked an average speed of 129.04mph. Martin was second. Michael Dunlop had also started well and was fastest of the Supersports, as well as being second fastest on the Superstock behind Gary Johnson.

It had been a promising start but practice rarely made perfect at the TT and so, as dusk fell and the riders departed, McGuinness to his motorhome, Cummins to his Ramsey home and Martin to his lock-up on the industrial estate, the TT prepared to take another of its horrible lurches into pitch black.

Stay out a bit later and back in by this hedge here. This point, Alpine Corner, is a complete and utter bastard. No other way to describe it. The big problem is you don't want to shut the power off, but there is a lift in the road, so you have to roll it as you go over the rise. It's one of the few early apex corners too, but because the bike is loose and the front wheel is in the air you have to wait for it to land and then lay it on its side. There is no pretty way through here. Feel the front go and ride the storm.

Sixteen

The Real Thing
1 June 2011

The weather on the Isle of Man can be Arctic at times and bipolar at others. There can be bright sunshine at the Grandstand in Douglas and torrential rain on the Mountain. The distances are relatively short, but the differences are striking. It helps make the TT the conundrum it is. Nobody, except perhaps Michael Dunlop and his inherent bullishness, wants to ride in the wet. So reports of a lack of adhesion at Ballagarey caused ripples of unease. Nevertheless, the third session got underway as planned. So people took their places. The Creg Ny Baa pub, with its perfect view of the Mountain descent, was full of drinkers, diners and watchers. It was the same story in the drinking holes of Ramsey, where the slow corner into the crossroads allowed fans to get a lingering look at the rebels. Others ignored practice and headed for Douglas promenade to party and watch *TT3D* being played out at the Palace Cinema.

Martin and Dunlop led them away again that evening at 6.29 p.m. Dunlop was marginally quicker and would overtake Martin on the road before breaking down at Ginger

Hall. It was hard to gauge too much from proceedings, but for the first time John McGuinness was not the fastest man on the circuit. Instead, Bruce Anstey, the 41-year-old Kiwi, was rolling back the years and perhaps making Philip Neill wonder whether he had done the right thing in discarding him and recruiting Martin. Anstey's average lap speed rose to 129.69mph, close to the magical 130mph barrier, with Martin second. Gary Johnson, a near-neighbour and sworn rival of Martin, was third on his East Coast Racing Honda. Johnson also topped the Superstock charts, as he had done the previous day. Hutchinson had been removed from the equation, although he was on the island and cut a miserable presence as he wandered around the paddock on duty for his sponsors, but new rivals had emerged.

Johnson was hardly an unknown – he had finished third in the Senior in 2009 – but he had disappeared in 2010 due to injury. He was an electrician who was struggling to get by. He had invested around £50,000 into East Coast Racing, which he said left him with 50 pence. 'I can only afford to get by because I'm living at home paying £10 a week,' he told Gary Pinchin, a journalist with *Motorcycle News*. 'I borrow a 12-year-old van from Lincs Lifting and I live off my start and prize money.' He was pushing 30 and had come close to quitting. 'I'd reached a point where I was totally sick of the job last year,' he said. 'The things kicked me from arsehole to breakfast and it was either stop or put my money where my mouth was. So I invested everything I had into this year's effort, made sure every detail was as I wanted it.' He had found another £30,000 for the current season, but needed a win to survive. If he went home empty-handed, that might be it. He might be back to wiring houses, providing electricity rather than feeling it.

McGuinness, meanwhile, was ninth in the Superbike charts, Conor Cummins a distant 24th that made you wonder whether it was all going to be too much for a man struggling against his body. Keith Amor, McGuinness' teak-tough Scottish teammate, nursed a dislocated shoulder after sliding off at Quarter Bridge. Where Barry Sheene had done the same and labelled the event a suicide mission, Amor picked himself up and vowed to ride in Saturday's opening race.

As the riders talked to their mechanics, did cursory interviews and headed off, the sidecars went out for their practice session. I had already sat down with Klaus Klaffenbock, the Austrian driver who had won the previous year's races with partner Dan Sayle. If TT riders had an inverted snobbery towards GP riders, sidecar men felt the same towards their TT peers. 'They look down on us for sure,' Klaffenbock said. He had been in the garage until 1 a.m. His hands were stained black. His eyes were yellow. 'But I know what I've achieved. If they say things about us it makes me laugh. Sidecars are more exciting than bikes because we are lower down. This is the real world. It's a real thing, a real sport. Sometimes questions are asked about the dangers. In Austria we have something called base jumping. We jump down in dark holes. But everything is calculated, every part of every second. Here, nothing is calculated. You can't calculate it. That's the real story of motorsport.'

Klaffenbock had lived several lives. He had won the FIM World Championship in 2001 with Christian Parzer. The partnerships of sidecars gave it that extra dimension, but the relationship with Parzer had flatlined three years earlier when he was caught speeding on the A1 in Austria. He had no registration papers and the police noted that Parzer seemed unduly nervous. They searched the car and found a stash of cocaine. He admitted to being a drug user and said he was ferrying the drugs to Upper Austria at the behest of his suppliers to whom he was in debt. He was sentenced to ten months and Klaffenbock was forced to state that he knew nothing about the incident.

'I have been doing sidecar racing for 25 years and have had three passengers,' he told me. 'It's like a marriage to someone. It works like a marriage. If you give the partner respect then you get it back.' Parzer was gone and so was the sponsorship deal with Dolly Buster, the Czech porn star who had tried and failed to become an MEP but had succeeded in penning a series of novels about a porn star-turned-amateur sleuth. Despite this background, it was hard to see sidecar racing as a world of sex and drugs. It was more wrecks and dregs as Klaffenbock and Co fought a constant battle for acceptance. 'We are the real deal but the truth is the world championship is dying,' Klaffenbock said. He sighed and looked at least his 42 years. 'I never did what other people did. I was always different. I never worked like a normal person. At 18 I was going round Europe on a coach and racing. They can laugh. Sidecar racing is dirty and grimy, but it is real.'

Klaffenbock was moving fast when news filtered into the press room, a small brick building at the foot of the Grandstand, bedecked by old paintings and a rarely working coffee machine. The session had been red-flagged. It is hard to explain the sense of foreboding that such a message provokes at the TT. Before long confirmation came through and, soon after, when the families had been informed, a statement.

ACU Events Ltd regret to announce that sidecar competitor Bill Currie, 67, from Ellesmere Port, Cheshire and his passenger Kevin Morgan, 59, from Shrewsbury were both killed during the second sidecar qualifying session at the 2011 Isle of Man TT Races following an incident at Ballacrye in the North of the Island. The session was immediately red flagged following the incident.

Bill was an experienced racer who first competed at the TT Races in 1969, when he recorded a third place finish. He finished eighth in last year's TT sidecar race in his fastest ever race time of 107.944. Kevin made his TT debut in 1984. This was the first year that the pair had competed together.

Bill was divorced with two children and Kevin was single with two sons. The ACU wishes to pass on their deepest sympathy to the family and friends of both competitors.

ACU Events Managing Director Jim Parker said: 'I have known both Bill and Kevin for many years and am deeply saddened by their untimely death. They were a huge part of the sidecar paddock and will be sorely missed by everyone involved in the event.' The Coroner of Inquests has been informed and an investigation into the circumstances of the accident is underway.

It would not be long before the tributes began. Currie's age would cause some to question the wisdom, even the morality, of letting pensioners take on the most dangerous of races, but he was also in love with the place, quitting his job as a telephone engineer at the GPO when his boss would not give him time off to try his luck at the TT. He went home without a job but with a third place from his 1969 debut, an unprecedented feat. Even a ten-year hiatus following an accident when he lost an eye at work did not stop him, and the previous year he had finished an impressive eighth with a different passenger. His brother, Les, said: 'They made him come back up through club level, which he did, winning trophies along the way. In fact, he won the European Formula Two Championship by winning every race. He just seemed to get faster with age. He was a quiet, understated person. To look at him, you wouldn't know he was a TT racer. But when he got on a bike he changed. He was focused and committed. A lot of racers lose their hunger over the years, but he never did. I used to worry about him, but he knew what he was doing and he was good at it.'

Bill Smith, a friend and four-time winner at the TT, said: 'People are upset about it but I take a philosophical point of view. Bill told me that, at his age, he would rather die racing than die from cancer. That might seem a strange thing to say, but it's the way racers think.'

I went back to the room I was renting in Derby Square that night and, like many before, wondered why they did it as much as how. I would get the definitive answer the following morning.

Run down into Ballaugh Bridge and up to sixth gear.
Come on, come on. Had a mechanical failure here one
year. Put it on the kerb but the big boy upstairs said,
'You're staying down there you bugger'. The crank case
exploded, oil inside my helmet and leathers, had to
slow. Braking into some 30mph signs. Real bumpy.
Bang, bang, bang. Don't want any heroics here or big
air. If you jump big at Ballaugh you won't finish the race
because the place wrecks suspension. Martin Finnegan
used to be the best through there. Out of Ballaugh and
through the gearbox as fast as you can. The biggest
jump on the circuit is this one here – Ballacrye. Sixth
gear. Fifty feet. I have smashed my screen and all sorts
through there. Such a handful. Turn down into Quarry
Bends. Second most important corner on the circuit.
Drive drive, drive.

Seventeen

Love Gets Dangerous
2 June 2011

It is almost a year since Paul Dobbs had died at the TT. Now Bridget Dobbs is sitting with me on the side of the stage of the press conference room. She tells me she met Dobsy, as she always referred to him, via her sister's boyfriend who ran a bike shop in Sydney. 'I met him within days of being in the country, but I was off on trips. I went to the Outback. But we got engaged soon after that and I knew it was right. I'd always had friends with bikes, and I got my licence, but his whole life revolved around it. He'd done three or four years racing in New Zealand. There was a whole bunch of guys – Ian Lougher, Joey Dunlop – who went out and raced there. He talked to those guys and they were full of the TT and that was it. He wanted to go. He'd heard of it, of course, but speaking to those guys made him want to go right there and then. But his boss told him to do some more racing down there. There was a job in Australia, so that's what he did. But it's there, isn't it? My family was not into racing, but bits are imprinted on my brain. It was in my consciousness, but I never felt it would be a major part of my life. But when we went to Australia, it became clear that he was going to go.'

An idea grew. Dobbs was a popular figure, with spiky hair and a bushy goatee. He had time for people and quickly found that the TT was different to all other motorsport. Part of that came from the danger, but a larger part from its almost mythical status and cultish camaraderie. These men, and women, were in the trenches together and the bonds that were formed were unbreakable.

'We married in England in late '98 and '99 was the first TT,' Bridget says. The way she told her story, with an almost unwavering voice and only the occasional welling of tears, showed how she utterly understood the worth of the TT. Know your value, Jim Moodie had told John McGuinness who, in turn, had told me. Jenny Tinmouth had not known whether she should ask for a wage, but she flipped the old adage and knew the value of a TT racer if not the price.

'I loved the Manx people,' Bridget says. 'I loved doing laps and reading out names to get a connection. All of that danger, it's mystical, the variation in the roads, going through the busiest town on the island, turning a corner and finding yourself in the pit lane. It's that transformation, that complete metamorphosis that happens every day.'

It was easy to understand that enthusiasm. The promenade was now thick with bikes. I had spoken to a café owner that afternoon and she could not stop smiling. The TT was not only a financial godsend, but it was a chance to catch up with old friends. 'We have the same people coming in year after year,' she said. 'I have one fella from Luxembourg who always has a black pudding sandwich and a can of Irn-Bru. I don't think they can get it over there. It's like a reunion.'

It was the same for Dobbs now. 'The anticipation cranks

up. When they had morning practices that sense of wonder would be stronger still because everything would be dark, people would be bleary-eyed, everyone yawning and drinking coffee, and then they would come down here and it would come to life.'

The first time they journeyed to the island was via the Kiwi grapevine. 'One of the guys in the workshop said he knew someone on the Isle of Man so we rang up. They put us up. Kiwis do that. We did put a tent up in the paddock so we had somewhere to prepare the bikes too. They looked after us for several years and they had their first daughter the same time we had ours. Now our girls can't wait to see each other.' The paddock life, with its peculiar sense of rivalry and commonality, was seductive. 'It was bohemian. I went through the whole thing of washing nappies in a bucket and then hanging them out on a line. You share showers and laundry, it's a close community.'

Of course, this being the TT, the community was strengthened by the knowledge that things could go wrong, and dealing with that determined whether you could stay in love with the place. I mention the sidecar racers, thinking how Dobbs scarcely needed anything to pour fuel on the memories burning bright. 'It's very, very hard, every time,' she says. 'Probably the one that affected us most was when it was the people opposite us in the paddock. Pete Jarman came off his Bultaco on the parade lap in 2003. That was the closest thing but, in a way, it would have affected Dobsy more. He knew the other riders far better than I did. Riders see things; riders go past debris; and worse. Yes, it all just carries on, but the riders don't just shrug their shoulders. The riders' response is very deep and genuine. It does hurt; it's like losing your next-door neighbour. Some riders don't mix that much, but you feel it just the same.'

She throws her head back as the crowds bustle by outside. It was more than mere sport and that was why it was so special. To deny that would be to mask what made this way beyond the British Superbike Championship and even MotoGP. Valentino Rossi came to watch and said it was crazy and he was right – it's a crazy little thing called love.

'People just have a way of getting on with life. Not everybody would choose to be a firefighter or an ambulance driver. Not everyone wants to see the nasty bits of life. We all buy our meat wrapped in plastic because we don't like to think about the animal that died. Nobody likes the idea of killing a rabbit or a chicken, not even a butcher, but you just get on with it.'

'I don't know if it sounds selfish, but we went into parenthood after a very quick conversation about what he wanted and what I wanted. He was not going to give up racing. He'd had a major relationship before me that had foundered because she did not like racing. I thought, "This is what we do, this is part of what we are". I said, "Sooner or later I want kids". He said, "So do it". That was it. We had the attitude that we had our lives and there is stuff we do. We were here first and we're not going to give this up. You have to show children that you can have passion. You have to give them something more.'

It is curiously uplifting to listen to a bereaved woman speak in such a way about her worst nightmare, but while the critics point to the deaths as conclusive proof that racing on the course was unjustifiable, Dobbs regarded it differently. To her, it was a loss not a waste. The alternative was a longer life half-lived. 'It was impossible to imagine him without racing. We did speak about what he might do after, when he was too old to carry on, because there would have to be something. We talked about doing a rally together. I like reading maps and I'm able to do that and not be sick in the car. But if anybody had tried to stop him racing they wouldn't have been able to. If he had stopped there would have been a meltdown. He was a very driven person. When he was not racing he was making stuff go faster – a bike, a car, lawnmower.'

Bridget watched a couple of TTs from the Grandstand, but she struggled with that and so she worked with Dobsy in the pits. As he improved, he got more crew and so she took a backwards step. 'Everyone had a turn in the pits. If it was not my turn I would go for a run; I could not handle the stress, the helplessness. I hated sitting and watching the pit stops. If you were down there yourself then you could deal with it because you did the best you could. I suppose there is an element of control freakery. After he changed the team around, he decided he wanted me there, so I opened the fuel cap, his visor, gave him a drink, told him the times. I'd do calculations on a bit of paper and listen to the radio.'

That was always the bit that was so hard to explain to outsiders. The TT is thrilling to see, but you only see snippets. The big picture was played out elsewhere, up the Mountain and in your head. There were no live action screenings. People sat on a particular corner and got the thrill of the rush, but they only kept track of the race order by listening to the radio or watching the screens with lists of names and times for each sector.

'You don't panic because there is human fallacy in the system,' Bridget says. 'But that day was different. Paul Owen was one spot apart from him and his dial did not move either. That was a bit of an alarm bell. It took so long for me to get the message officially. Part of me thinks, "Why did it take so long?" It was only the second race he had not finished in 11 years. That's what he did. He was a finisher. He had a reputation for bringing the bike home! He had done so in 27 of his last 30 starts at the TT. He had made the top ten in the lightweight classes and had a respectable best of 18th in the Senior. Even in 2010 it had been going well, an average speed of 120.8mph in the Superbike race, his fastest around the island.

'There are guys under the podium with phones and note-pads and they run messages. We did not get a message. I went to the guy under the podium and said, "Any news?" he said, "No 72 has stopped at Ballagarey". I said, "Okay, but what about No 31?" He said, "No news". I thought, "How the hell can they not know?" There's a number on the bike, there's a dog tag on every rider. I've gone through it in my head a lot, wondering why they didn't get the message, but within that half an hour, on some level, I knew.

'That evening or the next morning, they took me to a room I never knew existed. The room for grieving people. I've got to thank them for having that – comfy chairs, carpet, coffee machine, telephone. They talk you through it. I've never done this before, but they tell you what to do next. His parents and my parents, all the close people, they needed to be told. I went through the contact lists. It was 3 a.m. in New Zealand so it was rough. They said, "There are people downstairs in the race office asking; what do you want to tell them?" I wouldn't want people waking up and not knowing, and I've been on the other side of it when we've heard there's been a nasty incident and listened to the radio and heard nothing. Sometimes it's days. I wanted the message out there straightaway. I put out the statement because I'd seen occasions where the press had put words into the mouths of the family. And I was also acutely aware of how damaging fatalities are, not to the TT, but to the public image of the TT. There's always going to be part of the media that jump on to it and say, "Oh, look, let's ban the TT". I had a strong feeling about what was the right thing to do.'

That she could be so concerned about the event and the community and the other women hanging out nappies on the line showed a remarkable selflessness. But Bridget Dobbs was one of the extraordinary women behind the ordinary men, like Carole Cummins, Louise Dunlop, Becky and Zara. Like Guy Martin's fiancée, Steph, who was staying in a B&B on her first visit to the Isle of Man.

'I'm not bitter,' Dobbs continues. 'It's funny in a way. It's common knowledge what people go through in the grieving process. You're meant to get angry, but I can't see anything to get angry about. There was nothing wrong with the bike. Nobody did anything daft, whether it be a member of the public or another rider. There was nothing to blame. It was a pure racing incident. That's not that common. Often there's something like an oil leak or another rider doing something. He just got it wrong and that's all there is to it. In a way that's been a help. There is no bitterness; there is no anger.'

She speaks of Paul Owen, the rider whom Dobsy was closest to. Yet it was a relationship that lasted for two weeks a year. They trusted each other and would race hard against each other, knowing 'if you get something wrong then you could die', and then they would talk about it. 'I'd be in the paddock and listening to guys talking about the racing and that was almost as good as doing it. It makes people close, so it's strange that you don't stay in touch for the rest of the year.'

Now she was back on the island with her daughters, Eadlin and Hillberry, the latter named after a section of the course, and had issued an open invitation for anyone to attend a memorial service at Lonan Parish Church that coming Sunday. As we talked, the kids had been taken off for an ice cream. Dobbs' remarkably brave face masks an obvious pain, and she wonders whether her forthright defence of the TT has been innocently misappropriated by Dobsy's peers. 'Some of the compliments I have got have blown me away,' she says. 'But the cynical side of me thinks I have given them the okay to keep racing. You know people get in touch. "How are you?" "I'm doing good, thanks". "Oh, good girl". They have ticked the box.'

She did not mean that to sound ungrateful, and she was putting her energies into her children. She was not about to change her philosophy now and so the girls were riding bikes. 'They have always done that. The amount of risk you allow your children is different for every parent. We have stood back and let them take the falls, whether they be climbing stairs or in the playground. We were very aware of not doing the cotton wool treatment. One time we went out and found a massive dead tree. They started walking across the branches. I was having to take deep breaths and not let them feel my projected fear. If you see a kid fall off a bike on the other side of the paddock, you don't go sprinting over there. You head over but hopefully they have been taught how to pick up the bike. Some parents have radios. You think, "Let go".'

The children are nine and four. 'They are at that age

where they do something different every week. I've heard everything from they're going to be a doctor to a child-minder – "very proud of you, sweetie". Eadlin, particularly, wants to be her dad. When they sat down together it would be for Sunday motorsport on the TV. Eadlin told him, "I'm going to race bikes and sometimes I might fall off". He laughed. She'd taken it all on board. He hated watching them ride. He was terrified.

'I knew from day one that I wanted to come back. I did not know if I would be able to, because I did not know what the finances would be like, but it's like getting back on a horse, putting demons to bed, all those clichés. There's a hint of all that, but there are also the other guys I know from racing, not just the riders, and I wanted to be here and share in that again.'

It has been as heartfelt and as articulate an assessment of the whys and wherefores of TT racing as I have ever heard. A loss, not a waste. It is what they all feel. It is why so many cannot stop, from Dunlop to DJ to Dobbs. 'You don't stop because you win,' Bridget explains as a parting shot. 'You don't stop because you stop winning. You don't stop because you have a scare and you don't stop because you see some-one else have a fatality. None of those things change the fact that you love racing.'

That night the conditions were perfect but the practice session for the bikes was cancelled after an oil spill from a sidecar. It left the riders disgruntled and unimpressed at the shifting schedules. 'Nobody cares about sidecars,' one huffed as he marched out of his awning. But people did care. Bill Currie did. Everyone had their goals. It was, as Bridget Dobbs had said, almost mystical. It didn't matter whether you won or lost or rode a bike or a sidecar, the battle against your self and selfishness was the same for all. So Klaus Klaffenbock put a sticker on his sidecar, by way of tribute to Currie and Morgan, and carried on. 'The other day I said to someone I have to be self-confident,' he told me. 'I know I'll be safe around here, but I don't know if something will break on the bike or if there's a hare on the road or whatever. That's the danger and the danger is attractive. No doubt about that.' Dirty, grimy and unreal.

I'm looking for a helmet or a bike in the distance. If I see one I know I'm doing well. If not then they are closing in on me. Take a breath here. Chill out. You're taut and tense, but you have to take your breaks where you can. There are three places – here, Cronk-y-Voddy and the Mountain Mile where you can do that. Run through the speed trap. Fastest time recorded through here was Bruce Anstey, 207mph, in 2007. That bike had a full World Superbike engine brought over specially, but only lasted four laps before it self-destructed. All very well being fast. On the brakes for Sulby Bridge. Sixth to second, it comes up fast and you've been flat out for so long it's like 'Shit!' Down to Ginger Hall, over to the pub, the camber throwing me in the gutter, lovely corner, underneath the telegraph pole and out to the 50mph sign. This is where all hell breaks loose.

Eighteen

Red Squirrel

3 June 2011

It is the final day of practice and I go to see Guy Martin at his secret location at his lock-up. He is his usual chirpy self, but it is clear that he had been taken aback by the public interest in him. I had seen him twice in the paddock the previous day and he had perfected the art of keeping moving on his pushbike while apologising. He had signed hundreds more autographs than anyone else and his profile meant he was ripe for a kicking as far as some felt. On one occasion, he had been forced, due to pressure from the sponsors, not to sign a particular hat. The person waving the hat under his nose and demanding a signature was unimpressed. 'Piss off,' he spat at Martin.

The lock-up is owned by a friend of a friend called Craig. It is a normal garage, but in the corner sat the stationary engine that Martin had been given and would take to the Port St Mary Steam Fair during TT race week. He was enthralled by it, as he was his Martek turbo, which he had brought to tinker with in his downtime. He was sleeping on the couch in the tiny office at the back. There are assorted

253

DVDs around. *Tom & Jerry, Finding Nemo, The Inbetween-ers.* 'It's perfect,' he says. 'Just out of the way. Nobody knows.'

Hector Neill, the Irishman with the raucous accent and weather-beaten looks, drops by. They like each other. Both, in a way, are mavericks. Neill said they were both workers and was suggesting they go to Jurby and take advantage of the extra practice session the organisers had put on following the cancellation of last night's session. Martin is nonplussed by the idea. 'He's not one for scrubbing tyres,' Neill says as he leaves Martin to some spanner work in the back of his van.

Neill had been doing this forever, but he had never seen anything like Martin. He was, he said, a phenomenon. 'The paddock was blocked last night and they were all shouting for Guy,' he says. 'He came out of the truck and they all cheered. Normally he gets on his bike and he's away, but give him his due, last night he went down the line and signed them all. I sat back and thought, "Amazing". He's got some-thing. Hailwood got the same sort of treatment, but he was not a great man for signing things. He'd stick his head down and get away. I remember one photographer was trying to take his picture and he stuck his thumb on the guy's lens. With Guy, it's just going to happen sometime and if, by some luck, we happen to win a race then this guy is going to be completely mobbed. All that has let him down so far is the machinery, but I think he has a good chance to pull off a couple of races here. He's in good enough form and the bikes are in the best shape we have ever had them. He says that if we didn't get another practice session in then he could pick up the bike and ride it now. A lot of guys are struggling now but we're not, we're on it.'

Did Neill still get the same buzz, after all the years, the

wins, the losses and the tragedies? 'We got here and it was hard work. Pouring down with rain, putting the awnings up, thinking, "What am I doing?" Then the next day you get up, the weather's changed, you go along the prom, the sea is calm and you love it. A certain journalist told me five years ago that there would be one more TT and the Isle of Man would be finished. I said, "You're talking a load of nonsense". I see him now and he says, "You were right".'

The naysayers were out again when he recruited Martin. 'A certain official said to me, "I hear you're going to take on Guy Martin". I said, "We are indeed". He replied, "You'll never manage that man in a million years. You'll not last three months with him". Well, we're here. We talk the same way, from the bottom up. I have a nice place for him to stay, but he's quite happy living here. He says he's got a couch and TV. He says, "Boy, what more do you want?"

Did Neill, himself, sleep with the knowledge that the factory backers and Coca-Cola subsidiary were banking on success? 'I sleep alright. I had all my homework done in my head two months ago. I've been building up to this and you sort of sense in your head if things are good.' It would be the usual suspects, he says, as he runs through the opposition. 'There are about six riders. Dunlop and Johnson are flying and you can never rule out John McGuinness. But Keith Amor has a wee knock and he was going to be John's cover man. Guy and I have to go out to see the fairies before the first race, but with a bit of luck we could win it.'

Luck was only half of it. Neill was a shrewd operator with an eye for eking out every advantage. That had been the case all those years ago when he had changed the entire fuel tank during a pit stop. 'We filled it up and put it in the pits,' he says, the memory of his audacity softening his chiselled features. 'We covered it with pit boards and, when they all came in, I remember Phillip McCallen looking over, going mad and shouting. I had to ask Jackie Woods if there was anything in the rules that said you couldn't change fuel tanks. He said there wasn't. Within an hour the message came through that no fuel tanks were to be changed.' He helped Joey Dunlop win the Jubilee TT by borrowing an oversized fuel tank. He took it to a man in Crosby, himself, and told him to put 'two inches into it.' The man asked who it was for. Knowing Neill did not run Yamahas, he had to confess. 'But don't tell anyone,' Neill said. 'I told Joey that he would have to ride it carefully for the first lap because it would be a wee bit heavy on top, but when he missed his pit stop and went blasting down Bray Hill, I was stood at the back of the pit lane laughing. It held seven gallons but it wasn't illegal.'

Talk of Dunlop makes Neill reflective. 'I knew Joey really well,' he says. 'We had many a good session. I'd go home late at night and see the little light on in his garage. I go in and say, "What are you doing?" He'd say, "I'm just looking. Them boys from Honda built this, but I like to check things myself". The whole engine would be in bits and he'd be there until 4 a.m. the night before the race.' As he spoke, a few miles away, in a grubby tent at the back of plush paddock awnings, Michael Dunlop was doing the same thing – dismantling in order to rebuild. Martin, too, liked to be hands on, but Neill said there was no problem this year and he had handed over his trust. 'He's seen our workshops, he's seen the boys, and he says to me, "I don't need to touch this". He has every faith.'

'Do you want a brew, chief?' Martin says as he walks past. Neill declines, having made some arrangements for later and departs. I say yes and so Martin puts the kettle on.

'Aye it has been a bit manic', he begins. 'And yeah I suppose this is a bit Red Squirrel. I don't want the attention, really, because it's like, "I'm sorry to interrupt you but ..." – well, if you're interrupting then you're not fucking sorry are you? But they all mean well. The mither's not that bad. Well, it is.'

This was Martin's way. His meaning was sometimes drowned in that stream of consciousness and he had the remarkable ability to contradict himself within the space of a sentence. He admitted that his crash had been on his mind when he first rode past it on Monday. 'I did think about it, of course, but not in an "Oh hell, here I am again" sort of way. It was good to get it out of the way. The thrill is the little shocks you get and so it was a weird sort of fun.'

He could never stay serious for long and his scattergun mind unearthed a memory of his time partnering a rider called Karl Harris. 'I'm not the sharpest tool in the box, but Karl Harris! Lovely lad an' all, but I'm Einstein compared with him. Neil Tuxworth told him he had to go to this charity do and that, because Karl would be getting a lot of attention because he'd just won the British Championship, he would have to go incognito. Karl had a think and said, "Don't worry about that, I'll just go in the car". Martin was doing a loud chucking laugh now. "I'll just go in the car," he repeats. 'What a boy. No harm in him at all.'

Was he still enjoying it now that his fame had spread? 'I tell you, the BBC thing and this film thing have taken the edge off my racing, I've lost a bit of the enjoyment. I can't go to the shops now without someone pointing. But there is still a private place I have on the island. On the right day and at the right time it is the best place in the world for me. You know I haven't even watched any of the BBC programmes. Not interested. I couldn't care less what people think about it. I don't care if they think it's a bag of shit. 'My big goal is to win a TT and then go out as the undefeated champion of the world, like in boxing. I wouldn't want to be like Schumacher and come back and make an arse of myself. I wouldn't be able to let it alone, though. I know that. I need challenges. Need things. The BBC want me to do another job for them. I'm not convinced but I would like to get on my pushbike and ride from Hiroshima to Chernobyl. I was listening to Radio 4 and they were talking about this breed of horse, never been trained by man, and they put them in Chernobyl forests. Radiation never bothered them. Amazing stuff.'

His chances? 'You never know, do you? You never know. I respect John McGuinness. I respect them all. Conor's had his back all bolted so it will be a struggle for him. Michael Dunlop is wild and he is good, but there's a lot of pressure there, with the whole ... thing. It'll catch up with him. Not wishing bad on him, but you have the big one and it puts manners in you. You have to see the wood and the trees. I can't say I'm going to win. You can never say that. Never.'

That night Martin was back out for the final practice session. The times tumbled and the speeds increased. As the sun firmly set and the eve of the TT ushered in a new wave of anticipation, Bruce Anstey astounded everyone by posting the fastest time of the week in the last throes of practice, clocking 131.42 mph. That was almost a second faster than the next man, McGuinness, had managed all week. It was a gauntlet thrown down and reason to ruminate overnight. Martin was the third fastest and Dunlop fourth. All had topped 130mph. Cummins was 15th, but his TT would be a battle against frailties exposed in his 200-yard fall down the Mountain a year earlier.

Dunlop looked in fine fettle and topped the end of practice rankings in both the Superstock and Supersport classes. Gary Johnson, Bruce Anstey, Cameron Donald and his brother, William, made up the top five in the Superstock, with Martin sixth, McGuinness eighth and Cummins 20th. In the Supersport field, the order was Michael Dunlop, Donald, Anstey, William Dunlop, McGuinness and Martin, with Cummins 13th.

For all of them the waiting was over. Douglas promenade reverberated to its party by the sea. The neon flash of the funfair rides lit the black-blue sky. Paparazzi groaned with fans. Charley Boorman played the Gaiety Theatre. And the riders checked their bikes, tuned up and turned in. All had so much to prove – McGuinness that he was not over the hill, Cummins that he could climb back up the Mountain, Dunlop that he was not the third best rider in his family and Martin that a truck fitter could win this bloody race. He looked at his stationary engine, shut the door of the office in his lock-up and turned out the light. Even the ones who could not sleep dreamt big.

This is where you have to ride it like a horse, with your arms and legs as the suspension. Back up to sixth as fast as you can. Stay on the right and run down to Glentramman. People shut off because they can't see the road in front of them, but I have to tell them to keep it on. Stay out of the hedge. See the K on the tree. That tells me the kerb sticks out. Worst bit of the circuit and it really gets the heart going, 170mph, the bike floats around and throws me over. I fight it to get back to the right. Through the old town. Easy to tank slap through here so let the bike run right if it needs to. Then to the left, Milntown Bridge, click it back to sixth just before the jump to calm it down. Then get under the wall. As long as you don't hit your head on the wall you're laughing.

Nineteen

The Bastard Isle
4 June 2011

Midnight strikes and Manx Radio reports that the president of the Tynwald, the Isle of Man's Parliament, is to step down. There has been another fatal road traffic accident, this time involving a punter's sidecar and a parked car. A consultant psychologist tells how the TT is life and passion and how it would be wrong to take away the right of the individual to take risks. I suspect I am one of the few still listening to the radio at this time of night, but it feels like New Year's Eve, hope and anticipation ushered in on the airwaves. The consultant psychologist is the neurological Big Ben gong, ringing in a new year, bidding farewell to the departed. This is the day of the TT. New history to be inked.

I take breakfast alone in the guest room in Derby Square and walk up the hill to the paddock. Some fans shrouded by stale hangovers are loitering by the café serving bacon butties. Two marshals are getting their flasks out from the boot of a clapped-out old Mini. A priest walks past and smiles. Soon I am in the press room, ever-shrinking as journalists and photographers arrive from around the world. I am surprised to find James Toseland here. Twice the World Superbike champion, Toseland is currently the biggest name in British motorcycle racing after briefly vying with the best in MotoGP. He even threatened to become a mainstream success, playing the piano on the *BBC Sports Personality of the Year* show and flashing his panoramic smile at all comers.

'Alright kidder,' Toseland says. He looks gaunt, almost unwell, and he never ceases from flexing his hand, which is bound with tight blue plastic. I know he is suffering after a crash that had threatened his own career and think he has already had his unfair share of pain.

There had been high points. I remember him telling me how he had walked into the kitchen at his mother's house one day in 2004. He had just received a cheque in the post. 'Mum, do you know you've got a son who's a millionaire?' he said. 'We had a glass of champagne and looked at the zeroes on the statement.' So now he was a tax exile on the Isle of Man. But money and titles were tethered to God awful tragedy. His mother's partner, Ken, got him into bike racing, but he had gassed himself in the family garage when Toseland was 15. 'I later found out he was schizophrenic, but that night I rode to the top of an old slag heap, stretched my arms out and screamed.' He kept on riding in the CB500 series, but he had a bad crash at Monza and, that same weekend, his team mate Michael Paquay was hit by two bikes and killed. When he got back he crashed at Cadwell Park, wondered if he was paralysed and spent 45 minutes on the side of a track waiting for an ambulance. 'That tested my will to live.' Now he had what looked like an innocuous injury, by comparison, and yet it would be one that forced him to retire in another three months at the age of 30.

Toseland is positive about his prospects as he looks ahead

to the first race, the Superbike, taking place that afternoon. He is the honorary starter. He wears a designer leather jacket and dark shades; he looks like he belongs to a different subspecies of rider, but he is the same in most ways, fighting a battle against ailing body and belief.

The grid begins to hum with the heartbeat revs of engines. A bunch of fans with oversized Guy Martin sideburns take position. Others had hung a sign by one of the fast straights bearing the words, 'Fancy a brew, Guy'. Pit-lane reporters move among the riders and their wives and their girlfriends and mechanics.

'The bike's looking good, I'm feeling good,' says Bruce Anstey.

'What about John?'

'John's got a clear road ahead of him, but I do too.'

Conor Cummins is sitting on his bike. He is, as that old report said, abnormally tall and his inability to bend and flex and assume the biker's fetal position exaggerates his size. 'Get this first one out of the way and the job's a good 'un. Blissful isn't it? Should have gone sunbathing.' Cummins has been taped up by Cath Davis; Keith Amor by Isla Scott. It seems inconceivable that their bodies are being held in place by a souped-up version of sticking plaster, rugged dreams seeping out of raggedy seams.

Carl Fogarty is back. Like Toseland, he was the World Superbike champion too, four times in his case, and like Toseland, he was forced to retire after one mistake left him with an irreparable shoulder. 'There are four or five guys who could win. John McGuinness, maybe. Bruce Anstey. Those two are slight favourites.'

Guy Martin flashes a smile at a well-wisher. 'This is all I want to do,' he says. 'Ride the bike. Take it as it comes, boy.'

Someone mentions the sideburn crew. 'Them boys are legends.' Then he tries to debunk the hype as is his way. 'This is just a warm-up for tomorrow's steam fair.'

He is not kidding anyone, but everyone releases their pressure in their own way. It is left to McGuinness to say grace. 'Conditions are good so hopefully we can put on a good show and all get home safely.'

On Manx Radio, Charlie Lambert says:

One minute away.

The riders make their final preparations and line up one by one as multicoloured links in a chain. Toseland takes his position. Carole Cummins is with her daughter Roisin and Conor's girlfriend, Zara. Her eyes are filling up.

We are racing. And there goes John McGuinness.

He tears away down Bray Hill, the first bike to hit the track. He is focused on the task in hand, but he admits that there are times when your mind wanders when you are trying to cover six laps of a 37-mile course. Sometimes he thought about his dinner. Other times he might have fleetingly thought of his family. 'It's made me go faster and it's made me stronger, having another mouth to feed,' he had told me of fatherhood. 'The one good thing is my family is mint – no pressure, the missus is good. If anything did happen to me then nobody is going to come and repossess the telly. My little boy loves Lego. He's into his history, loves museums, it's a bit strange really because he's naturally been around bikes in the paddock, but he won't even have a pedal bike. He does not watch. He plays on his PSP when I'm racing.'

Always, he thought about absent friends. 'I have a pray before we go out on the bike and ask my mates who have been killed to look after me.' The course was marked by such mileposts. He asks DJ for help in Crosby. 'I don't know if he can hear me but I say, "David, look after me.

He had shared a room with Mick Lofthouse when they were newcomers. Lofthouse died at Milntown. Gus Scott was a journalist, motorcycle road tester and hugely popular. He crashed at Kirk Michael in 2005 when a marshal, April Bolster, crossed the road to attend another bike. If there can be different shades of black, Scott's death was darker than the others. The coroner recorded an open verdict, suggesting Bolster might have been prosecuted for unlawful killing had she not died too. It was another of the crashes that made people wonder if the TT was worth it and whether it could survive. It also made you understand Bridget Dobbs when she said that it was a small comfort to know her husband had made a mistake and nobody had done anything stupid.

Down Bray Hill went McGuinness and on towards Crosby. A lot of riders liked to follow others so they could reel people in and gauge their own speed. McGuinness preferred open road. So he gets ten seconds before the next bike starts. And then another. Hearts are held in mouths as the racers edge nearer to the front of the queue.

Ryan Farquhar is a non-starter after his accident at Keppel Gate last night. There's Michael Dunlop away. And Conor Cummins. Bon Voyage to him after his terrible off at the Verandah last year.

265

McGuinness is smooth and fast. The first section to Glen Helen is a favourite and he often destroys people over it. As the race takes shape, and the times are collated, McGuinness has a one second lead over Gary Johnson. Anstey is two-tenths down in third with Martin fourth. Michael Dunlop is sixth but will get stronger. By the time the final bikes have crossed the start line, there have already been retirements. A lap takes just over 17 minutes on these machines and by the end of the first circuit, McGuinness leads Anstey by less than a second.

Those two break the 130mph barrier, as do Johnson and Martin. But then it seems that it is slipping away from McGuinness. By Glen Helen on the second lap he is 1.5 seconds down on Anstey. It is a small gap but significant. A 41-year-old cancer survivor is denting McGuinness' belief. The speeds rise along with the stakes, the duellists pushing the lap speed beyond 131mph. Some people have offered the barbed compliment to McGuinness this week, suggesting he has never had to ride on the limit to win. Now he is and the bike is shaking under the G-force.

It goes wrong in the pits. The mechanics 'count the elephants' as the fuel goes in. They have to get it just right. Too much and the bikes will be slow; too little and they will break down. Anstey's lead disappears as he sits motionless on the bike. Martin's bike also struggles as he tries to move away.

Guy's having a problem. They had to push it to get it working. Now Guy is away but he is 12 seconds behind John McGuinness.

Their problems pale alongside those of Michael Dunlop. He sits on his Street Sweep bike as the fuel pump is attached. The seconds tick away; the elephants stampede. He gets off the bike and swears. Then he slaps the bike.

I think we will let him fester because there might be a few choice words.

Quickly, almost imperceptibly, the race has swung back to McGuinness. By the time Dunlop does get going again, McGuinness has a 12-second lead over Anstey. It is big but not decisive and anything can happen around this course. McGuinness knows it all too well as he sends up his little prayers to DJ and Mick and Gus.

Martin, too, is striving and straining every nerve and sinew. His eyes are starched open. 'That man doesn't blink,' shouts Jamie Whitham in the commentary booth. He is battling Johnson for second place, two Lincolnshire men with different approaches to life. The difference is less than a second. Everyone is fighting each other and themselves, praying that their machinery holds out.

Anstey is out at Quarry Bends. Bruce Anstey has retired at Quarry Bends. The news is Bruce Anstey has retired. The early leader is out and that gives a clear lead to John McGuinness.

The second pit stops take place at two-thirds of the distance with two laps left. Cummins does not make it that far. He retires at Signpost, his comeback safe and anti-climactic. He said that his TT would be won by completing the first lap of practice, but he is a racer and he has shifted the goalposts. After the start I had watched Carole, Roisin and

267

Zara walk back to the McAdoo tent. The paddock was all but empty, with everyone in the pits or on the course. They looked a lonely trio clinging on to each other for support. Cummins asks a spectator if he can borrow a phone. He dials the number. Back in the paddock Carole Cummins' phone rings.

> There has been an incident involving No 66, Mick Humberstone. He is conscious and talking to marshals.

The race continues. Johnson gets a 30-second penalty for speeding in the pit lane and so Martin looks safe in second place.

> We know it can be cruel at times ... it's been cruel to a few today.

> William Dunlop ... on course for his best big bike finish ... just keeping ahead of his brother.

> And Guy Martin is a retirement at Hillberry ... looked comfortable after Gary Johnson got his penalty ... now got it all to do again.

The field dwindles to leave the story of a revival. A couple of back markers wave McGuinness past, but he tells them to go on. He wants the open road to showboat and so he pulls a wheelie down Glencrutchery Road, past the helipad and pits and the Grandstand. He smiles the smile of the relieved. It is his 16th win. Not washed up yet. The anxiety floods from him as if from an open wound.

'That was just incredible,' he says as he dismounts and

hugs Becky and Maisie. Ewan is probably on his PSP, oblivious to the catharsis going on by the crooked stone wall that marks the paddock perimeter. 'I have been stressed all week and it took me all week to settle down. I got a pit board and knew Bruce was on a mission. I saw David Knight up over the Mountain, pulling a few moonies.'

He wins by almost a minute. The fans are delighted. McGuinness is popular because, he is not, as he points out, an arsehole. He wears his jagged smile. It contrasts sharply with Toseland's wide, white one. McGuinness is very much the working-class hero and Toseland the film star with the villa on the French Riviera. McGuinness hugs his childhood sweetheart; Toseland is dating the singer, Katie Melua, but the relationship is still under wraps and she is not here. One of these racers is a slightly podgy, well-worn former mussel-picker, the other all chiselled good looks with the tan of the globally famous. Yet only McGuinness is still racing. A decade older and still not finished.

Cameron Donald is delighted with his second place. Gary Johnson manages to fire off a Guy Martin brickbat, referencing his rival's post-race strop after his time penalty a year ago. 'I'm going to have a protest,' he jibes. 'I'm going to stomp my feet and go off to my van.' The official result is already fading as attention turns to the next race. McGuinness, Donald, Johnson, Amor, Michael Dunlop are the top five. William Dunlop was seventh and happy. Cummins and Martin will try again.

McGuinness gets back on the bike that night and takes advantage of an extra practice session. He rides with the bliss of the achiever. All those horrible fears about age and retirement and being left adrift by younger, better men are cast from the top of the Mountain. 'On Lap two I was blowing, panting, had a bit of forearm pump,' he had said in the press conference. But he had never lost on a big bike when he had finished since 2003, the year DJ had his accident. 'At some stage somebody is going to beat me and when that happens I will shake their hand,' he said.

But not yet. Life is good. This 600 bike feels good, even though his size and weight mean he is not a natural fit for the smaller machine. It has been a long journey. There was the time when he had won the British 250cc Championship. 'I was pissing my pants, being sick,' he recalls. Becky adds: 'Me and three mechanics tried to get you back to bed, but you were on your hands and knees crying.' Another time he had reversed down the motorway at 60mph and crashed into a 'Bikers Welcome' sign at Charnock Richard services. 'I had to leg it. No insurance. Three-point turn and off down the motorway with the back doors ripped off. I had no wipers for three years.'

It has been fun and hard and silly, but he has survived it all and now he is the king of the Mountain again. One race gone and one race won. Tomorrow is a day off. The pressure eases. And then during that evening's practice session, the island, that unforgiving, bastard isle, rears up and kicks him in the face, the windscreen shatters, he feels the air wrenched out of his body and blood begins to drip down his white leathers.

Beige wall on the right here is your braking point. Big problem with Schoolhouse is the manhole cover on the right side of the road that unsettles the bike. Some people use the lay-by. Into Ramsey itself now and the cross-roads, people everywhere, dead easy, like Quarter Bridge. You don't want to be falling off here. Bottom gear for this one. Slow as you can. Then up to May Hill. Lot of people crash here because it looks wide and open, but as they go round it tightens up and they overshoot. This is Coronation Park. There is a wall that runs at the back of it just in the trees. Where the wall meets the pavement and the green railings, that's your apex point. As long as you're looking for it you'll see it. That's the secret.

Twenty

Birdsong
5 June 2011

It is the day of the Port St Mary Steam Fair and Guy Martin is nervous. He is taking his 101-year-old open crank Amanco chore boy stationary engine down to the field on the south-west tip of the island. 'This is the big one. The rest of it's just playing.'

Martin loves his engines. So he drives down to Port St Mary in his works van, Moody International emblazoned on the side. A wizened old man takes money on the gate and the cars are lined up on a sloping knoll. The visitors get out and head for the exhibits. There is a long line of vintage lawn-mowers, a tea tent and a table for the raffle. It is so low-key it is almost subterranean. For all the talk of Martin being the TT's attention-seeker, he seems more at ease when just one of the rank and file. He admires the beautifully restored combine harvester that attracts most eyes, and he gets first prize in his class and is momentarily content. But then there are more autographs to sign and more well-wishers intruding on his oasis of anonymity. 'You just can't get away from it,' he says as he heads back to Unit 13 on the industrial estate.

I remember what John McGuinness had told me. 'I think if Guy Martin wins a TT then everybody's going to do a nude streak down Douglas promenade. The island will leap out of the sea.' I did not know yet what had happened to McGuinness the previous night and so merely considered that McGuinness had been wise and old enough to appreciate Martin's worth. Know your value, McGuinnness had been told. Martin had added to the TT's worth and so, by proxy, the other riders. Yet many of the others were less impressed. I had sat in the press room opposite Ian Hutchinson a day earlier and he had visibly bristled when Martin came on the radio and the announcer said the whole of Britain was rooting for him. I had also seen Hutchinson talk to Conor Cummins and moan dismissively about the lap times. He was a racer who was suffering by being force fed others' achievements while knowing he had done more and would probably be doing it again but for that bloody leg. Johnson's barb about going to sit in his van was pointed, and even McGuinness remembered the aside about him going home to polish his motorhome.

'Do you get that impression?' Martin asks when I suggest some of the other riders are jealous of his profile. 'Jealous heh?' It is as if he has never contemplated the subject. 'The only one not, I guess, is McGuinness.' Martin, too, was oblivious to the late night drama on the Mountain. 'You know, I have heard Steve Plater commentating and having little digs. Hutchy too. And Gary Johnson, I know he doesn't like me, but I think it's funny. They don't like it because I say I'm only doing it for a laugh. They all get stewed up about it. I don't give a shit.' He likes McGuinness and he likes Cummins. 'What a sound boy he is. Genuine. What a boy. God, he was withered. More meat on a butcher's shoe.

I was two weeks, he must have been six months.'

A few months later Martin would add more fuel to the ire of Hutchinson in an interview with *Motorcycle News*. 'Is he going to be strong enough to do the TT?' he asked. 'I've no idea.' He scoffed at Hutchinson riding in the British Superbike Championship. 'He's not going to win it is he? Maybe it'll make him sharper for the roads but he's had a factory bike for the TT before and didn't win then. He's not beaten me on a Superbike yet at the TT. I've done 131mph. He's done 130. What's the point in me worrying about him? I know Hutchy did five in a week – fair play to him – but he did get lucky. McGuinness broke down. Hutchy does like the talk though.' Hutchinson responded by saying the comments had enabled him to do his easiest ever gym session.

The Boat That Guy Built has spawned a monster. The money is 'silly', but so is the fallout. Martin does not want to be a mainstream TV celebrity and says he never felt natural in front of the camera. He also lets me know that his relationship with Mave, the buddy binding of the show, was not entirely ingenuous. 'My old mates have all drifted. No one left. Even Mave – I have not seen him since Christmas. You know how it worked for that show? They wanted someone to be on with me and asked if I knew anyone. I said, "Not really". They tried me with loads of other TV presenters. We did a pilot. They were all lovely people, but as soon as you put a camera on them they turned into different folk, not real people, just massive enthusiasm. One day me and Mave were out biking and I thought, "You'd be good at it". We were never best mates or owt. It was live and learn. He did get a bit starry-eyed because he could play up to the camera. I can't talk into the camera; it's a faceless piece of shit. But Mave can. He can just switch it on. I said, "Give the job to him", but they wanted me too. Trouble is I can't fake it. If they want me to be enthusiastic then they will have to show me something to be enthusiastic about. I would much rather have been at work.'

It is trivia compared with much of what has already happened. The families of Bill Currie and Kevin Morgan are coming to terms with the worst. As Martin displays his stationary engine, Bridget Dobbs spends a few quiet moments at Ballagarey. It was here where her husband and Martin had crashed the previous year. Then Bridget goes to Lonan Parish Church where John Coldwell blesses the tombstone. Later she would write a blog about her time back on the island. 'We had time to put some grass seed on Dobsy's plot before the first TT practice. Children are irrepressibly buoyant creatures and after we'd forked, raked and scattered compost and seed, it came to the treading stage. Passers-by might have been alarmed to see the three of us, barefoot, dancing up and down the length of the grave giggling, but I reckon Dobsy would have loved it for its innocent fun and hint of black humour.'

I had headed out to Lonan to pay my respects. I had not known Dobbs, but felt somehow that it was the right thing to do during this fortnight. I was too late for the blessing, but as the sun broke over the side of a green hill and ran down to jagged shore, leaping a drystone wall and mighty oak, you could not help believe that the island could, indeed, be a place of both innocence and black humour.

Back in the paddock there is a hive of activity beneath the Padgetts' tent. Bikes are being assembled and dismantled. They are the only ones striving under the aching sun. This is another family affair and racing dynasty. Peter Padgett was the British Clubman's champion in 1959. His son, Clive, was the British schoolboy motocross champion in 1974 and was forging a decent career on the Grand Prix circuit until he crashed in Belgium. After that the Padgetts threw their weight behind Clive's brother, Gary, who won two TTs. Now Clive ran the Padgett Racing Team, a respected outfit known for its work ethic and family values. There was no chance of Sunday being a day off for him, not after coming so close to winning the first race of the TT with Bruce Anstey. McGuinness had won, but he was on the Honda TT Legends bike for the Superbike race, and would not race a Padgett machine until tomorrow.

'Bruce got a lift back in the marshal's car,' Clive Padgett tells me of Anstey's retirement as we sit on the edge of a transporter laden with bits and boxes. 'We were down on the floor, but he came in and said, "Come on, boys, we've had a great day, we're on the pace, we can do it". He's chuffed to bits. He's 20 seconds quicker than he's ever been and he's never been a 130mph man in the past. In my heart I believe he can go quicker. He's working in this new zone and who's to say he won't find a new zone. I love John to bits, but in that class [Superbikes] he was not riding our motorcycle and I'd have loved to see Bruce peg him back. Unfortunately, he dropped out with a broken valve, not something anybody could see or take care of, just one of those racing things.'

Fortunes flamed or foundered on those racing things. Last year the Padgetts had won every race via Hutchinson's record-breaking feat. 'That didn't really hit me until this year,' Padgett says. He is a gentle, smiling man with a crook hand and weathered Yorkshire accent. 'Four weeks ago I stopped and thought, "Gosh, we didn't do bad last year". Afterwards we spent two days loading and unloading and went to the next British Superbike round. We were busy and we're not a family that looks backwards. We don't have scrapbooks and pictures.' He then rekindles memories of the lost treasure in Joey Dunlop's sandpit. 'I once found some trophies buried in my dad's back garden,' he says. 'We must have left them there when we were kids.'

He does not look back but he is proud of his family history. He was effectively raised in the paddock. 'I remember Phil Read coming over and winning the 350cc race on my dad's bike. I remember the noise. I was a wee kid running around the paddock and Phil Read, this big star, said to me, "Fill my jerry can with fuel". My dad said, "You're bigger than him – go fill it yourself".'

The Padgetts were also embroiled in the TT's most fabulous tale of all. In 1978 Mike Hailwood, the much-beloved star of the island, decided to make a comeback after a ten-year hiatus. Hailwood had it all, Joey Dunlop's earthiness allied to Barry Sheene's flamboyance. He was like a brass-tacks Gatsby, leaving a sulphurous trail of vodka and broken hearts in his wake. His legend was interwoven with the winding lanes of the island, from the time he vied with Ago in 1967 and, in the Italian's words 'we were one, black and white,' to the time he flew down Douglas Head in his white Jag and took Pauline, his future wife, to see *A Kind of Loving* at the Palace Cinema, where *TT3D* was now playing. He had left bikes and moved to Formula One and was good on four wheels too. He was brave to boot, pulling an unconscious Clay Regazzoni from a flaming cockpit in the 1973 South African Grand Prix. He had ignored the fingers of fire and plunged into the body of heat. He returned to the pits and jerked a thumb at Pauline to signify they were leaving. They departed on his motorbike. It was only the next day when Pauline read the newspaper that she realised what had happened.

'Why didn't you tell me?'

'Oh you know, it was nothing much. Anyone would have done it.'

He got the George Medal for that, but never enjoyed the hero status he had on two wheels. 'He found it frustrating going from being the best to being very good,' Pauline said of his switch. Things trundled on. They had a son. 'And then he went to the Nurburgring and that changed our lives.'

The crash was a bad one. 'His heel had shattered into so many fragments and lodged itself up around the ankle joint. He lost about an inch or so. They could not get the heel back down and had to put staples around it just to hold the pieces together. He had a huge plate down his leg as well. The outer bone had split downwards. That had to be bolted back together. The other leg was broken too.' It was 4 August 1974, the day of the Big Slide.

He asked Pauline if she could still love him. She told him her love ran deeper than leg length. They got married but he was unfulfilled. A business venture came up in New Zealand. They sold two houses. By the time his old manager, Denny Hulme, pulled out, everything they owned was on the high seas bound for New Zealand. They went anyway. Hailwood grew depressed and existed until the idea of the TT comeback surfaced.

The first stage of the plan was a clandestine practice in 1977. Peter Padgett unloaded a 750cc Yamaha from his van at Jurby airfield for a test. The bike was a beast and Hailwood had been away for so long. Padgett looked on. 'He's enjoying it now,' he mused. 'The lad's having a grand old time. Just look at him – he's lost nowt of his old flair. And there's no way he's going to let that bugger beat him.' Hailwood had already decided there was now way he could ride that buggery bike in a race. 'It's like a bloody aeroplane,' he griped after dismounting. Padgett, though, had the gift of the gab, a blunt Yorkshireman well-versed in the nuances of rider neuroses.

So Hailwood did practice at the Manx Grand Prix, as Clive Padgett well remembered. 'I was a young teenager when Mike rode dad's bikes,' he says on the back of his transporter, the memories transporting him back three decades. 'Dad jacked it up for him to ride at the Manx. He had no leathers so we borrowed some from Uncle Don's shop. We tried to disguise him. We taped a stopwatch to the tank. He came back in and said, "I think I could do this again. I can come home". The rest is history.'

When Hailwood went on to win the TT in 1978 it was as emotional as anything the island had seen in 100 years on the Mountain Course. Age was temporary, class permanent. It was why Padgett was convinced McGuinness could keep on going. 'John's not a gym person but he's relaxed on a motorcycle and that conserves energy. It's experience that counts at the TT. Joey Dunlop, bless his heart, did his fastest ever lap around here on his very last lap at the age of 48.'

Anstey is older than McGuinness and he brings us back into the present. 'I get more nervous now,' Padgett says. 'It's 17 or 18 minutes of waiting nervously for the guys to come back. It's better now because there are six check points and the live timing is better. I visualise in my head where they are. The first I heard of Bruce breaking down was on Manx Radio. I knew he was late going through Ramsey. I did my own arithmetic. John says our bikes finish races. I'd like to think it's because we work harder. You get out what you put in. A simple thing broke that nobody could foresee, but I heard Guy dropped out because his seat fell off; now let's be fair, that should never happen.'

Anything can happen, though, as the cracked windshield in the corner proves. Padgett explains what happened the previous night. McGuinness had been celebrating his win in the Superbike race taking Padgett's Supersport out for a spin. That was when he saw the flash of movement directly in front of him, heard a huge crack and felt something deliver a right hook to his shoulder. 'Lucky man,' Padgett said. Bloody lucky, as it turned out, as McGuinness admits when I catch up with him. 'I hit loads of tweeties and things, sparrows and stuff,' he says. 'But this was not normal. I think it was a partridge or something. I just saw this big black-brown lump come smashing through the screen and belt me in the chest. There was blood and guts everywhere. I hit a lot of stuff. Maybe it's being the first man on the road. I hit something in the first race and cracked the fairing, but when I hit this one I thought, "That could do some damage". If it had been a bit higher and hit me square in the face then God knows?' His eyes drift for a nanosecond and we shudder at the thought. 'I saw it coming so I braced myself. I gripped the bars and thought, "This might take me off". It was like being punched hard. It gave a good old clatter. It shook me up.' It is yet another facet to the TT. 'I've seen dogs and cats and rabbits on the track,' McGuinness adds.

Elsewhere in the paddock Nick Crowe is working on the engines of his sidecar team. Crowe has a prosthetic hand after an accident two years earlier, when his sidecar had crashed after a hare ran into the road. Klaus Klaffenbock, meanwhile, is basking in the dirty, grimy afterglow of winning the first sidecar race the previous afternoon. Like he said, you could know that *you* are safe, but you could never trust the course. And on the Mountain the amateurs, or one-day heroes as McGuinness referred to them, are taking advantage of Mad Sunday to sample the course. Even on a day off at the TT there is no respite. 'I know it sounds a bit silly,' McGuinness says 'but half a dozen scarecrows wouldn't go amiss.'

Right-hand bend here is my favourite corner on the circuit. You're not going to make much time here but the camber is with you so really lash it in. That fires it out to the walls and straw bails. See how steep this is now. Into Ramsey hairpin. Nightmare. This is where the Mountain climb starts. Really damp, dark and slippy. Careful. Towards Water Works, revving it out of third gear and back on the gas. Down a gear, balls out, very bumpy, nice wheelie. Tower Bends. Three bumps. Bruce Anstey crashed on the first one a few years ago.

Twenty-One
Nobody Told Me
6 June 2011

They had done away with morning practice years ago. In sepia days Conor Cummins set his alarm clock and rushed out, 'snot running down my face, freezing my nads off', to watch Joey Dunlop race by. It was a romantic image leant a hazy sort of magic by the morning mist and deceptive calm. Now the races were in the afternoon and the practices at night, but another Dunlop had got up early and gone back in time. Michael followed in the footsteps of his father by driving around the circuit prior to the action with a can of paint and a brush. Stephen Davison went with him. Every so often Dunlop would get out of the car carrying his can. He would then mark his braking point on a wall or fence or concrete pillar. It was his way of remembering where he was going and where he was from.

The second race of the TT is the first Supersport race, run over four laps. Dunlop is many people's pick, but he is barely over the disappointment of the first race. 'One of those frustrating things,' he says to Craig Doyle, the ITV frontman. 'We could not get the tyre on. I got off and swore away at anyone that would listen to me.' When the team did get the tyre on, one of them told him not to ride because his head was too clouded with anger and adrenaline. He ignored the advice, rode on and broke down. 'Gutted,' he spat. Now it is the 600 race and he feels he has a better chance. Nobody had been on the 600 bike as much as Dunlop in practice. He topped the charts. 'I will be there,' he predicts. 'I know it. I think everybody else knows it too.'

On the grid the cameras shine on a string of faces.

'It's holding up really well,' Cummins says, divorcing himself from his injuries in the way a racer always does.

'I love the 600. It feels like a 250 which is where I come from,' says Bruce Anstey.

'Go like heck,' says Cameron Donald when asked what his game plan is.

They all go like heck. Dunlop is fast and aggressive. So is Donald. They circulate at mesmerising speed. From the corner of his eye Dunlop sees the bright white markers that he painted days ago. All just want to drag their bodies for the maximum; all want the rush. The fans' heads move from side to side as bikes flash and roar past. People watch them go on and go back to their crosswords in *The Sun* and morning cans of beer.

Dunlop looks good, and all around the island people are wondering if this will be his day, when they forget the caveats about his previous win in 2009, when he was lauded for being braver, but not better, than the rest in the wet. But then he breaks down. Guy Martin hurtles down the Mountain to the Creg, where the balcony is full of drinkers. They get a perfect view of the riders' descent from the Mountain, while taking advantage of the steak and ale special. The landlady, Sandrina, rarely has time to catch sight of a bike heading towards her front door at breakneck speed. It is a supposedly safe corner but Martin manages to misjudge it. He comes off the bike and hurtles into the safety barriers. He gets back up and remounts. 'You can't go mate,' a marshal says. He comes back to the pits bemoaning his fate and saying that it was not a crash as his hands did not leave the handlebars. He is not lying but he is totally wrong, as the video will prove. Indeed, Martin flew off the bike and landed around ten feet away on a grass verge in front of a thick phalanx of spectators. 'He should not be coming off there,' says one to his young son. 'Way off line.' Later, when confronted with this incontrovertible evidence, Martin will concede it was a crash. But much will have happened by then.

Donald is the one making hay in the sunshine. He sees a pit board that says plus 20. He is flying on Wilson Craig's bike and the lead is big. And then the red flags come out. There is an accident at Gorse Lea. The TT falls back into its information vacuum. Manx Radio cuts to music. It is eerily reminiscent of the scene in *The Truman Show*, when Jim Carrey breaks into the voyeurism that allows viewers to follow his every waking moment and the live coverage is suspended.

The race is due to be restarted. Riders have negotiated the crash scene and know it is bad. Everyone gets to know that the accident involves Derek Brien. In the age of Tweets and texts, the danger is that family and friends will find out via half-truths and gossip. Brien has a partner, Sarah, and would take her son, eight-year-old Oisin, to his football matches at Loughshinny United at the weekend. That domestic happiness has now been torn asunder. In the press office, the Irish are explaining how good Brien is. Certainly, he was looking good here, rising to ninth place on the first lap. But as ever, the riding is only half of it.

The vista has changed. For Dunlop and Martin there is good news to be dragged from disaster. They can join the restart and set off in the new, abridged three-lap race. They have 113 miles to go and the pit stop strategy will be key. Dunlop has kept his focus. He clocks 170mph through the Sulby speed trap. He looks easy on his R6 Yamaha and leads Donald by 0.9 seconds. Donald is showing no signs of his Big Slide at the TT two years earlier. Martin says it messed with his mind, but Donald is catching Martin on the road. 'Guy Martin the lorry mechanic,' Steve Parrish says for the ITV commentary. 'He will be wishing he was back there working on the lorries.' John McGuinness is toiling away with the comfort of knowing his TT is already a success. 'Like having jam on his back,' Jamie Whitham says with a flourish. 'All the bees are swarming all over him.' Whitham turns to Dunlop and defends his style. 'I have not seen him miss an apex yet.' Maybe it is the paint.

McGuinness, the first man on the road but no longer the race leader, enters the pits first.

It's going to be a splash and dash.

Donald comes in and hits trouble. The fuel cap will not come off. Seconds tick by, advantage gained is lost. Dunlop keeps his head down and tears by the pits. He is not stopping and so his opening lap of 125.8mph gives him a six-second lead. Donald and Gary Johnson look like the only men capable of stopping him. Then his bike expires again at Ballig Bridge. He edges off the course, gets it going again and tears down an unused country lane. His race is run, but his sense of anger and injustice are ratcheted up to blistering levels.

After two laps Donald is leading from Anstey and Keith Amor. But the TT is not finished yet and spits more savage fortune at the riders. At Glen Helen on the second lap Johnson leads by a huge 37-second margin.

Briefly, Cummins is up to fourth place, although he has still to pit, and he does not get the chance because his bike fails. Donald also retires at Kirk Michael. Johnson's pit stop strategy backfires and, when the stops have given clarity to the order, Anstey leads. He rides the bike like one of his old 250s and takes the flag with the fastest lap of the race.

He parks his bike, gets slapped on the back and gushes into a camera. 'What can I say? Padgett bikes are so reliable. I knew Cameron's bike was fast but I was not too sure that it was going to make it to the end. I was useless in the first race and needed the restart. I rode like a wuss but got my finger out.'

Keith Amor is delighted with second place, just three days after being in hospital following his crash in practice, while Martin has scrambled third thanks to the failures elsewhere. 'Cameron went past us and I thought I'd stick on his back wheel. He blew up in a ball of flames and that nearly ended in tears.' Donald, himself, is phlegmatic. 'It's motorbike racing. You have to cop it on the chin.'

Anstey pops the champagne on the podium and smiles broadly. Then, as he comes off the podium and makes his way to the press conference, someone drags him to one side and whispers something. Anstey's face drops. He edges into the press conference and is quick to apologise for spraying the bubbly in unbridled joy. 'Nobody had told me,' he says.

The vacuum would soon be filled and another of those horrible formulaic statements issued.

Following the red flag during the first run of the Supersport 1 race, the following statement has been issued.

ACU Events Ltd regrets to announce the death of Derek Brien, 34, from Co. Meath in Ireland who was killed during the first Supersport race at the 2011 Isle of Man TT Races following a high-speed accident at Gorse Lea. The race was immediately red flagged following the incident.

Derek was an experienced road racer who first competed on the Isle of Man in the Manx Grand Prix in 2007 and competed in the TT Races in 2009 and 2010. He had a highest TT place of 13th in the 2010 Supersport 1 race.

Derek had a partner, Sarah. The ACU wishes to pass on their deepest sympathy to Derek's family and friends.

Jim Parker, Managing Director, ACU Events, commented: 'Derek was a very talented road racer and achieved a number of notable career highlights including his Manx Grand Prix victory. He will be sorely missed.'

The Coroner of Inquests has been informed and investigation into the circumstances of the accident is under way.'

Now Anstey knew that his actions might have looked awful. But this was the TT and life did go on. It was one of the things that struck outsiders. The grief of Brien's family was raw and unfathomable and yet the race had been re-run. Now there was another one due. The Superstock race had now been shifted back until 6.30 p.m. Paddock life went on, but as Bridget Dobbs had explained, the riders' response was deep and real. It was just that the emotion would be suspended for racing. Was that crass or inhumane? The anti-lobby felt so although some left themselves open to counter-allegations of opportunism by calling for a ban while the grief was at its rawest. 'Ritual sacrifice,' one critic posted in cyberspace. Another spoke of how when the race was red flagged the riders at Glen Helen passed a mobile phone between them, ringing their loved ones to sate nerves.

No 58, whose life was worth as much as No 1, had just finished his first race in 39th place, or second last, on his borrowed Triumph 675cc. Like all the riders, Vernon knew about death, but he shelved it into a dark place that he rarely unlocked. It had been 'gutting' when Paul Dobbs had been killed. 'There's not a lot you can do about it. I never think about it when I'm on the bike. It's only when you come home that you think, "Bloody hell".'

'Do you know what a spatchcock is?' says Guy Martin. He is sat in the TAS section of the warm-up area before going out for the Superstock. Steve Parrish, working for ITV, looks bemused by the question. 'It's a baby chicken,' Martin adds, his eyes spinning and sparkling. Steph is sat next to him, impassive, as if such non-sequiturs are natural in her life. 'I thought it was something to do with a massage parlour.'

It is safe to say Derek Brien is not dominating thoughts. It is not evidence of a flippant approach to life, but a means to an end. It is how you get through. Rare is the rider who can race and win when grief is seeping into his veins. It is the mental oil leak that can wreck everything. So Martin talks spatchcocks. Rare is that rider, but not extinct, as Michael Dunlop showed when he won that North West 200 in 2008, when his grief was almost crippling.

They queue up again for the third time today including the restart. The Superstock will be run over four laps. These are the bikes that are near identical to the bikes punters can buy in the shops. In some way it is a purer race. John

McGuinness is No 1 and the first away again on another Padgett bike. The start numbers had been decided by the race organisers, but racers could put in requests and past wins and lap speeds counted. McGuinness wanted to be the first bike out because he loved open road. And he is fast again. Behind him Martin has banished thoughts of spatchcocks and is on the pace, just two-tenths of a second adrift. William Dunlop is third, but by the time they get to Ramsey his brother is in the lead. By the time they make it back to the Grandstand at the end of lap one, past the wall of plaques with new names to be engraved, Martin is leading.

Guy Martin is in the lead. I think everybody wants him to win this one.

Ian Hutchinson, no doubt, begs to differ. Anstey drops out on the first lap, a few hours separating triumph and disappointment, and Martin becomes embroiled in a duel with Keith Amor. Martin has the lead on corrected time, but they are side by side on the road. Inevitably, duelling costs seconds and Martin cannot concentrate on putting in fast laps when he is vying for position on the road. He defends his line but not his lead and the close proximity of the duo sees him drift backwards. After the second lap Dunlop is 13 seconds clear of Martin who is two clear of McGuinness.

Watching Dunlop was always a sort of history lesson. You would find yourself flitting back to the past, re-imagining Robert and Joey and the Armoy Armada. The roots of road racing were emblazoned on both sides of Michael's helmet with its tributes to dad and uncle. You had to like his bullishness, especially when you realised he bled like everyone else. 'I fear nobody,' he had said beforehand. 'I hope they fear me. I've not done all that fancy training you hear some of those boys talking about, but I'm good for six laps round the TT course. People say I'm overweight. They don't have to carry me on their backs so why should they worry.' But he carries the weight of his family on his back. He goes home and sits in the memorial garden, now linked by its pathway. Sits and thinks and craves to be more than a bit part in this odyssey. They are history, he is the legacy.

McGuinness gradually closes in on Martin, but the race is within the head and engine of Dunlop.

Gets a lot of criticism for being too aggressive and you don't need to do it over those jumps.

They climb 1,382 feet to the top of Hailwood's Heights. Past Joey's. The course is a memento mori, a walk of fame. Martin and Amor are still side by side. Commentators wonder why Amor is trying so hard when the distance between the two in time is far more than that on the road, but Amor is helping his friend and sometime teammate, McGuinness, by distracting Martin. A spatchcock is a chicken split down the back and grilled. It is how he feels. Behind them William Dunlop and Dan Kneen indulge in the same sort of white-knuckle contest.

Michael's lead grows to 17 seconds. It is unbridgeable if he stays on board and his bike holds. It is now a question of concentration and faith. McGuinness is still the leader on the road and has eked out an advantage over Martin. They circulate. On the television it looks almost sedate; in the flesh it is almost awful as they miss a thousand disasters by inches, finding the pencil line, stepping over it and drawing back.

The names are checked off.

Bungalow – where the old Bungalow Hotel, with its tin roof and ugly façade, had nestled against the course, occasionally tripping riders, and where a statue of Joey Dunlop, an identical version of the one in Ballymoney, sits astride his bike.

Windy Corner – where Tommy Robb broke his neck and where Ago had broken down to enable Hailwood to win what for many was the greatest battle of all in 1967.

Creg Ny Baa – where I had attended a sponsor's meal earlier in the week and watched a monosyllabic Ian Hutchinson wish he was somewhere else.

Hillberry – which Paul and Bridget Dobbs used as a name for their daughter.

Past the uphill swoop of Cronk Ny Mona and past Signpost Corner. Dunlop passes The Nook and Governor's Bridge and now he is so close that the dangers suddenly seem magnified tenfold. The last stretch of the 37.73-mile course is Glencrutchery Road. Even here, on this straightforward stretch seemingly bereft of dangers, things could happen. It happened to Uncle Joey in 1981. Dunlop ran at record breaking speeds in the early laps, but ran out of petrol and had to freewheel to Governor's Bridge. He had to push it back to the pits and only managed it by taking one telegraph pole at a time.

Now Michael comes down Glencrutchery Road. Nothing can stop him. He crosses the line. He stops and whoops and hollers. Emotions he might not even recognise pour out of him.

When the times are collated McGuinness is almost 20 seconds back in second. Martin is four seconds further back in third. It is his 11th podium but he is still to win. With three races gone, the chances are dwindling. William Dunlop is an impressive, career-best fifth. And behind them all, three minutes behind the winner, comes Cummins. He finishes the race in 12th place out of 43 finishers. It is a victory of sorts.

Drive, drive, drive to the Gooseneck. Wave to the fans. Up to the 26th milestone. Out towards the white line and then back under the hedge. The secret coming up to the 26th is you have to roll the throttle, you can't take it flat. Up to Guthrie's, the third most important corner. This is the big boy. Three left-hand bends and immediately afterwards you have a right and a left on the exit. This is the steepest part of the circuit. I take a lot of the newcomers up here on my pushbike and that makes them realise just how severe it is. Look after the first bend and the second two will look after themselves. Flat out into the first, 170mph, into the second and out to the white line, back into number three. Pull the bike straight and down three gears. By the time you've done that you're on the next bend over the rumble strip. This right has a trap and it's easy to highside on the exit. That's why there are all these holes in the hedge.

Twenty-Two

Awakening

7 June 2011

Michael Clague is glad to see Conor Cummins come by. 'I'm so glad he is on the mend,' the marshal says. 'He was cautious through the Verandah but he did not noticeably slow down much.' Cummins did not like to make much of his mindset, but he admitted the crash had been lodged in a dark corner, a semi-dormant nagging. 'I told myself to be extra cautious in that first mile before the Verandah, first time around,' he says. 'It was there. It has to be doesn't it? But that was it. I tiptoed a bit, but then did not slow again.' The semi-dormant was put to bed.

Seeing Cummins back is a sort of validation for Clague. 'I enjoy being able to help. I have seen some nasty things but I have had some marvellous times too. Where else could I get this view? It can be grim and forbidding up here, but the view can be spectacular. You know I could go down and stand by the roadside in Douglas, but I really feel I can help up here.'

The contribution of the marshals had become a news story during the week. There had been some disgruntled comments from the Mountain marshals about how long they were left atop the grim and forbidding summit before the roads were reopened. That had prompted a curt reply from Eddie Nelson, the clerk of the course. 'Stop your whingeing about nothing,' he said over the Tetra radio system used by Clague and his peers. That message was quickly passed on to the media and there were even calls for Nelson to resign. On Manx Radio, former racer turned presenter Charlie Williams read out an email. 'Your management skills are lacking and I would like you to come to the Tetra radio and give an apology. Remember without the goodwill of the marshals you would be out of a job.' Knowing he had made a gaffe that had alienated hordes of volunteers, Nelson did indeed make his apology. 'I just want to apologise unreservedly for the comments made last night,' he said. 'It was inappropriate and I regret very much saying the words I used in the heat of the moment. I fully applaud and respect the work marshals do for the TT and I fully understand we could not run the event without any of them.'

By the end of the week Nelson would be embroiled in more controversy, but the apology was grudgingly accepted and the TT went on. Clague, less militant than some, said he thought the notion of a strike had been fanciful. 'I have never complained about being stuck up there,' he says. 'It can be bad. The worst thing is at night, if practice is delayed, but then it's usually only if there has been an accident and then you feel sorry for the person, not for yourself. There has been trouble this time, but as long as there is somewhere to get out of the weather and somewhere to sit then it's not that bad. A lot of people complained and said they would walk off. They think about the other guys at Balla-garey who have already gone home, but I don't honestly think they would have quit. They love it too much. Warts and all.'

It is Tuesday of race week. The winners are celebrating while thinking about the next ride tomorrow. For Michael Dunlop the monkey is off his back. He tells the journalist, Gary Pinchin, one of the few he is prepared to talk to, what happened. 'On the start line I'm really fired. Then when I leave the start line my head turns blank and everything turns to madness.'

He would tell me how much he needed this win. 'I didn't think I needed to prove anything, but other people did. They would go on about only winning in 2009 because it was wet. Well, that was dry and everyone was there. I beat McGuinness and Guy Martin, all them boys. I would have cried if I hadn't won. We've been having such crap luck before. I feel mentally tired. You feel fine during the race, but by the end you're bollocksed. Stupid things were going wrong. A wire went in one. I was fuming. The Superstock had not been happening either, but I thought, "Have a go and see what happens". I got my head down. I was leading to Signpost then dropped a couple of seconds behind Guy. Then I was plus 1, plus 9, plus 12, plus 15, plus 18. All the time I'm thinking this is going to stop. I had a year like this before when the bike just kept stopping. I resigned myself to it. I said, "I know this thing is going to end". Even on the last lap I thought something would go wrong, run out of petrol or something. But it didn't. I did a good pace. I beat everybody I needed to. I feel huge relief. A lot of boys have put money into this and now I've paid them back. Relief is the main thing. I'm glad the Dunlop name is still riding up there at the front, but it's a relief – winning a TT is a constant battle.'

And life and the TT go on, even in the wake of Derek Brien's death. Dunlop and Brien shared a sponsor and the race winner said he was dedicating his triumph to his compatriot. Sometimes those sort of knee-jerk tributes felt hollow and pointless, but not this time.

They tried to make it safe. It was why the riders had to know the ten different flags that could be waved during a race. It was why they all had to wear dog tags, bearing their name and date of birth on a metal plate that was between 20 and 25 millimetres. It was also why you could not race unless you did six laps in practice and posted a time that was no more than 115 per cent of the third fastest time. But you could do anything and you could never make it safe.

Like Dunlop, Bruce Anstey was also getting to grips with winning a TT race. He was an intriguing figure, short and sleepy, not downbeat but remarkably relaxed. I recalled McGuinness telling me that Anstey's prospects depended on what side of bed he got out of. He was mercurial and eccentric. 'I don't like this side of it,' he says in the bowels of the Grandstand where, a day earlier, he had needed to apologise. He means talking about himself. He is a man of action rather than lethargic words. 'Clive Padgett has to wake me up a lot. I like to go for a snooze in my motorhome. If the race is at 10.30 a.m. I will probably get out of bed at ten. If it's an afternoon race I'll get up around midday. I don't do a lot. I watch TV, have dinner and go to bed.'

Anstey had ridden for the TAS Suzuki team in 2010. The previous night I had watched Philip and Hector Neill beneath a black awning laughing. They were amazed by the queues outside the TAS work area across the gravel path, where fans were gathering for a glimpse of Martin, their beloved bridesmaid. They laughed about how Anstey was now winning and Martin having to make do with podiums. It paid to be philosophical in this game. Philip gave Anstey the news that he would not be kept on via email. 'He said he could not bring himself to call,' Anstey remembers. 'Trouble is every day now, when he sees me, he keeps apologising. All the boys were sad to see me go because we were together for such a long time and got on well. Now we're next to each other in the paddock and it's weird.'

He knew anything could happen in the next two races, the second Supersport and the Senior. 'Two years ago, on the Superstock bike, just before Ramsey, on the bumpy section, I had a massive tank-slapper. That was a scary moment. Nothing I could do.' And his apology the previous evening showed the jarring incongruity between triumph and disaster. 'You just don't think about it, you stick it somewhere in the back of your mind. In any other sport they would cancel the event. I sprayed the champagne but nobody told me. I apologised, but one of his pit crew came up and said, "You spray as much champagne as you want". We don't really think about that part.'

He is savouring these days because it will soon be over and he will go back to Slough and a life of relative anonymity. 'It's bad when the TT ends. It's so intense and full on for two weeks and then it all stops. I go home and it's a terrible low. I'm in a bad mood for weeks on end.' Klaffenbock had told me the same. He said he, in turn, had spoken to Hutchinson who said it took him 'five weeks to get back to normal'. It was a domino effect of dulled senses. For the punters it was the same. The previous night I ended up walking down the promenade in Douglas. I had a drink in a cavernous marquee and got talking to two fans from different spectrums. One, Simon Bryant, said he was a City banker. 'It's all gone tits up, though,' he said. 'This recession is going to last for years. It's why I like it here. It's normal.' Of course, it was anything but normal, but people came to escape. The TT was Steve McQueen's silver motorcycle. Terry Lee was an East End florist with an old Norton. He had been coming for years. When the foot and mouth saw it cancelled a decade ago it had ruined his whole year. 'It's like a fix that keeps you going for another year,' he said. I left them to it, unlikely brothers in arms.

Now I leave Anstey to his life less ordinary. He is a high-speed racer and part-time somnambulist. He has no idea why he was riding like a wuss in the race before Derek Brien's accident. Maybe he had just got out of bed on the wrong side. Interview over, he is suddenly enlivened and moves quickly to his preferred existence. It will not be long before he is back in bed. 'People keep asking me if I've seen this new TT film,' he says. 'I say, "No". I don't like going out. I can't be bothered.'

Still climbing. Onto Black Hut bend. Come down one gear, ride the bump, back on the gas and cross the line into the Verandah. There are four bends in the Verandah. No 3 is the important one. This is where Conor lost the front end. Just here. Straight over that one. Jesus. Fourth corner and sixth gear on the exit, 150mph. Run up to the Bungalow and Hailwood's. The steepest point on the circuit. The bike feels so slow. Come on, come on. Fourth, fifth, sixth, as fast as you can. Down to the 32nd milestone. Three left-hand bends. Ignore the first one, close the throttle for the second, out to the white line and drive it through. Head behind the bubble. Awesome corner. That's what you tell people about.

Twenty-Three

Rainmen

8 June 2011

I have breakfast alone in Derby Square. I have yet to see the two bikers who are sharing a room across the hallway. I don't know if they are late-night revellers or early risers. Either way, I get to have first crack at the croissants as the TT builds inexorably to its finale. There are other mysteries too, more questions to be answered. Will Conor Cummins be able to drag his ailing body to the finishing line? Will Guy Martin ever win a TT? Who will truly write their name into legend by winning the Senior race? And, as the shades in Derby Square fail to mask portentous clouds and the whole sky turns off white, will the Supersport race be run today?

There is an air of resigned disgruntlement in the paddock. Grounded riders are like caged animals. They prowl and stalk and frown. Biking is an escape, a form of alchemy. It can transform John McGuinness from a salad-dodging man approaching middle-age and fast-track him to his youth. I remember Roald Dahl writing about how he would shun the country walks favoured by his school friends and ride through the middle of Repton village, 'sailing past pompous prefects and masters in their gowns and mortar boards.' He recalled that, if he was caught, he would be punished with 'a savage beating that drew blood from your backside.' But Dahl rode on, disguised by goggles and helmet, risking being 'thrashed within an inch of my life' for the thrill of riding close to the bricks and mortar boards. 'I never told anyone, not even my best friend, where I went on those Sunday walks,' he wrote. 'I had learnt even at that tender age that there are no secrets unless you keep them to yourself, and this was the greatest secret I had ever had to keep in my life so far.'

Racing bikes is a private matter made public. These riders were a different breed and far away from the careerists on the short circuits. It meant the parade lap, due to take place today, was an oddity. Famous names would ride famous bikes around the circuit while waving to the crowd and receiving warm applause. There were TT legends aplenty, but the riders who drew the biggest headlines were the GP ones. They were the motorcycle racers who were truly famous. In the past Valentino Rossi had been here. So had Jorge Lorenzo. Now Nicky Hayden and Mick Doohan are being feted in the hospitality suite behind the wall at the back of the winners' enclosure, neighbouring the start-finish straight.

Nobody, other than Guy Martin, would pretend that racing GP bikes is like driving round Morrisons car park in comparison with the TT. Doohan had ridden the blood-spitting two-stroke 500cc GP bikes and landed himself five world titles. Hayden had only one but it had been as dramatic as anything I had seen in sport. In the penultimate race of the 2006 season his Honda team mate Dani Pedrosa took them both out. 'Fucking bullshit!' Hayden, a country boy from the Midwest, howled in a gravel pit in Portugal.

Pedrosa looked over his shoulder, thought about apologising, and then shrugged and walked off. Hayden said he felt like killing Pedrosa. Newspapers printed WANTED! posters emblazoned with Pedrosa's mug shot. It was the mother of all finales, but the title seemed to have been handed to Rossi by Hayden's own team mate. And then, in the next race, Rossi, the king of MotoGP, master of mind games and flawless executor, inexplicably slid off his bike on the fifth lap and gifted the world title back to Hayden.

I speak to some riders as they mill about and they are disgruntled that the likes of Doohan and Hayden would be riding around the circuit before the race. 'If the weather's going to be bad let's get the race over with first,' one says. 'They are more bothered about a bit of showboating than racing.' Another says the parade lap was just 'eye candy' for the female fans. GP riders did have a tendency to be better-looking than their TT counterparts. GP riders were testosterone drips, jet lack hair, perma-tans and neat-fitting teeth. TT riders were waifs and strays, with unkempt hair, chipped, black fingernails and the look of men who had been sleeping in lock-ups on industrial estates. They were similar and yet entirely different.

Ian Hutchinson goes on the parade lap to rattle the nerves of some watching. Hutchinson is not fit to race and still has the external fixator on his damaged leg. Yet he squeezes into his leathers, a flap cut in the leg to cater for his cage, and gets on the bike. 'It's madness,' one journalist mutters to me. 'If he comes off then he might never ride again. And for what?' He has a point, but Hutchinson needs his fix, even if it is a watered-down one. He is the rebel racer version of Dahl the schoolboy, needing to escape the humdrum, grounded existence.

He does not fall off. Hayden waves. Doohan pulls a wheelie. Finally, the preamble fades away and we edge towards the race. They play the national anthem on the tannoy and Craig Doyle, the ITV presenter, ponders whether they might be doing it again later for Guy Martin. 'I think he's got his hands full today,' Steve Parrish says. They speak about the other riders. McGuinness and Bruce Anstey, old stagers on the reliable Padgett bikes; Michael Dunlop – 'kind of took his brain out in the wet in 2009'; Cameron Donald and his Wilson Craig bike that is super fast but rarely lasts.

The start is delayed and, by the time the riders gather on the grid, they are consumed by a miasma of uncertainty and confusion. There is an impromptu meeting of top riders. Martin says they are considering refusing to ride. 'McGuinness, Anstey, Amor and me; we're saying if one of us is not going then none of us are. We want it to be safe. It's hard work going round here at the best of times, let alone when it's wet.' Keith Amor shakes his head. He has already been in hospital once at this TT. 'If you tip in at 150mph and it's wet coming out the other side, full angle lean, then it's over,' he explains. 'We're doing it for the danger, but if they are throwing in things like damp patches ...' Anstey, never-knowingly roused to excitability, raises his eyebrows in incredulity. 'You can see black clouds over the Mountain. It will be peeing down when we get there and they are going to stop it. What's the point?'

Gary Johnson says what many are thinking, that he is glad he is not No 1 and the first man to test the circuit. At the TT there is no warm-up lap, no sighting lap, they ride blind and rely on radio reports about the rain. The first man out will be the guinea pig. The first man out will be John

McGuinness. Parrish and Jamie Whitham debate the issue. 'John McGuinness does not want to be racing,' Whitham says. 'All these riders can say they don't want to go, but there is a lot of pressure from sponsors, teams and fans.'

The insistence on running the parade lap means the clouds are now spilling black ink and a suspension looks inevitable. But still there is no word of another delay. Eddie Nelson, the beleaguered clerk of the course, will explain: 'I think it's a part of the TT. I am sure in days gone by they didn't have weather forecasting.' In days gone by, he says, they would hang a piece of seaweed out the window. If they listened to the riders, and only ran races in the dry, then there might only be one race a day. What would the fans and promoters make of that? 'They would not be getting value for money.' Know your value, Jim Moodie had told McGuinness. But with 16 TT wins and knowing his worth outweighs riding in the wet for the sake of promoters, McGuinness still twists his wrist and the staccato noise of the engine signifies no respite. They will race whether it is wet or not.

By his standards he is moving slowly. The dark patches under the trees are treated with care. He is tiptoeing round in his words. Amor and Martin feel marginally more confident and they make up time on the road, catching McGuinness by Ramsey. However, they are bystanders compared with the Dunlop boys. The Dangerous Brothers show no regard for the damp patches at all and pin their bikes through both light and shade. Maybe Michael had 'taken his brain out' again. Maybe, he just knew he was better and bolder in the wet than the rest. Maybe this was what someone had meant when they told me that Michael did not have a death wish per se, but that he 'just thinks it's inevitable.'

Being from Northern Ireland the Dunlops were used to

the wet. By the end of the first lap Michael leads William by 1.9 seconds. The rest are another ten seconds back. It is all about the sibling rivalry, the one that had caused Michael to say his brother had 'screwed' him the previous year, the one that saw William damn his brother as 'stupid', and the one that sees them joined in a blood pact.

Amor's bike appears to cut out, but he gets it going again and rejoins his battle with Martin. And then they come to Union Mills, an elongated S bend framed by stone walls and a Spar shop. The first man through is Cameron Donald, but he lurches out of his seat and veers horribly off line. Immediately behind him, Martin is bounced from his seat and his legs flail in the air. Seconds pass and then McGuinness comes through. He sits up in the centre, clearly mystified by what is happening in front of him. Luckily, he cannot see what is happening behind, where Amor slips off his Honda. The bike crashes into the wall on the left, ricochets to the right and then spins in the middle like a pirouetting ice skater. Amor, somehow, misses the walls, his bike and McGuinness. Amor gets up and shakes his head. Ahead of him McGuinness, unaware how close he had come to disaster, slows. The rain is falling. Surely now the race will be stopped.

Michael Dunlop hopes not. He passes William on the entry to Kirk Michael, the village that shrinks the road and exaggerates the sense of speed. They are in their own world. Michael takes his hand off the handlebar and gives his brother a thumbs-up. They are fighting in the playground. If a TT race gets to half distance before it is stopped then the result is called. There are only 23 miles left. The Dunlops are closing in on one-and-a-half laps. It is going to be a family affair. And then the red flags come out and the race is stopped. On his bike Bruce Anstey sighs.

When they get back to the paddock the bloodletting begins. 'Cameron had a huge moment,' Martin says. Sweat drips from his brow and his hair is a febrile mess. 'I ran over my own leg and was picking which bit of wall to go into. Somehow I saved it and pulled up next to John at Sulby. He looked at me and said, "By 'eck".' Amor is the most outspoken, but he has reason to be. 'I don't like gambling with my life,' he says. He goes into one of the TV vans to have a look at his crash. There had been an onboard camera. Knowing he survived, it was visceral drama, but it had been close to footage that would never be aired. 'I saw Guy's feet come off the bike. I lost the front. If I let go too early then I was going to go straight into that wall and that would probably be it. Lucky? Tell me about it. And that's two in a week.'

Martin is just happy to be back in one piece. 'That race shouldn't have gone,' he says when we meet up. 'I was talking to McGuinness and he's the most experienced round here. He didn't want to go. Keith didn't want to go. Bruce Anstey didn't. We got on the line and I went to McGuinness and said, "What do you reckon?" He said, "I'll just go steady". That's why I went. If he says that then it's alright for me. We could do with a bit of a union, but they don't make us do it. They don't *make* us do anything. But the clouds were as black as fuck and it was pissing down in Peel so they should have known. Maybe it's the pressure of getting the TV out and all the other pressure. But first things first, the main thing around here is safety. To get good racing you need decent conditions. What's the point? Or maybe I didn't see the board at the start saying there's ten squillion pounds and a world championship at stake. Yeah, I must have missed that.'

Martin cannot comprehend how Dunlop had approached the conditions. 'Fair play, he is fast. He's a good rider, but he's wild, the general way he goes about things. I'm a bit outspoken in interviews, but he effs and blinds. I've spoken to him, though. He's not a bad person. I just think, "Bloody hell, I thought you'd have grown out of all that".'

Michael is understandably irritated. He knows how close he was to a win. 'Me and William were first and second and we'd done a lap-and-a-half. We only needed to do another half lap and that would have been the win. So they made us put our lives on the line for nothing.' William agrees. He does not like the TT, but he is not about to suggest the damp had made it unrideable. 'I was disappointed with the decision. Michael had just passed me and I thought, "Here's a chance to learn something". I mean, really, it was not that bad.'

Michael interjects and goes further. 'It was dry. There was absolutely nothing wrong with the circuit. I'm not just saying this, but on the first lap I was not going madly, I was backing off. Then, for some reason, someone stuck a hand up [to signify rain]. That was more dangerous. The next thing I remember is coming out of Handley's flat out and them boys were sitting up. On this section I'm lying in the bubble going 170mph and they are doing 50 or 60. They were trying to get the race stopped because they were not happy, but they could have pulled over to the side. That was the most dangerous thing. It's crap. The conditions were far worse in 2009 when I won and nobody pulled out that day.'

It is not long before they cancel racing for the rest of the day. The sidecars are put away too. The rain has won. William Dunlop goes back to the home that Wilson Craig has got for him, Michael to his tented awning where he will check over the bike before the rerun tomorrow. Keith Amor shakes his head once more as he feels the intimations of mortality. It had been too close.

Windy Corner. Named for the fact the wind comes at you from two different directions so you will be blown one way or the other even on a Summer's day. If the flags are going on the Grandstand then it will be as windy as hell up here. Used to be third gear, now fourth. Run down into the 33rd, kiss the orange sign and then get back under the fence. Fast but gorgeous. Keppel Gate, looking for the white hut, brake two gears, back it in. This is where Cam crashed a couple of years ago. Missed a gear and made him run on. One little mistake can do it for you. Past Kate's Cottage. Got to drill it. Can't take it flat out and down to Creg-ny-Baa. Back up through the gears towards Brandish. Proper TT corner. If Carlsberg made TT corners then this would be one of them.

Twenty-Four
Old and Crooked
9 June 2011

'I was all for going out,' Conor Cummins says in his soft Manx brogue. 'I was picking my way through the field and I was up to fifth. I thought I might have a sniff of a podium. I thought I must be pretty good in the rain. Then they stopped it. Gutted. I wouldn't say I'm known for riding in the wet, but I certainly like having a spin. It's another skill of road racing that you should have in your locker. It's a leveller.'

He needs a leveller. Cummins' body is barely holding up. His foot-pegs and seat have been altered to compensate for his lack of movement. The bikes sit on their stands in the awning. Cummins sits behind a screen with his mechanics and mother. Cath Davis flits about and departs briefly to answer a call from Cameron Donald. Cummins' knee is a criss-cross pattern of blue tape. 'It's like a sticky fabric that you strap onto the skin and it lifts the skin and improves the blood flow,' he says. His knee still looks horribly misshapen. 'Cath is a fantastic woman. She and Isla spend two weeks here, working all hours to get the likes of me ready.'

Cummins' results have been modest by his standards.

He has failed to finish the first two races and been 12th in the third. For a man who had been at the front of the action when he fell off the Mountain, and had done more 131mph laps than anyone else, it is a bitter pill to swallow. At least he knows he is not unique. He has met Rico Penzkofer, an older German rider down the gym. 'He had two big scars down his back, different sections of the spine. There was a lot of metal work in there. He actually gave me a bit of relief because here was someone else in the same situation. You see people who think they know everything. Then you see someone like Rico, who has been through the same thing, and he's back riding the same event. It gave me a bit of extra motivation.'

He is also looking forward to seeing Marcus de Matas, his spinal surgeon, who is flying over from Liverpool to watch the Senior race tomorrow. It has been a team effort to get the broken man back on his feet and bike; meat and bone, wing and prayer.

Carole watches from the side of the grid as he shuffles towards the start. He is No 10 and so their hearts race as others throw their bikes down Bray Hill and suck the rabbits out of hedges. John McGuinness, Guy Martin and the Dunlops have gone by the time Cummins sits on the start and counts down the seconds. I glance at Carole and her eyes have a teary glaze. And then he is gone.

The words of Keith Amor resonate. 'Could have been four of us lying in Nobles Hospital,' he had said on the grid. 'It would not be a bad thing if the riders had a voice around here for once.' Cummins and Martin are familiar with Nobles. So are Amor and Cameron Donald. 'Ready?' Donald had been asked moments before he put on his helmet and slammed the visor shut. 'Born ready,' he replied.

In the commentary booth for Manx Radio, Charlie Lambert, with his soothing voice, watches Michael Dunlop closely. 'He's thrusting himself off the pegs. He's so determined.' Seconds pass. 'And there goes Conor on the McAdoo Kawasaki.' Lambert counts them out. Cummins concentrates. He knows the track so well, but you can't relax. There are places where you have to remember to breathe and suck in some air, but every corner has its trap and he will have to negotiate more than a thousand of them by the end.

'Without a doubt I would be running up the front if it wasn't for the crash,' he had told me. 'My bike is like 100 per cent, but this is winter training for me. Now I can go to the gym and hit it hard, but everything is delayed. It's holding me back. I have to keep pinching myself because it was only the end of January that we thought, "Right, let's have a go at this", but I suppose you get greedy. I have no right to be pissed off but I am. Excuse my language.'

He circulates at speeds that numb the senses of those watching. He passes Ballagarey, where Martin had crashed the previous year, and does not hold back. He rings the throttle so hard that his wrist aches. Through Kirk Michael, where the road narrows and the fans are perilously close, putting all their faith in the skill of the riders. They are dragged into the action by the noise, smell and colours that linger in the air. Cummins completes the first lap at an average speed of 121.7mph. McGuinness had been surprised when he had reached his first pit board to be told he was in the lead. But it was a false dawn. He led only because Gary Johnson was starting down in 11th place and had not been included in the rankings. When he is, he is a class apart. The man, who openly dislikes his Lincolnshire colleague Guy

Martin, is almost ten seconds clear by the end of the first lap in a race that is usually one of broad scope and fine margins. Johnson's lap speed is 125.5mph.

Behind him the subplots thicken. Michael Dunlop had been half a lap from victory when robbed by the rain yesterday. Now he breaks down and spends an age repairing his bike. It means that he takes 45 minutes to complete a first lap that has taken the leaders 17. His average speed is 49mph. His race is run and yet something makes him carry on in last place, two places adrift of Sam Dunlop, his cousin and another branch of the family tree. William is seventh and Cummins ninth.

By the end of the second lap Johnson's lead has increased to 15 seconds over McGuinness, who is riding in splendid isolation. 'I didn't see one bike the whole of that race,' he would say afterwards. 'It was really weird.' Donald and Martin scrap for third place, while Cummins settles into a rhythm, despite being overhauled and shunted back a place by Ian Lougher.

God, he loved this place. 'This has been the biggest hurdle of my life,' Cummins had said when we met in one of the TT's downtimes. 'But everyone has a blip on the radar. Character building? You're not wrong there. I will never moan about the cold again. I had never been so bashed up so it was all new. I had no reference points.' He keeps going. The bike has let him down already this week, but Cummins is a magnanimous man who sees the bigger picture. His mechanics do all they can for him. If that is not enough, or if someone makes a mistake, it is life. 'Nothing to be gained from spitting your dummy out. They want to win races as much as I do. Yes, it's a bugger, but they didn't do anything deliberately. I've done stuff wrong at times and they don't come down on me. We've been together since 2008. It's a family. We get some backing from Kawasaki UK, but it's not massive. Essentially, we're going up against real factory efforts like HM Plant and Relentless Suzuki and we're sticking it to them. That's great. It gives me a kick.'

He is not sticking it to them now, but he is doing well enough. Back in the paddock, Carole watches the times flicking by and wonders. Maybe she spared a moment's thought to think again on how it all began. 'I remember the night,' she had said. 'The night when he got the call saying he had the ride in the first TT. It was late. Can I enjoy it? Yes, but I have to be there. That's the way I cope with it. I need to be there watching him do well, because I know he can do well.' There were lots of memories that segued into one another and painted the picture of a proud parent. Carole and Billy did not live in the past but they could not be divorced from it when its dark tentacles wound their way into the present. 'I remember Billy just knowing. I don't know how he did, but I remember that day when he said, "He could be bloody good on a race bike".'

By the end of the third lap Johnson leads by more than ten seconds from Donald, who is the fastest man on the circuit. McGuinness is eight seconds clear of Martin and still in splendid isolation. William Dunlop and Cummins are eighth and ninth.

Manx Radio coverage cuts away to one of its many announcements. 'It's the 100th anniversary of the TT Mountain course and you may be tempted to celebrate by hitting the bars,' the voice intones. 'But if you drink leave your bike at home. An Isle of Man driving ban applies in the UK too. TT 2011: love it, respect it. Brought to you by the Department of Infrastructure's road safety team.' A man's voice then takes over. 'Would owners of domestic animals and livestock adjoining the TT course, please ensure they are secure during practice and race periods.'

The last lap changes much. Donald is assured of a podium if he can make it to the line, but he cannot. His Wilson Craig Honda expires at Signpost Corner, barely two miles from the finish. William Dunlop's machine also fails on the last lap within sight of the line. The order is reshuffled.

I think of what Cummins had told me. 'Fate?' he pondered. 'That's a difficult one to describe. Basically, if your number's up, your number's up. Sounds harsh, but I don't want to get to 60 and be a crooked old bugger.' He said he did not really think about death or near-death things. Motorsport was selfish, he said, and things happened. He mentioned Daijiro Kato, the Grand Prix rider, killed when he ran into a wall in Suzuka in 2003. 'This week it's been nice to hear the support from the crowd. It's nice to have them fighting your corner. Don't get me wrong. People have been through a lot worse than me this week. I'm just grateful to get a second chance.'

The bikes cross the line. McGuinness is the first to pass the Grandstand but he knows that, when the rest of the field does the same and the times are totted up, it will not be enough. He is sure of second place, though, and beams a wide smile. Not bad for a bloke who is supposedly no good on the little bikes.

'Nothing stops,' Cummins had continued. 'It's just a bash-on job. I'm sure my mum's nervous. But everybody's held up. Everyone has been solid. I think they realise that if they seem emotional before a race then that might have an affect on me. But I am sure they feel that way. I can see it on their faces. I want to win one. But I don't want to win just one,

I want to win lots. Next year I will be as fit as a butcher's dog and ready to have a proper crack. The trouble is once you start progressing nothing is ever enough.'

Johnson is a clear winner from McGuinness who is 13 seconds ahead of Martin. However, Martin is fuming inside his black helmet. He had seen a red flag at Union Mills and slowed. He lost close to ten seconds on Donald before he realised nobody else was stopping. Had his mind played tricks on him? Was it a red coat or bail? He finished the race confused and simmering, in front of Amor and Bruce Anstey.

Cummins finishes sixth. A year after he hurtled down a valley and bounced over a drystone wall, he is back in the elite of the most dangerous race in the world. He gets off his bike and smiles. 'Not bad,' he says. Later I find him and he elaborates. 'My main goal after the last TT was getting to the next one. The first night of practice. That was what it was all about. All those hand exercises, the endless exercises, the frustration, the feeling down. You know my bikes have taken a hammering as well. Blow-ups. This is the TT. It's the ultimate test of man and machine. That's a cliché, but it's also true. When I finished that practice lap it was like the whole thing had been put to bed. My physio said, "This is the start of the new chapter". That's what it feels like. Everything from here on is great. This is where we start.'

The aftermath is a mix of farce and drama. Johnson is collared by Manx Radio in the winners' enclosure and told how fast he had started the race. 'I was not pissing about was I?' he says. This being the TT, where truth is the bedrock of the event, nobody feels the need to apologise. Having spent so much and come so close to quitting, the win would change his life. 'Cars are pulling up in the street,' he would say soon afterwards. 'Blokes are shaking my hand. I went to the butcher's and a bloke comes out all starry-eyed and wants to talk about racing for half an hour. I've never had that before.' He makes a thinly veiled V-sign to Guy Martin. 'Not bad for a bunch of civil engineers sticking a bike together in a shed.' It is a version of Martin's 'I'm just a truck fitter' mantra that so annoys his rivals.

Martin is still fuming when he enters the press conference. A red flag had been waved in error at Ramsey and that prompted another at Union Mills. A red flag means stop and often because of a bad accident. Martin had sat up on his bike and cruised before noticing nobody else was. 'It's not right is it?' he says. 'We shouldn't be doing this until it gets sorted. It needs sorting before we go any further.' As his sense of injustice grew, so his words speeded up. 'I saw it at Union Mills. I saw a bird in the road, a feathered kind not the one in skirts, and I thought, "Was it that?" Look, nobody wants an ear-holing because we'd be knackered without the marshals, but it's not fair on a lot of lads, not just me. Mistakes do happen but that was a big one. It will all come out in the wash won't it?'

McGuinness steals the show and manages to lighten the mood. This is his 50th finish at the TT and his 32nd podium. He speaks of his quiet race in isolation and how he had feared he had lost his way on the 600 bikes. He gives a few platitudes and then says: 'I had no problems apart from when I got to the bottom of Bray Hill my foreskin rolled back and there was a bit of chafage for the next hour and ten minutes. It's a fact. I'm not swearing. But there is a hood on there and it came back and for the next hour and 15 minutes it was chafing on the zip. Maybe I'll get Becky to check it out later.'

The watching Murray Walker guffaws at the spectacle. The TT is different alright, from the candour to the ardour. Later that day I sit with Cummins in the press room and he casts his eye over the time sheets. Ian Hutchinson, his face still as portentous as any Manx cloud, sits next to him perusing them too. They are awaiting the call to move next door and take part in the BBC's *Bike Night* special, hosted by Murray Walker. Hutchinson is damning of the times and the personnel, suggesting that with all due respect, nobody wants to come and see Gary Johnson win. Cummins, too nice and generous to follow suit, knows that he can do much better. He is sixth with all these injuries and lack of racing. He is already thinking about next year.

Martin comes in and sits down with me. 'Who's seat is this?'

'No one's. Why? Is it warm?'

'Noooooooooo.'

He talks about the red flag again, still mystified by its presence. 'I thought I was seeing things, but Keith Amor said he saw it too. Then the marshal says, "Yeah, the flag was out". Normally the race is stopped and the result doesn't count. I mean, I'm on the podium so it's not too bad, but there's a lot more of them boys further back. Today is like a no-brainer.'

He talks about Michael Dunlop again. I tell him he reminds me a little of John Belushi.

'Who? Never heard of him.'

'John Belushi. Was in *Animal House*. Have you heard of that?'

'Heard of it,' he says unconvincingly. 'Not seen it. Noted.'

'You seem down.'

'Down? Noooooo. I'm not down.'

'It's been a struggle though?' I persist.

'I have enjoyed it but only because I stayed out of the way and come into the pits only when I need to. If I hadn't stayed in the lock-up I don't think I'd have ever come back. You know, I love the racing and it's brilliant an' all, but it will catch up with you. I mean, I aren't afraid of dying.'

'But you'd rather not.'

'I'm not bothered. Maybe I don't want to win one because when I do I'm not coming back. I'm packing it in.'

He is close to the win and retirement. He has one DNF and a hat-trick of third places from his four races. He is consistent. Cummins has two DNFs, a 12th and a sixth. Dunlop a fifth, two DNFs and a win. McGuinness is the star with a win, two seconds and a fifth. The other three have achieved much of what they wanted. Only Martin is still wholly unsatisfied.

Murray Walker walks past on his way to the empty coffee machine.

'Alreet Murray.'

'Keep smiling,' he says.

And he does. Through the thick and thin and the crash that nearly killed him to the near-miss at Union Mills. He has one more chance.

It's quite easy to scare yourself. The bike feels dead. This is Hillberry. In Spring you can see the road goes right but in June it's a wall of green. Now it's Cronk-ny-Mona, three bends. Too much front brake and you're going to go down. Nigel Davies crashed about three times because of that. Down to Signpost and into Bedstead. This was the hardest corner for me on the circuit. I could nail every other corner, but I was always indecisive here. I went too early or too late. It's a bugger because it's blind and steep. So fast and quick but now you're nearly home. The mind starts to twitch and a lot of people crash. You come to Governor's Bridge and you know you have to slow, but it is still 120mph and can bite you on the bum. Out to the gatepost. Out to the kerb. Quick blast of power. Close now. I have watched Guy through here and he takes a totally different line to everyone else. Guy comes through here with a closed throttle. John drives through it and is precise. It's as if Guy scares himself.

Twenty-Five

Last Chance

10 June 2011

It is the last day of the TT. The riders and fans awake with the same sense of anticipation, even if the hangovers are restricted to the latter group. The Senior is the big one, the prize that is craved far and above all others. If you win the Senior TT you are a made man on the Isle of Man, afforded lifelong respect and free dinners.

The sidecars finished off last night. It had looked like another win for Klaffenbock and Dan Sayle until they hit mechanical trouble. A huge 17-second lead evaporated and John Holden and Andrew Winkle took the victory. The duo had previously been second on five occasions. They were, in effect, the Guy Martin of the sidecar world. Klaffenbock and Sayle were naturally disgruntled, but they did not begrudge the winners their maiden triumph.

Sidecar racing hurt. Sayle recalled how he had once sucked in endless fumes when riding with the legendary Dave Molyneux, and as a passenger he spent most of the race tucked behind Klaffenbock with his head down. He felt the rush but did not see it. The previous year, which had

327

been the Austrian's first time at the TT, he had tried to teach him the ropes. 'I told him to do two laps as fast as he could. I created a rod for my own back because I've never been so scared. He was all over the place.' Klaffenbock rode one kerb with both front and back wheels. 'Everyone's entitled to hit the kerb now and again,' Sayle said. 'But then he did exactly the same thing on the next lap.' Luckily, he was a quick learner and Sayle emerged bruised, bloodied and victorious. The ugly truth was sidecar racing was physically horrible. Being so close to the ground meant there was effectively no suspension. You were on a tea tray. You rolled with the bumps and punches. A friend who had once been taken around the track on a sidecar admitted to me that he had 'been pissing blood for a week' after the experience. He never tried it again. If the solos shared a link then the sidecars were blood brothers, and so Holden and Winkle were roundly applauded.

But the sidecars are gone now as I walk along Douglas prom and dip into an art gallery with some canvases showing the likes of Mike Hailwood and Joey Dunlop. I leaf through a book about the Ace Café, the legendary London bolt-hole for bikers, its black and white logo reflecting the rebel racer's pragmatic approach to life. There is a section on the 59 Club, a gang set up by a biker priest, Father Graham, who wanted to divert the leather-clad quiffs from a life of loutishness. The church-based youth club sprouted and membership ran into the thousands. Each year the 59 Club would base itself at St Matthew's Church Hall in Douglas, with around 50 bikers bedding down and sometimes adhering to the no-alcohol rule. I think for a moment about Father Brian and whether he will be out at Cruickshanks again, praying for Conor Cummins and the rest.

It is a frustrating day. The weather is again mixed and sunshine in Douglas is tempered by hail on the Mountain. It causes a protracted preamble. Marcus de Matas walks through the packed paddock and breathes in the smells and sights and sounds. Petrol merges with burger grease, weathered leather, beer and coffee. The Red Torpedo stand, selling Guy Martin T-shirts, has sold out. De Matas edges into one of the huge awnings selling official merchandise and buys a TT raincoat. He has already been to the McAdoo tent to meet Cummins. 'It was only then, when I saw him in his full regalia, sitting on a bike weighing half a tonne, that it struck me,' he says. 'For him to be there, only a year post surgery, with his knee flex at 90 degrees, it was just incredible.'

The riders try to idle away the hours. Bruce Anstey goes back to bed. McGuinness sits in the Honda Legends truck and sips a cup of tea. Guy Martin gets on his pushbike. The red flag from yesterday is still a red rag to bullishness. 'That shouldn't have been a result,' he says. 'Not when one half of the field gets a red flag and the other half doesn't. Paul Phillips is a cracking lad, but I didn't go to the podium because it's a fucking joke. It's not fair. It's a bit amateurish round here at times. I take it to heart. I made a bit of a fuss for an hour or two and then let it flow under the bridge. Those that know, know, and those that don't, don't matter.'

That is straight out of Martin's own version of *Zen and the Art of Motorcycle Maintenance*. It has been a week flushed with intrigue and subplots. The wet race still festers away too. 'There was no pressure from the team to get out there, but from the organisers. We should not have gone. Keith came off and, fuck me, I saw that alright. I looked behind me and thought, "There's a dead man there". Mental.

329

Then I had the biggest moment of my life coming out of Union Mills, picking which bit of wall I was going to hit. That's not a nice thing to do. There was no skill involved.'

The Dunlops disagreed. So did Cummins. That was what made running the TT such a thankless task. Opinions were split about the intricacies of the event and on the status of the event itself. Some wanted it banned because it seemed wrong that they were seeking glory when three racers had been killed in the past 11 days. Others felt it was the last bastion of the pre-PC world.

Philip Neill was on Martin's side. 'I felt for John McGuinness that day,' he says of Wednesday's wet race. 'He was the first guy on the road and so the first to hit the conditions. Someone has to go first, but it was a tremendous thing to put on someone. The decision was not informed. The clerk is a gentleman and does a real good job, but for that decision he could not have had enough information from a full lap. When human life is at stake I think riders should be the first point of consideration.'

McGuinness has seen it all. He witnessed the aftermath of DJ's crash and he had felt guilty about Gus Scott's death because he had advised him to try the TT. 'I would never say to anyone now, "Go and do the TT", he told me. 'Not after Gus. I was on the podium spraying the champagne around. Then I got off and someone told me, "Gus is dead". I thought, "Oh no".' He has seen enough to err on the side of caution as much as anyone riding at 200mph can. 'If in doubt put a flag out. Better safe than sorry. That might take 20mph off your corner speed and that might make all the difference.' He had not appreciated being sent down the road blind in the wet race. 'The TV and radio came to me and said, "You're the most experienced rider. What do you think?" It was not fair on me. I didn't want to go, but if we had to then I would ride around like the district nurse. I was No 1. I was the test jockey. Keith passed me, then Guy and Cameron. The next thing I know Keith's off and those two are nearly upside down. I'd rather wipe my backside with a broken bottle than do that again. We feel more pressure from the sponsors than we probably get, but there's a lot of money gone into it. If we all said no then I think they'd take that, but it's a hard one. A double-edged sword. What I do know is that if we didn't go then we would get slagged off for it.'

As the hours pass and the weather improves, so does McGuinness' mood. He is glad to be the No 1 now that the track is drying. Keith Amor might catch him on the smaller bikes and drag him along, but he does not think he will be able to get to him on the big bike. 'I don't like being near anybody when I'm riding at the TT. I hate it. I want to ride this track on my own. All that diving under each other, it's not me. At the North West we were wheel to wheel, but everybody has different styles; somebody might brake a bit later here; peel a bit earlier there. I don't like having to trust people because, normally, if someone crashes you follow them off the track.' He pauses. 'And, anyway, I've been racing long enough to want to keep a few secrets.'

The other races begin to fade away as the day progresses. The Senior is the finale and the farewell. Steve Plater, the 2009 winner, speaks into a microphone, his arm in a sling. 'Obviously, John McGuinness, 16-time winner, confidence growing,' he says when asked to pick a favourite. Plater predicts Anstey will be close too. And then there is Martin. 'He will be pushing hard for his first win and is probably a bit down in the dumps after his fellow Lincolnshire man, Gary Johnson, won his first TT before him.'

Finally, at 5.15 p.m., half a day late, it is time. The bikes edge their way to the starting arch. There are six laps and 226.38 miles to go. McGuinness has been out already on the Yamaha 50th anniversary parade lap and so is confident in the conditions this time. It had been right to sit and wait. Better late than never. He twists his wrist, the Honda roars and he disappears at a speed that defies all logic. The others follow at ten-second intervals – Amor, beaten up from two near misses; Martin, with an island yearning for him; Donald, fast and unlucky so far; Anstey, newly awoken. There is no No 4 because that is Ian Hutchinson's number, but there is a No 7, Ryan Farquhar, lining up despite the injuries that have ruled him out of all the racing so far. Then come the Dunlops, seeking their first Senior triumph, and Cummins, a year on from the crash that has changed his life.

Philip Neill has hammered home the message to Martin. If he wants to beat McGuinness then he has to beat him to Glen Helen on the first lap. If McGuinness gets off to a flyer then there will be no catching him. It all comes down to this first sector. There is never much margin for error at the TT and now there is none.

Marcus de Matas had walked to the bottom of Bray Hill. 'I stood there having a cigarette with my father-in-law. I'd never had any inclination to go to the TT, I preferred Formula One, but the bikes went by and I realised this was the most frightening thing that you can watch. To see them go round the bend at 140mph with stone walls three feet away, it was mind boggling. I'd seen an interview with Guy Martin and he said, "I do this because I might die". I watched them go by and thought, "You might, actually". I rang my wife. I said, "This is making me sweat just watching this".'

By the time they have all got to Glen Helen, Martin has

defied the odds to lead. Nobody beats McGuinness over that first sector on the Superbike, but Martin just has. He does not relent either. He charges towards Ballaugh Bridge and records the fastest ever time over that sector. By that point he has clawed the ten seconds back on Amor and is right behind him. He leaps over Ballaugh Bridge, reminding me of the time Ron Haslam said he had jumped so high that he could see inside the commentary box where a man was screaming at him for being so reckless. The lead is two seconds. His exhaust spits fire like a black dragon. A friend waves a board as he comes out of the Gooseneck. All around the island, word filters through via gossip and radio. Guy Martin is flying and leads the Senior. After all the years of trying, one year on from his own crash, he is ringing the neck of his bike and dragging the hidden depths. The noise is thunderous.

This time, maybe this time. That would shut up the knockers, Simon Buckmaster, Hutchy, Steve Plater and the rest. He is not some comedy sideshow. He is a racer. Better believe it. As he comes past the Grandstand for the first time, sagacious sourpusses in the press room exchange quizzical glances. Martin is seven seconds up on McGuinness. Anstey has taken second place and is 4.48 seconds back on Martin. The race is on. 'I did have a think when I went through Ballagarey in the Senior', he said later. 'That was one year on, the same race. I was lucky. I know that. I did have a second or two, but you can't get too deep and meaningful when you're going at 170mph.'

His fiancée, Steph, is suffering like all the other partners and parents. Martin had long maintained that he would not get married because he did not want the distractions. He would never forget Martin Finnegan, his friend killed months after his wedding. He did not want the mortgage, the kids and the responsibility, but now he *was* getting married. 'She obviously understands,' he had told me earlier that week. 'She's not weird *but* ... ah, the subtext of that "but" is that she is weird I suppose, so how do I get out of that one? She's on my wavelength so she must be weird. I've had loads of crossroads over the last year – girlfriends, jobs, the TV, the team. Sometimes I suppose it's nice to not just have me' self to talk to.' He had fallen out with father over the job situation and he said his family was not close. 'They're all nice enough people, but we're not that great at talking.' Yet his sister, Kate, had worked as his mechanic for years, as he had worked for his father. They were probably closer than he knew.

Carole Cummins had filled up when she heard the cheer that her son had got on the start line. 'It was very emotional,' she said later. 'The start was the hardest bit, knowing he was going out onto the line, and that it was the anniversary.' They were a close-knit family. Billy had cried when he had seen his son in hospital, but now he was back out on the course and hoping. Conor alternated between sleeping in the lower paddock and at home in Ramsey. 'You can't beat your own bed,' he said. 'You can't beat normality. I still live with my mum and dad. If I can get my own place then spot on, but your family is your bedrock. I'm lucky because I have a family I can talk to. I would rather not talk about racing, though. I want to see how they are. It gives me a fresh head.' It was a comment that reminded me of something Carole had said when it was put to her that she must be proud of Conor. 'I'm proud of all my children,' she had replied instantly.

McGuinness' father is at the TT too. He has travelled

334

over and is staying in a campsite. He is proud of his son but rarely says it. Northern men often left such things unsaid, but McGuinness knows. His dad cares, as had been obvious from the time when John had endured a torrid race and John senior left for the ferry without even taking his tent down. 'Be careful and make sure you win,' his mother said – the impossible conundrum that he is wrestling with as Martin speeds away.

For Michael and William it is a different family affair. 'Mum, she doesn't say much,' Michael said, and how could she after all that had passed under this extraordinary family bridge. 'I always give her a ring after the race. That's all she asks.' Michael was more concerned with William. Sometimes it made it harder. 'I have to think for the two of us,' he told me. 'Well, I don't have to but I do. It's always a worry. That's why, sometimes, I like racing away on my own. Half the fears.'

Half the fears but twice the glory. Gary Johnson is not threatening the lead this time. His East Coast Racing team have changed the forks on his Honda and it has not paid off, but he is already delighted to have won a TT, thrilled to have got one over on Martin. But now Martin is charging in his sleek, black livery and yellow helmet – like Dunlop or Senna. Elsewhere, everyone is fighting. Dan Kneen, another Manxman, loses control of his bike. It begins to shake violently as if fitting. Kneen holds on, but only when a bike loses the smooth racing line does the danger rear up and bludgeon the senses. The bike wobbles, his legs fail and then, somehow, impossibly, shape and speed are restored and Kneen goes on.

The Guy Martin fans, in their fake sideburns, and the admirers with their 'Fancy a brew?' sign, lap it up. Their man is winning. The promoters are licking their lips too. The TT has never had a character like Martin and, if he wins, he could take the TT into the mainstream. That will open up a new can of worms, because it is its outsider mien that appeals to so many of the spectators, but that is a debate for tomorrow. For now it is all about the bloody brilliant moment and the fact that, as the bikes come in for their first pit stop at the end of lap two, Martin leads by 4.15 seconds from Anstey. McGuinness is just another second back. The rest, led by Michael Dunlop, are almost half a minute adrift. It is a three-horse race, two old stagers and the apprentice.

The pit stops are long. Far longer than anything you might see in Formula One. Including the entry and exit, McGuinness' stop is timed at 52.27 seconds. Martin's is 55.58 seconds.

> He's lost three seconds in the pits has Guy Martin and, when the race is as close as this one, that could be critical.

With over a third of the race gone, Martin still leads, but the gap is being bitten into by McGuinness who is now enjoying having the open road ahead of him. He has the knack of making it look effortless. 'You have to relax and breathe and try to get your heart rate down. A lot of people put a right load of effort into it and sometimes you don't need to. It's hard to explain, but on the bumpy sections you have to let the bike do what it wants. Let it run. It's like flying a helicopter in the wind. There's no point fighting it because you will not win.'

Martin was always fighting. He had more to deal with at the TT than other riders and, if much of that was of his own making, it did not make it any easier. Deep down, he felt he was a more rounded, honest person than many at the TT. It was why he struggled with bits of the TV presenter role. 'There were three directors. One lad, James, was brilliant. He knew what to say to me. Yet he would sign to do other things. He would quit the BBC then present *World Sheepdog Trials* with Barry Davies on Channel 4. 'Still old-fashioned things. From the mid 1880s to the 1900s. I get to travel around. I'm not into money but they are paying a lot more than the BBC. I like to do things my way and Channel 4 are a bit more leftfield. I'm happier working with them. The BBC are all nice people, but it's jobs for the boys there. It didn't go down well with the BBC at all. They think you're honoured to work for them.' He had more strings to his bow. He said he thought his life would make a good yarn and that he would like to try a bit of stand-up storytelling. He recalled how he had been in the grain store at the farm one day and he had started walking on top of an RSJ. He was a long way up. 'I wouldn't mind giving tightrope walking a whirl. I reckon that would definitely flick my switch. It can't be that hard.'

Michael Dunlop only had racing. It was the only thing that flicked his switch. It had been a mixed week. His bikes had a depressing habit of blowing up, but he had got a win. That was what counted. Nobody remembered the failures. He had stuck two fingers up to all those critics who had pigeon-holed him as a loose cannon and demeaned his 2009 win because it was wet and so the others were, to use McGuinness' terminology, riding round like the district nurse. 'Everyone thinks it's all down to dad, but he was the master of the little bikes so couldn't tell us too much about how to ride the big ones. I'm just his son. A sack of dough. I've never been much good at anything. At school I was such a waste of a seat. But I put my neck on the line in that wet race and won. And people said it was only because it was wet. Well, it's about being comfortable and I enjoy the TT circuit. I make things harder for myself. I build bikes. I'm hands on. The factory teams have more stuff and I just make do. But I'm happy making do. Doing it on my own has been the key to success.'

This race is not going to end in success. The Senior has slipped away in the wake of Martin and McGuinness' battle. The latter overhauls Anstey on corrected time and the gap is a shrinking slither of grey road. It is less than a second with more than half the race to run.

Cummins feels the bike crumble beneath him. It is not a dramatic finale as it had been the previous year, but it is terminal for his chances. He knows it is the suspension. Bugger. He passes the Verandah for the last time in 2011. 'You need the little kicks up your arse', he had said. You don't need 'the armchair racers' telling you what you should and shouldn't be doing. He has made his point to them. 'It's been such a long road. There were times when I was cheesed off, depressed, wondering what was the point. My arm was shrunk to bone, I was drugged up and I was getting nowhere with my hand. But then it all came together.'

The irony was that the turning point had come the day that Ian Hutchinson's world was wrenched off its axis. The gaunt giant went to the British Superbike round at Silverstone as a gloomy spectator living a half-life. He heard about Hutchinson's accident. The pair would never really debate their crashes, but the date would have huge significance for both. 'I was sat in my mate's car on the way home from the race and my wrist twitched momentarily. It gave me a sign of good things to come.' Carole Cummins and Cath Davis would wonder whether the flashes of optimism were wishful thinking or real, but the proof is now on this road, passing Michael Clague and the green-stained cat's eye and the drystone wall.

'When did I feel normal again? When I got back on the bike. In Cartagena. That night when you were with me and we were having pizza in Paparazzi. The call came through. The scans were okay. All the time I was thinking, "Is he going to let me ride?" In fairness, I would probably have thought sod it and ridden anyway.'

He had worried about his body, his biking and his job. He half expected his sponsors to desert him. 'I thought they would say, "Enough is enough". It's not easy in this economic climate. But they stuck by me. On the first night here, one of my sponsors Joe said, "The big man's back". That meant something.' He had been to visit another of his sponsors, Kenyon Crowe, during the TT. He was 89 and unwell. Crowe was a wealthy man who had made his money in farming, but he loved motorcycle racing. He sponsored a number of riders, including world endurance champion David Knight and now Cummins. However, he hailed from a different era and the notion of quick-fix fame was alien to him. Some of his financial support was given on the proviso it went unreported. 'He does not get the recognition he deserves,' Cummins said, but some people did not do it for the recognition. They did it for something higher. 'He just wants to help people,' Cummins said. When Crowe died at the end of 2011, there would be plentiful tributes from his beneficiaries and his cover would be blown.

Cummins passes the Bungalow. McGuinness had once broken down here and ended up being press-ganged into action, helping the paramedics carry a stretcher-bound rider to the helicopter. It is that sort of a race, a cauldron of fear and hope and bonhomie. Cummins has cried a lot along the way, but he is not an unduly emotional man. He is happy with his sixth place, but he wants more. He pulls into the pits for the last time and dismounts. Carole heaves a sigh of relief. Cath Davis is proud of him. 'He's just done phenomenally well,' she says. Davis has been helping other riders during the TT, but she always tries to give Cummins the first hour after a race and the last one before. 'I think he needed it and so did I. I have learnt a lot. It's been great, great work. I feel really privileged. How long will he have to see me for now? Probably forever, or at least until he gets bored of me.'

He is not a freak, as Marcus De Matas knows better than most. He and Jo Banks had fixed him, but there would be others with different stories and the same anxieties. De Matas remembered Cummins talking of crashing for the first time with his rods in situ. The big smile when he stood up. 'Somebody else got it that day,' De Matas mused. Now Cummins walks away. He is safe. For now. He already knows what his future holds. 'I want to be 10mph faster up the road,' he says. He can go around the TT at more than 131mph after all. Only McGuinness has gone faster and not from a standing start as Cummins had managed last year. He is the fastest Manxman, the first Manxman to top 130mph. He feels blessed. 'I shouldn't be doing these speeds yet,' he admits. 'That's not me being big-headed.' A less arrogant man you could not find on the island. 'It's just I've done the speeds before. Next year I will be on it. This year I feel like I've missed out. It's like having your train set pulled away from you.'

Cummins is gone and Michael Dunlop is off the pace.

And quickly and smoothly, McGuinness begins to exert his dominance. Martin has rattled him with his start, but now McGuinness is flying. He keeps his nerve because it is not all fun; he had never got over a mishap at Ballacrye a decade earlier, and there was the bump in the road at Kerrowmoar where he had 'the biggest tank-slapper ever' in 2000; the fairing was shattered and he had that horrible nanosecond of resignation – 'This is going to be big' – before he survived and forgot. 'That SP-1 had me in tears, terrified me, had my body black and blue, tank-slapping, arms slapping. Then we switched tyre brands and ended up on the podium behind Joey. From being in another planet to being on the podium the day after, you think, "Is it me, have I got the wrong style, can I ride one of these things?" Then, all of a sudden, you find the problem and we're back in the hunt.' Even so it had not stopped him lying in the road trying to discern where the bump was. 'I've still not worked it out,' he admitted. 'It scarred my brain.'

But by the time they get to Ramsey on the third lap McGuinness has turned the deficit into a 0.9 second lead. It is small but the tide has turned. By the Grandstand and the start of the fourth lap, he is 2.56 seconds ahead of Martin.

There is always pressure. Even back in 2007 when he had become the first man to break the fabled 130mph lap barrier. 'I had wanted to do it in practice, but I did 129.6mph and was disappointed. I did that again this year. I was fastest in practice. Becky said, "130.6". I went, "Oh". Then Bruce did 131.4, a lot faster than me. I was like, "Fucking hell, we're going to struggle here".' He said the crowds had been noisier than ever this year. Even with his plugs and the wind and the engine, he could hear people cheering all the way round. 'I've never had that before.'

They keep circulating. Dunlop runs on at Ballacraine and loses more time. McGuinness then swings the hammer. People kept talking about how he rode within himself, but he was the fastest man around the course in 100 years of racing on the Mountain. And now, he puts in a blistering 131.2mph lap. Martin struggles to respond. He clocks 129.7mph, still dizzying and dazzling, but not enough to close the lead. The TV cameras catch Dan Kneen at the same spot where he had almost come to grief.

'Much better this time,' Steve Plater says.

'It would be,' Jamie Whitham adds.

'Better for his underpants too.'

They come into the pits at the end of the fourth lap and McGuinness sits up in his seat. His visor is changed and he swigs long and hard on a bottle. Anstey has now crept past Martin into second place.

'Look at Bruce Anstey,' McGuinness had said to me. 'He's 41. He's older than me. But the man's a complete weirdo. He wins or he's eighth. I mean, how can you be eighth in the first part of the 600 race, then it gets stopped because the boy gets killed, and then you go out and win. All that's happened is he's had a ham sandwich and a kick up the backside from Clive [Padgett]. He's the most naturally gifted rider on the planet. He just sleeps all day, gets on it and wins.'

His father suggested that perhaps Anstey grew demoralised quicker than McGuinness realised. Either way, McGuinness is now wary of the fact he has both Anstey and Martin behind him. The gap is healthy, up to 12 seconds, but much can change. Even out in front, with a supposedly clear road, there are back-markers, mechanical issues and those damned birds.

The front of the TT Legends bike has turned from white

to grey with the remains of flies, but it is the bigger animals that concern McGuinness. He had almost come to grief in practice after his Superbike win and he had suffered again in the Superstock race. 'I've never hit so many birds during a TT fortnight. The Isle of Man wildlife community has really got it in for me this week. I hit one in the Superstock and some of it started cooking on the exhaust. There was this awful smell. They say Hondas have got wings and this one really did. There were bits of it everywhere. It was burnt to a cinder after a bit.'

Martin makes up four seconds on Anstey in the pits and still believes. What he does not believe in is destiny and fate and such nebulous concepts. A few years ago he had stated his opinions when debating his New Year's resolutions. 'What a load of old tripe. Luck and resolutions and all that crap. I went to ask for some luck at the Fairy Bridge last year and what did that do? Sod all. I'm making my own luck now.' He loves this bit of the TT. The rest of it can be a pain, but the sensation of riding so close to the edge is peerless. He likes Hector and Philip too. They take care of the bikes and so he no longer has to juggle everything else with dissecting engines. They do not try to 'reinvent the wheel' like his chief mechanic of old. So Martin had been down to the Villa Marina for the prize-giving this week. It was a tedious affair, with everyone receiving their trophies all the way down the field. 'It goes on and on and there are 101 other things I would rather be doing, but I went for the team.'

Slowly, something small grows into the semblance of a conclusion. As McGuinness improves, so Martin fades. McGuinness is only half a second quicker over the fifth lap, but it is enough to increase the lead to 13 seconds. It will take an engine failure, a bird strike or worse to deny him now. He wants respect and had feared it might ebb away if he had another barren TT, but it looks easy now. On the last lap they all up the pace. McGuinness clocks a 130.04mph lap. Martin will not be browbeaten into a submission that would underscore every nod, wink and innuendo, and responds with 130.8mph, the fastest man on the circuit. It scythes into McGuinness' lead, but as dusk moves in, the Morecambe man has daylight. Keith Amor manages his first 130mph lap to round off an eventful TT for him. Battered, bruised and fifth, he will soon announce his retirement from the sport, two falls and a submission.

McGuinness knows that he has won as he indulges in a long wheelie down Glencrutchery Road. Martin is second, seven seconds adrift. It has been a hell of a last lap, but again, it is not enough. Anstey, Donald and Amor complete the top five. Michael Dunlop is sixth, brother William eighth, yesterday's man, Gary Johnson the meat in that family sandwich.

There are quick interviews in the winners' enclosure. 'The man's class,' Martin says of McGuinness. 'The icing on the cake,' the winner says as he hugs Becky and Maisie. They stand on the podium and then move into the press conference. They are given ice creams by Stephen Davison, the photographer. Anstey plants his on McGuinness' head; McGuinness puts his in Martin's face. They stop laughing and Anstey admits the later race probably suited someone who treated mornings as something to be missed. Martin is asked about the crowd noise when he had led after the first and second laps. 'I'm a bit shy and have been hibernating away all week,' he says. 'A fella leant me a lock-up.' I knew from Cummins that some of the riders struggled to believe this and thought he was in a hotel. 'That's all I hear from the anti-Guy Martins,' he had said. But that was the thing with Martin. He was just a bloke who liked racing bikes and yet there was even a name, the *antis*, for those who did not buy into his ordinariness. Both he and his knockers felt he was nothing special and yet they used that shared belief to form contrasting opinions. In a more reflective moment, he had spoken to me of Steph. 'I really don't know what she sees in me.' He meant it. 'I like the idea of getting married, but I'm not sure about everything that goes with it. I hate routines.'

In the press conference, Tim Glover, the compere, tells Martin that the fans adore him. 'Crackers,' Martin says, almost blushing. 'I could hear stuff through my ear plugs out there. Crackers. But to beat John on the first lap or even to beat him to Glen Helen was an achievement. I can go to bed fairly happy.' He pauses and counters. 'Still haven't won the fucker, have I? To beat him on the first two laps, I could not do anymore. Happy camper. Just got to come back next year and beat the bugger.' McGuinness interjects. 'Yeah, it's about time you won one.' It is gentle and not boastful, but given that McGuinness has two wins in a week and 17 in total, while Martin still has none, it hurts.

McGuinness admits he has never ridden harder. When he realised he was fourth on the first lap, it had been a shock. 'It's the first time in a long time I've had to push like that. Nearly broke into a sweat.' He is only joking, but I feel for Martin as he contemplates another year of debate.

It is the conundrum that Philip Neill was also wrestling with. The TAS Suzuki boss would face a frantic few months as he plotted the next assault on the TT. Tyco replaced Relentless as the title sponsor and he needed riders. He wanted Martin. He was still intrigued by him. He could not understand why Martin could record the fastest ever sector time from Glen Helen to Ballaugh Bridge and not repeat it. 'He clocked 3.04 for that sector when 3.07 is the norm. Then he went back to 3.07 for every other lap. Why? It's not like he could cut the course anywhere. If he does 3.04 on every lap then he's won the race. I have nothing but respect for John, but he said he turned up the wick and created that victory. I don't believe he did. John turned on the pressure, but at the same time, Guy had a couple of weak laps. The only thing that could be down to was the bike, the tyres or Guy. Well, there was nothing wrong with the bike or tyres. He will get there. He will crack the TT and we will be the team that takes him there. I told this to Guy and you could see the wheels turning, but then, very quickly, he probably went back to thinking about potato picking.'

It would be a few months before I saw Martin again. He was still in the old blacksmith's cottage, still wearing his old green shorts and still building his Martek turbo. Things were changing. Soon Neill would complete his deals, first with Cummins and then Martin. It was a dream partnership, the local hero and the people's champion, both back from the brink, both searching for their first win.

When we met, Martin was out of action because of a new injury. 'I can't race,' he lamented. 'I've got a blood infection. It started under the patella [kneecap] and became borderline septicaemia. My mate took me to the hospital. If not for him I'd have thought grin and bear it. They said if it had got worse they might have had to take it off. In my job I'm always cutting and nicking my hands but they said it wasn't an oil infection.' Yet the oil and the grime and danger were under his nails and in his blood. There was no way out. 'Yeah,' he said. 'I've got to go back now. I've got to win one and then quit. Get out. Try something new.' He talked of the

Salzkammergut, the toughest one-day bicycle race in the world. 'Climbing 250k, 7,500 feet, I was the first Brit home.' But he had already decided what he would do after the TT. He needed the buzz and the danger and so he had come up with a plan for life after that near-death thing. 'Base camp on a mountain bike and then to the summit. Costs you 15 grand to the Nepalese government before they get a Sherpa to go up with you. I have to do it. Need to do a few peaks first. Will take two years. But that's it. Once I get over this TT thing I'm going to climb Mount Everest.'

On the last night of the TT I watch as all the riders gather in the pit lane and the prizes are handed out. It is late, due to the delay, and most of the punters have wandered off down the hill into Douglas for a Friday night of drunken recollection. The riders stay. There are mementos for all of them. Their names and numbers are called and they traipse up, the winners, the stars and the journeymen doing it for kicks on a shoestring.

No 58, Lee Vernon, walks up. He was 39th in the first Supersport race and 31st in the second. That was his TT. He is heading down to Colours nightclub with its faded grandeur, garish interior and restorative beer. He would get in at 7 a.m. the following morning. 'I got the boat at four o'clock in the afternoon,' he would recall. 'So did everyone. All the riders must have been booked on that boat, all hungover, all reeking of beer.' He would soon be back in Stoke, working in Manchester, dreaming of the island. And the bitter reminder of the downside would be delivered back here, at the Manx Grand Prix, in two months' time. 'It was bad when Wayne Hamilton got killed,' he would tell me much later. 'We parked next to each other at the Ulster two weeks before. He stayed at our house a few times. He wins the newcomer prize at the Manx and you think, "Great, he's on his way, now he'll take it steady". Then the worst thing. Still, if you've a smile on your face it's better than sitting at home being miserable and drinking beer.'

Conor Cummins stands with his mother and girlfriend. He wanders through the crowd, shakes a hand and the brotherhood claps. He has climbed the Mountain and gets the Spirit of the TT award as a result. 'Well deserved,' his mother says. 'After all he has been through.' Cummins is pleased but he hides his emotions well these days. 'One to show the grandchildren,' he says to me. A pause. 'If I make it that far.' He smiles and lopes off. He loads all his gear into his van and takes Zara for a ride up to Onchen Head. They look out over the sea and eat pizza.

Slow in, fast out. That's the key to the TT circuit. The last bend and there's a trap. Well, you wouldn't expect anything else would you? The old road meets the new and there's a big lump. Too apprehensive and it will fire you out of the seat. Back up through the gearbox and that's a lap of the TT course. You've got to love it.

Afterword

I went back a year later. It was the summer of the Olympic Games, and back on the mainland, and especially in the world of sports writing, we were tangled up in red, white and blue. On the island the only sound was the heartbeat revs of engines and the rain on the roof. Nothing else mattered.

I met Derek Redmond, who merged both worlds. He was co-owner of the Splitlath Redmond motorcycling team, but he used to be a 400-metre runner. He was good enough to win European, Commonwealth and World Championship medals but was best known for what he did when it all went wrong.

'I had not run pain-free for four years before the Olympics in Barcelona in 1992,' he told me as he took a break from preparing his bike team. 'I had 16 operations in that time but, to coin a cliché, I got to Spain in the shape of my life. I thought, "This is it." I breezed through the first and second rounds without breaking sweat. I told myself to keep a lid on it. I was so excited. Then, in the semi-final, I pulled my

351

hamstring after about 150 metres. The disbelief, I can't tell you. I went into denial and hit the floor.'

What happened next would become one of the iconic Olympic moments. Redmond staggered to his feet and began hobbling. His father, Jim, wearing a baseball cap and a T-shirt saying 'Have you hugged your foot today?' broke through the security cordon and rushed to his son. Together they made it to the finish, an act of defiant failure that would resonate with 65,000 people in the stadium and millions around the world. Redmond rested on a railing by the paddock tower and told me it took him years to get over the incident that both made and broke him.

'It was the most frustrating and disappointing moment of my life,' he sighed. 'What made me get up once I'd gone through the initial pain was I wanted to see where the other athletes were. I thought, "I'll catch them if I start running." But then at 200 metres I looked over and saw they had finished and that was like someone plunging a knife into me.

'Then I felt stubbornness, disappointment and annoyance. I said to myself, "I'm going to finish this race if it's the last effing race I ever do." I was pissed off. My old man arrived and said, "Derek, you don't need to do this." He wanted me to stop because we did not know how much damage I'd done and there was still the relay. I said, "Get me back in my lane," and he could see he wasn't going to stop me, so he tried to take some of the pressure. I just remember saying, "Why me? Why me? What have I bloody done to deserve this?"'

He was 46 now and used his experience in motivational speeches, but he always turned away when the film showed his hamstring snap. Soldiers had told him he was a hero. Like Guy Martin, he was uncomfortable with such remarks, but dealing with the dark side of sport certainly came in useful for anyone running a road-racing motorcycling team. He had found out when his team 'lost' Mark Buckley at the North West 200.

'We lost Mark and carried on, not because we are cold-hearted so and sos, but because if we could talk to him for ten seconds he would tell us to,' Redmond said. 'I was in the pits for the Superbike race on Saturday and waiting for the start. The three-minute warning came, and the riders all put their lids on. It was amazing to watch, because they look into each other's eyes and give warm embraces, wish everyone luck. They don't say it, but they mean, "Just in case you don't come back."'

That Superbike race had been won by John McGuinness. He was still doing the business. He had a lead of six seconds by halfway and, even though Cameron Donald managed his first ever 130mph lap, the result was a done deal. Afterwards, there was the usual mix of honesty and medical reports, further evidence that for all their gladiatorial machismo, these men were brittle bruisers.

'I got a bit emotional when I went through the Creg on the last lap, as it reminded me of how I used to wave at Joey all those years ago,' McGuinness said. It was natural that, with the passing of the years, he would grow more nostalgic, and the rest of the week would show that others, too, were becoming tuned to their mortality.

There were no racers killed in 2012, but five people died in road accidents. And there were injuries aplenty, Simon Andrews being taken to hospital after crashing in the Superbike race. He had broken bones but the official statement said none of the injuries was 'life-threatening'.

Conor Cummins was injured, too. I had seen him during

the winter and knew how confident he was going into 2012. Then he fell off his bike at the North West 200 and broke two bones in his right hand. During TT week, he came down to the Lexicon bookshop in Douglas to help me sell copies of *That Near-Death Thing*. He did not need to do that, and it was an act of generosity that was much appreciated by both me and David, Lexicon's owner. In my head, I had always thought Conor was the real hero of the book, so it was good to see him sign copies as we launched the thing, but I kept my real feelings to myself when he showed me his hand and said he still planned to race in the Senior. Horribly swollen and scarred, it looked impossible. Just like last time.

McGuinness also won the Superstock race to take his tally to 19 wins, but the thriller was the Supersport. Michael Dunlop appeared to have it won, bludgeoning his way to a 22-second lead, but he failed to finish, and an exhilarating fight was played out in his absence. The lead ebbed and flowed into a win for Bruce Anstey. The margin of victory was a mere 0.77 seconds. It was the second-closest race in the history of close shaves, the third win of the week for men over 40.

The boy racers were back in the second Supersport race when Dunlop won. I remembered McGuinness saying that, when it all came together, Michael would be just about unbeatable, and so it was beginning to prove. Life after McGuinness looked increasingly likely to be dominated by the nephew of the man he had idolised.

Sadly, the 2012 TT would end in crushing disappointment when the rain led to the Senior being cancelled. Only world wars and foot and mouth had stopped it before. For Cummins it was a horrible kick in the teeth. He had toiled for months to restore his body to potentially winning ways and had sat out the whole of TT week thus far, leaving Cath Davis to work on his hand and the Hyperbaric Chamber to do the rest, the racer nodding nicely at the endless procession of punters who asked if he would be racing this week. 'I'll be out there for the Senior,' he would say. 'No bother.' Pull the pin and see what happens.

Now it was another year gone, but he had time. For Guy Martin it was beginning to run out. He had a fourth, fifth and eighth to round up a dismal week. I caught up with him late in 2012, when the Olympics had finished, and, for all his contrary protestations, he was about to launch a new TV series called *How Britain Worked*. He explained that it was about the grafters and the forgotten, which seemed apt.

He had not changed at all. Affable, eccentric, hairy and recklessly honest, he was still wrestling with the same old problems when he met me in the café at the Design Museum on London's South Bank. He had the final proofs of his 2013 calendar with him. There were pictures of cars and tool boxes and engines, but none of Martin; nobody could call it a vanity project.

'The TV people are lovely, but they are arty-farty,' he told me. 'I'd do a day's filming, but it's not work, is it? I come home from working on trucks and I'm knackered and covered in shit and that's satisfaction. Do a day's filming and I've not achieved anything.'

He was still scraping up against his rivals, too. Ian Hutchinson, who had returned to the TT with his battered body that summer, had indulged in mockery by social media. 'I'm not into this twitting or tweeter, what's it called?' Martin said. 'He slagged me off and fair play, old boy. They take offence because I'm earning a few quid on the side. What's that they say about the Manx crab – he tries to get out of the bucket and the rest pull him back in?'

He sighed and took a swig of his tea. 'The thing is I love my work. I love my spanners. The trouble these days is there is no enthusiasm for going to work. Sports people want to get to a certain level and pack it in, but you can do both. Course you can. I don't understand why schools want everyone to become an astronaut or a brain surgeon. What's wrong with getting your hands dirty? It's looked down on, I know, but nobody has a trade any more.'

The favourite part of Martin's new programme, which he said looked beneath 'Brunel, Stephenson, Watt and superstars of the industrial revolution', saw him help a crew renovating Llandudno Pier. 'These lads must have thought, "We've got one of these TV dickheads coming down. We'll show him." There were no namby-pamby risk assessors, no health and safety. I was thrown in the deep end, 4 a.m. in the morning, pitch black, abseiling down the side of it, burnt a nipple, hard-core. It's good for you, though. People in this country, in sport and everything, have forgotten the working man.'

He was warming to this theme as his tea grew colder. 'When my first TV programme came out, and then the TT film, I just wanted to smash my head against a brick wall. I never wanted to be famous. I mean, do you think The Beatles or The Stone Roses made music to be famous?' He stopped himself, paused and saw a contradiction. Most sports stars I'd met would have buried it, but he just blurted it out: 'But I'm the one who is here doing an interview for *The Times*, aren't I?'

Banging his head against a metaphorical wall and smashing it against real ones. We went back to his crash in 2010. 'Made out to be worse than it was,' he said. 'But there is a line, and there is a time and place for crossing the line. When you do that you might crash, but if I killed myself battling for the lead of the TT then no bother. What a way to die, eh?'

He said he was more affected by a crash at that year's North West 200. 'I hit the wall head first at 120mph and was lying in the road thinking, "Why?" I've been racing for 11 years and done a lot of crashing, but that was the first time I didn't know the cause. I'd knackered "me sen" and then I had to go to the TT not knowing what had happened. That did play on my mind. Yes, it did.'

The TT did not change but the riders did. After all these years, McGuinness got married to Becky. Martin took Steph to Cuba. 'We ended up in what we thought was Guantanamo Bay, so I suppose we're doing well to be here now, but we both came back a bit wiser on the whole idea of communism and the balls that Castro and Che Guevara had.'

Cummins' mum thanked me for the book when I bumped into her. 'You told it as it was,' she said. It meant a lot. Dunlop signed to ride alongside McGuinness for TT legends in 2013, the old and the new, bound together in red, white and blue.

The book got some nice reviews and was up for a big award with a £25,000 prize. It lost to *The Secret Race* about doping in cycling. In some ways that was right, because the TT racers are still outsiders, doing it for kicks. This is the real secret race. I thought it amusing that the winning book had contributed to bringing down Tour de France legend Lance Armstrong, with its tales of EPO-taking, while Guy Martin had gleefully admitted he had taken the same stuff. The difference was cyclists took it to cheat, and Martin took it to stay awake while doing shifts down the docks. It seemed to sum up the chasm between the pampered, twisted world of elite sport and the TT grafters.

Back in that summer of 2012, the cancellation of the Senior TT had not met with wholesale approval. McGuinness had said, 'Rider safety is paramount.' A poster to the official TT website countered, 'They have all gone soft. Paramount safety bolllocks.' It was staggering that some people still did not get it. Some TT fans had complained about the title of this book. I understood why, but I never intended to glamorise the danger, because the utter lack of glamour is what the TT is all about. I remembered all those discussions about going out in the wet in 2011, when riders felt they were playing Russian roulette with each circuit. I also thought about the excitement and bemusement on Derek Redmond's face as he tasted the TT and told me, 'Courageous acts will always outweigh medals.' Like it or not, it is a near-death thing . . . and that is close enough.

Photo Credits

John McGuinness (©Pacemaker Press International)
Guy Martin (©Pacemaker Press International)
Conor Cummins (©Pacemaker Press International)
Michael Dunlop (©Pacemaker Press International)
Guy Martin (©Marc Aspland)
That Near-Death Thing (©Marc Aspland)
The old stager (©Pacemaker Press International)
'I'm so proud of him.' (©Pacemaker Press International)
The eyes have it (©Pacemaker Press International)
'He spiralled up in the air.' (©Isle of Man, DED/North One
    Television)
The Verandah (©Isle of Man, DED/North One Television)
'I'm not scared of dying.' (©Noel O'Reilly)
The luckiest (©Noel O'Reilly)
Happier days (©Marc Aspland)
The sorcerer and the apprentice (©Pacemaker Press
    International)
Brass tacks (©Pacemaker Press International)
Father and son (©Pacemaker Press International)

Sibling rivalry I (©Pacemaker Press International)
Sibling rivalry II (©Pacemaker Press International)
'It was black with people.' (©Pacemaker Press International)
'I'm not a flash bastard.' (©Marc Aspland)
'The pencil line' (©Pacemaker Press International)
The broken man (©Pacemaker Press International)
Tea (©michaelpowell.com)
& Sympathy (©Pacemaker Press International)
A family odyssey (©Pacemaker Press International)
Go for laughs (©Pacemaker Press International)
One year on (©Pacemaker Press International)
'Crazy' (©Pacemaker Press International)
Breaking down barriers (©Pacemaker Press International)
Craggy Island (©Pacemaker Press International)
Back to the drawing board (©michaelpowell.com)
Woman's world (©Bradley Ormesher/*The Times*)
'The place was on its arse after DJ.' (©Pacemaker Press International)
The most dangerous race in the world (©Marc Aspland)
Back to his best (©Pacemaker Press International)